国际贸易实务
双语教程

刘红英 程 杨 主 编

中国财经出版传媒集团
中国财政经济出版社
·北京·

图书在版编目（CIP）数据

国际贸易实务双语教程：汉文、英文 / 刘红英，程杨主编. -- 北京：中国财政经济出版社，2025.7.
ISBN 978-7-5223-4114-9

Ⅰ. F740.4

中国国家版本馆CIP数据核字第2025UR3838号

责任编辑：彭　洋　　　　　　责任校对：胡永立
责任印制：史大鹏

国际贸易实务双语教程
GUOJI MAOYI SHIWU SHUANGYU JIAOCHENG

中国财政经济出版社 出版

URL：http：//www.cfeph.cn
E-mail：cfeph@cfeph.cn

（版权所有　翻印必究）

社址：北京市海淀区阜成路甲28号　邮政编码：100142
营销中心电话：010-88191522
天猫网店：中国财政经济出版社旗舰店
网址：https：//zgczjjcbs.tmall.com
涿州汇美亿浓印刷有限公司印刷　各地新华书店经销
成品尺寸：185mm×260mm　16开　22.25印张　705 000字
2025年7月第1版　2025年7月河北第1次印刷
定价：68.00元
ISBN 978-7-5223-4114-9
（图书出现印装问题，本社负责调换，电话：010-88190548）
本社图书质量投诉电话：010-88190744
打击盗版举报热线：010-88191661　QQ：2242791300

编委会

主　编　刘红英　程　杨
副主编　纪向岚　刘敏姣　邹　文

前 言

从事国际贸易是一项专业性和技术性都很强的工作，面临着众多的挑战，包括来自不同国家的政治风险、市场的不确定性、不同国家的监管要求、支付问题、运输延误以及复杂的贸易流程和满足不同国家的单据要求等。与此同时，在经济全球化深度调整与数字技术革命双重驱动下，国际贸易面临着全球价值链重构、国际产业转移和制造业向发达国家回流的冲击，中国对外贸易下行压力增大。因此，培养兼具国际视野、数字素养与外贸技能的国际贸易人才，具有紧迫性。

国际贸易实务是国际经济与贸易专业的核心基础课，采用双语教学具有必要性。本专业最早在2006年开始探索该课程的双语教学，2012年课程被立项为校级双语示范课程，此后持续采用双语教学至今。本书编者均为多年从事国际贸易实务双语教学的国际经济与贸易专业教师，积累了丰富的双语教学经验。在2023年，本课程立项为省级一流本科课程，为此我们对本专业省级规划教材《国际贸易理论与实务》进行修订，结合课程组多年的双语教学经验，将国际贸易实务的内容以双语形式编排，以契合当前外贸形势对地方本科院校高素质、复合型、应用型人才的需求，着重培养学生的外贸技能和英语应用能力。

本教材的编写融合了最新有关国际贸易的法规和国际惯例，并结合了编者从事国际贸易实务课程的教学体会。与其他教材相比，本教材具有以下几大特点：

第一，本教材的排版便于双语学习。已有的同类双语教材大多采用中英文逐段对照的排版，这种方式对外贸专业的学生完全没有必要，因为学生并非一句英文都看不懂，他们只是部分词汇或句子看不懂。还有部分教材采用英文在前，中文翻译在后的编排，由于中英文相隔太远，使得学习者要耗费大量脑力在英文和中文之间进行搜寻和匹配，降低了学习效率。基于多年的教学经验，本书采用了部分双语的形式，仅对可能造成学生阅读障碍的重点词汇、术语或表达进行了中文标注，这可以降低学生双语学习的负荷，并摆脱对母语的视觉依赖。

第二，本教材结构合理、内容完整。本教材以国际贸易流程为主线安排章节顺序，依次阐述开展贸易前的准备、商务磋商与签订合同、国际贸易术语、商品条款、国际货物运输、货物运输保险、出口价格核算、国际货款支付、合同中的一般条款、进出口合同履行、数字贸易实务。其中，数字贸易实务是本教材根据全球贸易发展新趋势而增设的章节，为读者概述了数字贸易、跨境电商的实务知识。为方便教学，本教材配套设计了课后习题，题型除了常规的判断题、选择题、案例分析题外，还设计了网上信息搜索题和小组任务题型，体现了本教材的专业性、特色性和趣味性。

第三，本教材充分反映了国际贸易惯例与规则的最新发展以及国际贸易实务的最新做法。例如，本教材介绍了最新版的《国际贸易术语解释通则》，采用了最新版的《跟单信用证统一惯例》（UCP600）和《托收统一规则》（URC522）的内容进行阐述，详细介绍了《中国保险条款》（C.I.C.）最新版内容和英国伦敦保险协会《协会货物保险条款》（ICC）最新版的内容，以及《联合国国际货物销售合同公约》（CISG）等内容，使本书富有时代气息。

参加本书编写的分别有：刘红英（第二章、第三章、第七章）；程杨（第一章、第六章）；纪向岚（第十章、第十一章）；刘敏姣（第五章、第九章）；邹文（第四章、第八章）。在本书编写过程中，我们吸收了有关专家、学者的最新研究成果，在此，一并表示最诚挚的谢意。

由于编者才疏学浅，书中不当之处在所难免，希望读者反馈各种意见和建议，我们将会不断完善和提高。

编者

2025年7月

CONTENTS

Chapter 1 Preparations for International Trade — 001

    1.1 Designing and Making an International Trade Plan — 002
    1.2 Be Familiar with International Trade Laws and Regulations — 012
    1.3 Obtaining the International Trade Qualification — 027

Chapter 2 Business Negotiation and Signing the Contract — 035

    2.1 Contents and Forms of Business Negotiation — 035
    2.2 General Procedures of Business Negotiations — 036
    2.3 Signing Sales Contract — 043

Chapter 3 International Trade Terms — 052

    3.1 International Trade Terms and Its Basic Rules — 053
    3.2 International Rules for the Interpretation of Trade Terms 2020 — 059
    3.3 Clauses Commonly Used about the Trade Terms in Contract — 083

Chapter 4 Terms of Commodity — 089

    4.1 Name of Commodity — 090
    4.2 Quality of Commodity — 091
    4.3 Quantity of Commodity — 101
    4.4 Packing of Commodity — 109

Chapter 5 International Cargo Transport and Shipment Clause 122

- 5.1 Means of Transportation 123
- 5.2 Major Transportation Documents 140
- 5.3 Shipment Clause 150

Chapter 6 Cargo Transportation Insurance and Insurance Clause 161

- 6.1 Fundamental Principles of Cargo Insurance 162
- 6.2 Marine Risks and Losses 166
- 6.3 Cargo Clauses of Marine Cargo Insurance of C.I.C. 171
- 6.4 Coverage of Marine Cargo Insurance of ICC 179
- 6.5 Insurance Terms in the International Sales Contract 185

Chapter 7 The Calculation of Export Price 193

- 7.1 Price Components of Export Commodities 194
- 7.2 Calculation of Export Price 198
- 7.3 Export Quotation Accounting in Trade Practice 206
- 7.4 Price Terms in Sales Contract 209

Chapter 8 Terms of Payment 212

- 8.1 International Trade Payment Tools 213
- 8.2 Modes of International Payment 220
- 8.3 Other Methods of Payment 237
- 8.4 Payment Terms in Contract 241

Chapter 9 The General Terms and Conditions in the Contract 251

- 9.1 Commodity Inspection 252
- 9.2 Claim 260
- 9.3 Force Majeure 264
- 9.4 Arbitration 267

Chapter 10 The Performance of Export and Import Contract   278

    10.1 General Procedures of Export Transaction   281

    10.2 General Procedures of Import Transaction   290

    10.3 Documents Needed in Export and Import Transaction   292

Chapter 11 Digital Trade Practice   313

    11.1 Overview of Digital Trade   314

    11.2 Overview of Cross-Border E-commerce   317

    11.3 Differences between Cross Border E-commerce and Traditional Trade   332

References   338

目 录

第一章　开展贸易前的准备　001

　　1.1　制定国际贸易计划　002
　　1.2　熟悉国际贸易法律法规　012
　　1.3　获得对外贸易经营者资格　027

第二章　商务磋商和签订合同　035

　　2.1　商务磋商的内容和形式　035
　　2.2　商务磋商的一般程序　036
　　2.3　签订销售合同　043

第三章　国际贸易术语　052

　　3.1　国际贸易术语及其惯例　053
　　3.2　《2020年国际贸易术语解释通则》　059
　　3.3　合同中使用的贸易术语　083

第四章　合同中的商品条款　089

　　4.1　商品的名称　090
　　4.2　商品的品质　091
　　4.3　商品的数量　101
　　4.4　商品包装　109

第五章　国际货物运输及合同中的装运条款　　122

  5.1 运输方式　　123

  5.2 主要运输单据　　140

  5.3 装运条款　　150

第六章　国际货物运输保险及合同中的保险条款　　161

  6.1 保险的基本原则　　162

  6.2 海上风险与损失　　166

  6.3 中国海上货物运输保险条款　　171

  6.4 英国伦敦保险协会的海运货物保险条款　　179

  6.5 合同中的保险条款　　185

第七章　出口价格核算　　193

  7.1 出口商品价格构成　　194

  7.2 出口商品价格核算　　198

  7.3 实际业务出口报价核算　　206

  7.4 合同中的价格条款　　209

第八章　国际贸易支付及合同中的支付条款　　212

  8.1 国际贸易的支付工具　　213

  8.2 国际贸易的支付方式　　220

  8.3 其他支付方式　　237

  8.4 合同中的支付条款　　241

第九章　合同中的一般条款　　251

  9.1 商品检验　　252

  9.2 索赔　　260

  9.3 不可抗力　　264

  9.4 仲裁　　267

第十章　进出口合同履行　　　　　　　　　　　　**278**

  10.1　出口业务流程　　　　　　　　　　　　281

  10.2　进口合同的履行　　　　　　　　　　　290

  10.3　主要进出口单证　　　　　　　　　　　292

第十一章　数字贸易实务　　　　　　　　　　　　**313**

  11.1　数字贸易概述　　　　　　　　　　　　314

  11.2　跨境电商概述　　　　　　　　　　　　317

  11.3　跨境电商与传统贸易的区别　　　　　　332

参考文献　　　　　　　　　　　　　　　　　　　**338**

Chapter 1
Preparations for International Trade

第一章 开展贸易前的准备

◆ Learning Objectives

• Understand the significance of developing an international trade plan

• Understand the basic concepts of commonly used international trade laws and regulations

• Master the process of developing an international trade plan

• Understand the essential requirements for conducting international trade

    International trade, also known as foreign trade, involves the exchange of goods or services between two or more countries in a fair and deliberate manner. While the success and failure rates for those venturing into international trade may not be explicitly documented, they likely mirror those of general business endeavors. As such, thorough preparation is crucial before engaging in import or export activities.

    First and foremost, it is essential to have a deep understanding of both the product and the market. Identifying a product with strong market potential is key. This involves conducting comprehensive **market research** to assess opportunities and threats, and then establishing or leveraging an appropriate import/export organizational structure to

国际贸易

市场调研

develop a viable international trade strategy.

Secondly, engaging in import and export requires a solid foundation of **specialized knowledge** in international trade. Although there have been few changes in the laws governing international trade contracts in recent years, the widespread adoption of e-commerce, along with advancements in transportation and communication technologies, has significantly altered many procedures, rules, and documentation requirements. Particularly, documents that are closely tied to the internet must be updated promptly. Therefore, it is imperative to be well-versed in **international trade conventions, customs,** and relevant national **laws and regulations.**

Finally, once the preparatory work is complete and you are ready to embark on international trade, you must navigate a series of **procedures** to obtain the necessary qualifications. For certain goods, securing the appropriate **quotas or licenses** is a prerequisite before commencing import or export operations.

专业知识

国际贸易公约、惯例和法律法规

流程

配额或者许可

1.1 Designing and Making an International Trade Plan
制定国际贸易计划

Can I do international trade? This question is essentially the same as "Can I start my own business?" which is a dream shared by millions. Of the countless entrepreneurs who try, many fail, some succeed to varying degrees, and only a few achieve great success. Therefore, to start any kind of business, we need to plan and prepare carefully, considering all necessary aspects.

1.1.1 Preliminary Considerations before Business Plan
贸易计划前的初步考虑

This chapter will discuss the preliminary considerations that anyone intending to export or import should consider. Before beginning to export or import, a number of considerations should be addressed to avoid costly mistakes and difficulties. Those companies that begin doing international trade or continue to do trade without any preparations will run into problems sooner or later. Therefore, it is very important to have a solid business plan before you start your company. Such a plan will help your business better and determine whether it is likely to be profitable. Advice on preparing business plans is available from **the Small Business Administration of Ministry of Industry and Information Technology of the People's Republic of China** and from small business development centers, books, software, and the Internet.

中华人民共和国工业和信息化部中小企业司

Usually, the contents of trade plan include the types of trade and products; potential markets, market segments, and competition; promotion and sales plan; organization and personnel; **import/export logistics**; schedule of start-up activities and so forth. To develop such a complete plan, the first thing we should do is the preparatory work before carrying out international trade, also need to conduct market research, and then consider how to finance, how to find a supplier and set forth the agreement, understand the regulations of foreign trade, how to avoid import and export fraud and so on.

进出口物流

1.1.1.1 The Basic Conditions for Carrying out Trade
开展贸易的基本条件

Importing and exporting require expertise in purchasing, marketing, finance, and entrepreneurship. Aspiring traders should take courses or read books on starting and managing small businesses. Initial capital is needed for registration, office setup, and operational costs. If buying goods, upfront payments for merchandise, transportation, and storage are often required. Agents or brokers may reduce capital needs but still incur communication and office expenses. Savings or loans (with experience and collateral) are essential for living costs if transitioning from a job.

Global knowledge is crucial, including geography, international relations, and currency strengths. Stay informed through newspapers like China Daily or news platforms like BBC. Familiarity with foreign cultures and languages is vital to avoid miscommunication. Use clear, simple language, avoid idioms or slang, and respect cultural norms. Learning basic local language or hiring qualified translators ensures accuracy in communication.

坚持不懈
注重细节

Success in international trade demands **persistence** and **attention to detail**. Early stages may involve months without orders, requiring patience and stress management. Regularly evaluate customer pipelines and adapt strategies if losses persist. Detail-oriented planning is critical, as international trade involves complex logistics like shipping, customs, and compliance. Understanding customer needs and precise product specifications is key to building trust and long-term relationships. While sourcing products is important, selling is often more challenging; having a buyer with clear specifications simplifies the process. Delivering exactly what buyers want ensures success in this competitive field.

1.1.1.2 Market Research

市场调研

Market research is vital to carry out international trade. Even if you have some experience in international trade, it's unwise to rush into the market that has not been investigated. Most small business are started with inadequate market studies or with none at all. Yet a market study is almost the only way to support your income projections and your marketing plan. Market research can help us analyze the realization of income, and can help us complete the market research program. Market study before trade will help to analyze how to market them and to whom to sell them.

The following Table 1–1 is a typical outline for a report on the market for any product being export from one country to another. If you can produce or buy this kind of information before you begin, you might decide to try another product or another market. If you decide to go ahead, your chances of success will be increased considerably. Moreover, a solid market study looks very good to potential investors and lenders.

Table 1.1 Example of market study on an exporting product

Basic Information
· Product name and HS number
· Country of origin, exporting country, importing country
Regulations
· Exporting country controls and taxes
· Importing country controls and taxes
· Import restrictions, quotas, and so forth
· Import duties
· Marketing and labeling laws
· Other regulations
Supply and Demand
· Availability of supply in the exporting country
· Domestic production less imports in the importing country (five years' statistics)
· Imports for consumption (five years' statistics with trend calculation)
· Percent of product for consumption that is imported
· Industry experts' perception of current and future supply and demand in the importing country
· The perception of selected buyers with the same business scope
Competition
· Survey of producers in the importing country
· Description of selected producers
· Sources of imports (countries), with import market share of each
· Average FOB, CFR and CIF prices from each country
Target Market
· The market and market segments
· Characteristics of important market
· Kinds of industrial users
· Main industrial users and a brief description
Product Description
· Main types/varieties of the product
· Required or desired product characteristics
· Required or desired packaging and labeling

continued

Distribution
• Normal distribution system in the importing country
• Principal importers and wholesalers
• Principal industrial distributors

Pricing
• Representative prices and markups at each level in the channel
• Price trends
• Discounts used in the trade

Promotion
• Methods of promotion used in the trade
• Promotional assistance usually provided to the exporters
• Approximate costs of this assistance

Logistics
• Steamship lines and airlines serving the route
• The usual transport mode for this kind of product
• Availability of vessels (planes) and cost of shipping
• Shipping term normally used
• Payment term normally used

Other Considerations
• Local laws on the product, label, distribution, pricing, promotion
• The distributor's and consumer's attitudes of acceptance to new suppliers
• Image of exporting country in the importing country

1.1.1.3 Sourcing International Trade Leads and Seeking Trading Partners
国际商贸信息的搜集及寻找交易伙伴

Here are some methods for sourcing international trade leads and finding trading partners.

公司网站

Company Websites: Establishing a professional website with product details and manufacturing facility images enhances credibility and attracts international buyers. SEO optimization is crucial for visibility.

B2B跨境电商平台

B2B Platforms: Registering on cross-border B2B platforms (e.g.,

Alibaba, Amazon, Global Sources) increases exposure and provides access to global trade opportunities. These platforms also improve supply chain efficiency.

Search Engines: A primary tool for finding suppliers, with 42% of international buyers using them. Advanced search techniques, such as combining product names with country-specific domain suffixes, can yield targeted results. 搜索引擎

Trade Associations: Industry-specific organizations provide valuable resources, including member directories and networking opportunities. They are more detailed and active in developed economies. 行业协会

Yellow Pages: Both traditional and online yellow pages offer categorized business listings. Online versions are increasingly popular and can be accessed globally. 黄页

Trade Fairs: Attending trade fairs (e.g., Canton Fair, Exhibitions in Germany) is an effective way to connect with potential partners, learn about markets, and gather industry-specific contacts. 贸易博览会

Embassies: Chinese and foreign embassies provide trade-related information and can connect businesses with local agents or procurement needs. 大使馆

Social Media: Platforms like Facebook, LinkedIn, and Twitter are essential for brand-building and sourcing leads through interactive engagement and networking. 社交媒体

Customs and Commercial Databases: Reliable sources of trade intelligence, offering detailed import/export transaction data. Some B2B platforms also provide high-quality business contact databases. 海关数据库和商业数据库

Other Sources: Inspection institution websites, forums, publications, referrals, and competitor analysis can also yield valuable trade leads.

In summary, leveraging a combination of digital tools, industry networks, and traditional methods is key to effectively sourcing international trade leads and finding reliable trading partners. Creativity and persistence are essential in this competitive field.

1.1.1.4 Establishing Business Relations
建立商业联系

To build business relationships, exporters typically start with **email direct marketing**, as it is the most convenient and cost-effective method. Other approaches include adding connections on social media, sending faxes, making international calls, or attending trade fairs. When making phone calls, prepare a list of topics in advance. For trade fairs, selecting the right event, preparing thoroughly, and following up promptly are crucial for success.

电子邮件直接营销

Key principles for effective email communication are as follows:

Subject Line: Draft a short and attention-grabbing subject line.

主题行

Conciseness: Keep the email body brief and to the point.

简洁性

Strengths: Highlight your strengths succinctly.

优势

Simplicity: Use simple language, especially if the recipient is not a native English speaker.

简单性

Call to Action: End with a clear call to action.

行动号召

In summary, emails should be straightforward and concise, catering to the short attention spans of international buyers and cultural preferences for **low-context communication**.

低语境沟通的文化偏好

1.1.2 Main Contents of Trade Plan
贸易计划的主要内容

1.1.2.1 Issues to Be Considered in Making Trade Plans
考虑因素

Starting an international trade business involves addressing several key issues to ensure success. Below is a condensed overview of the essential considerations:

Objectives: Determine why you want to start an import/export business. If your goal is to make money, focus on detailed financial planning. If you're experimenting or gaining experience, a less formal

目标

approach may suffice.

Necessary Conditions: Assess if you have the required skills and resources, such as business training, capital, product knowledge, buyer contacts, travel experience, or foreign language proficiency. Decide whether to focus on importing, exporting, or both initially.   必备条件

Types of Trade: Choose between self-support trade (directly buying/selling goods) or acting as a commission agent/broker. Self-support trade requires significant capital and involves higher risk, while brokerage offers flexibility but may lack formal contracts. Consider legal structures, liability, and taxation when registering your business.   贸易形式

Target Market: Identify a specific and reachable market. Focus on customers with appropriate income levels, lifestyles, and geographic locations. Use B2B platforms (e.g., Alibaba), attend trade fairs (e.g., Canton Fair), or explore cross-border e-commerce (e.g., Amazon) to reach your audience.   目标市场

Product Selection: Choose products you know well or have a market for. Ensure the product is available in sufficient quantities and can be transported and cleared through customs. Research domestic competitors to find your niche.   产品类型

Sources of Supply: Work directly with manufacturers to reduce costs. Consider factors like a country's reputation for quality, cost structure, transportation, and customs duties when selecting suppliers.   供应商

Shipping Methods: Decide on shipping methods based on cargo size, value, and fragility. Options include couriers, airfreight, sea, or land transport. Understand international shipping terms like FOB and CIF.   运输方式

Payment Methods: Use secure and cost-effective payment methods, such as letters of credit, document against payment, or modern options like PayPal. Be cautious of fraudulent buyers.   付款方式

Regulations: Comply with national and international laws, including bilateral and multilateral agreements. Stay updated on   贸易惯例及法规

regulations from both exporting and importing countries.

营业场所　　***Business Premises:*** Start with a home office to save costs, especially for small businesses. Equip it with essential tools like a computer, phone, and printer.

服务商　　***Service Companies:*** Engage professionals like accountants, attorneys, and insurance brokers. Use freight forwarders, customs brokers, and courier services as needed. Seek guidance from industry associations as your business grows.

资金来源　　***Capital and Profitability***: Calculate start-up costs, including equipment and operating expenses. Project sales, income, and expenses to determine profitability. If short on funds, explore financing options.

By addressing these issues systematically, you can build a solid foundation for your international trade business.

1.1.2.2　Making a Trade Plan

制定贸易计划

As mentioned before, it is very important to make a useful and reliable business plan before starting a business. Such a plan will help you plan your business better and determine whether it is likely to be profitable. The preparatory work before carrying out the international trade is a very complicated process. It involves a lot of research and analysis about their company and target markets. The following Table 1.2 is a suggested outline for an import/export business plan, with some annotation. We can find other outlines in books on business planning and on Internet.

Table 1.2　Examples of Trade Plan

Cover Page
Table of Contents
Executive Summary （This should give the highlight of each of the sections that follows. Most people who read business plans look through the summary and then read other sections only as needed for clarification or additional details.）
Narrative Section （This section of the plan describes in words, with graphs if you wish, how your business will be set up and operated. It can be from 12 to 15 pages in length.）

continued

Cover Page
• Type of trade and products
Whether you plan to import or export, and your sources of supply, types of products, and product characteristics including packages, labels, and brands.
• Potential markets, market segments, and competition
A description of the likely consumers of your product, the channels of distribution through which you will reach them, and your main competitors.
• Promotion and sales plan
Your anticipated strategy with regard to pricing, promotion and selling, that is, how you actually cause your customers to buy your product.
• Organization and personnel
A description of the company's managers, employees, and sources of assistance, such as your advisers, accountant, banker, and attorney.
• Import/export logistics
How you expect to handle the functions of packing, shipping, insurance, documentation, and so forth.
• Schedule of start–up activities
A list of steps in starting the business with a target date for completion of each, and a final target date for opening the doors and beginning to operate.
Financial Section
This section of the plan shows, in numbers, what you expect in the way of sales, income, expenses, and other financial aspects of the business.
• Schedule of start–up costs
• Proforma income and expense statements
• Proforma cash flow statements
• Proforma balance sheets
• Main assumptions used in preparing the financial projections
• Financial analysis
Supporting Documents
This section can contain any document that will establish that the information in your plan is correct or that will be useful to the reader, for example:
• Pictures of your products
• A summary of your market study
• Sample promotional literature
• Owner's resumes

continued

Financial Section
· Detailed costs for a sample import or export transaction
· Lease agreement for office space
· Detailed sales forecasts
· Letters of intent from suppliers

1.2 Be Familiar with International Trade Laws and Regulations
熟悉国际贸易法律法规

国际贸易公约，国际贸易惯例，各国的商业法律法规

The legal system of international trade mainly consists of three parts: international trade conventions, international trade customs and practices, national commercial laws and regulations. In the process of international trade, the parties wish to adopt the law applicable to the country that they are familiar with. But because people come from different countries or regions, it may be controversial on which national law should be used. Therefore, in the long-term trade practice, we are willing to adopt a generally accepted international trade contract or practice, and sometimes willing to apply the law of a certain country in the contract. So international traders should be familiar with international trade conventions, international trade customs and practices, national business laws and regulations.

1.2.1 National Business Laws and Regulations
各国法律法规

The existing international commercial conventions and practices are still not complete uniform rules about all the fields of international trade, and even the existing conventions and rules of international trade have not yet been recognized and adopted by all countries and regions. When a person or enterprise is engaged in economic and trade activities across the border, it may also choose a national law applicable to the settlement of contract, dispute according to the rules of conflict of laws. Therefore, the national law has a great influence on the international sale of goods.

1.2.1.1 Understanding Anglo-American Law System and Continental Law System
英美法系和大陆法系

At present, **the common law system and civil law system** have a great influence on legal formulation of international trade and economic cooperation. In the countries of continental law system, the commercial law is mainly used in the form of codification. The layout is divided into two: one is the separation of civil and commercial form, that is, the civil law and commercial law were compiled into two laws, in such a country generally compiled the sale of goods acts into the civil code, included a special section or in the chapter on debt which to be explicitly stipulated in the civil law. In addition, it is also specified the special matters of transaction in the code of commercial law. Countries that adopt this approach are France, Germany, Japan and other countries. The other is a combination of the civil law and commercial law which separated in some states. Namely, there is no separate commercial code, and the commercial law, including the content of the civil code is incorporated into the civil code, such as Italy and other countries. In the countries of Anglo-American law system, commercial law mainly take the form of specific regulations. Precedent is an important source of commercial law in the countries of Anglo-American legal system.

> 普通法系和大陆法系

1.2.1.2 Chinese National Law on International Business
中国国内关于国际商务的法律

In China, after **the Civil Code of the People's Republic of China** officially came into effect on January 1, 2021, the Contract Law was integrated into the "Contract" section of the Civil Code, becoming a part of it. The "Contract" section of the Civil Code further refined and optimized the provisions of the Contract Law, making it better

> 《中华人民共和国民法典》

suited to the needs of modern socio-economic activities. There are some other important laws and regulations about international economic and trade activities, which have covered a very wide range of fields, such as **Maritime law of P.R.C.（1992）, Company law** of the People's Republic of China revised in 2018, **the Law of the People's Republic of China Note** revised in 2004, **Insurance law** of P.R.C. revised in 2015.

海商法，公司法
票据法，保险法

1.2.1.3　The Legal System of Chinese Foreign Trade Control
中国对外贸易管制的法律体系

China's foreign trade control system is mainly composed of **Customs supervising system, tariff system, foreign trade operators' management system, import and export licensing system, the Entry-Exit inspection and quarantine system, foreign exchange management system, trade remedy system,** etc. In order to ensure the implementation of the system of trade control, China has basically established and gradually perfected the legal system of foreign trade, which take the Foreign Trade law of the People's Republic of China as the core, promulgated and implemented in 1994, revised in 2022, and implements the foreign trade control independently in accordance with the relevant provisions of these laws, administrative regulations, departmental rules, and China's implementation of international conventions.

海关监管制度，关税制度，对外贸易经营者管理制度，进出口许可制度，出入境检验检疫制度，外汇管理制度及贸易救济制度

Currently there are some laws on management of foreign trade in China, such as **the Foreign Trade Law of the People's Republic of China, the Customs Law, the Law of the people's Republic of China on Import and Export Commodity Inspection Law，the Law of the People's Republic of China on the Entry and Exit Animal and Plant Quarantine,** the Law of the People's Republic of China on the Prevention and Control of Solid Waste, the Frontier Health Quarantine Law of the P.R.C.，the Law of Wildlife Protection

对外贸易法，海关法，进出口商品检验法，进出境动植物检疫法

of People's Republic of China, the Drug Administration Law of the people's Republic of China, the Law of the people's Republic of China on the Protection of Cultural Relics, the Food Hygiene Law of the People's Republic of China.

Moreover, there are some **administrative rules and regulations** related to foreign trade control in China, such as Regulations on Technology Import and Export Administration of the People's Republic of China, Regulations on Technology Import and Export Administration of the People's Republic of China, Regulations of the People's Republic of China on Import and Export Duties, Regulations on Customs Protection of intellectual property rights of P.R.C., Regulations of the People's Republic of China on the Protection of Wild Plants, Regulations on Foreign Exchange Control of the People's Republic of China, Regulation on Countervailing of the People's Republic of China, Regulations of the People's Republic of China on Anti-dumping, Regulation on Safeguard Measures of the People's Republic of China, etc.

行政法规

Furthermore, there are a lot of **ministerial rules** about the management of international trade in China, such as Management Rules of Goods Import License, Management Rules of Goods Export License, Management Measures on Cargo Automatic Import License, Management Measures on Verification of Export Proceeds, Measures for the Administration of Imported Drugs, Measures for the Administration of Radioactive Drugs, Measures for the Administration of Import and Export Licenses for Dual-Use Items and Technologies, etc.

部门规章

All kinds of **international treaties or agreements** to which the People's Republic of China is a contracting party or participating party, although they do not belong to the category of domestic law of our country, in terms of its effectiveness they can be regarded as one of the sources of law in our country. Mainly include: the relevant bilateral or multilateral trade agreements signed by China during the

国际条约或协定

accession to the World Trade Organization, International Convention on the Simplification and Harmonization of Customs Systems (also known as the Kyoto Convention), Convention on International Trade in Endangered Species of Wild Fauna and Flora (Montreal protocol for short), International Convention on Substances that Deplete the Ozone Layer, International Convention on Psychotropic Substances, London Guidelines for the Exchange of Information on Chemicals in International Trade, International Convention on the Prior Informed Consent Procedure for Certain Hazardous Chemicals and Pesticides in International Trade (also known as the Rotterdam Convention), the Basel Convention on the Control of Transboundary Movements of Hazardous Wastes and Their Disposal, Convention on Establishing the World Intellectual Property Organization, etc.

1.2.2　International Trade Conventions
国际贸易公约

1.2.2.1　Convention Relating to Contracts of International Sale of Goods
有关国际贸易货物销售合同方面的公约

(1) United Nations Convention on Contracts for the International Sale of Goods (CISG)
联合国国际货物销售合同公约

Status: United Nations Convention on Contracts for the International Sale of Goods (Vienna, 1980) (CISG) | United Nations Commission On International Trade Law (这是一个网址)

The United Nations Convention on Contracts for the International Sale of Goods (CISG; the Vienna Convention for short) is a treaty that is a uniform international sales law. As of the end of 2024, it has been ratified by 94 states that account for a significant proportion of world trade, making it one of the most successful international uniform laws. Turkmenistan was the most recent state to ratify the Convention, having acceded to it on April 5, 2022.

The CISG was developed by the United Nations Commission on

International Trade Law (UNCITRAL), and was signed in Vienna in 1980. The CISG is sometimes referred to as the Vienna Convention (but is not to be confused with other treaties signed in Vienna). It came into force as a multilateral treaty on January 1, 1988, after being ratified by 11 countries.

Generally, the CISG is deemed to be incorporated into (and supplant) any otherwise applicable domestic law(s) with respect to a transaction in goods between parties from different Contracting States.

The CISG has been regarded as a success for the UNCITRAL, as the Convention has been accepted by states from "every geographical region, every stage of economic development and every major legal, social and economic system".

The objectives of the CISG are: To adopt uniform rules governing contracts for the international sale of goods; To adopt uniform rules that account for different social, economic, and legal system; To contribute to the removal of legal barriers in international trade; To promote the development of international trade.

The CISG is divided into four parts: Part I: Sphere of Application and General Provisions; Part II: Formation of the Contract (Articles 14-24); Part III: Sale of goods, obligations of the seller, obligations of the buyer, passing of risk, obligations common to both buyer and seller; Part IV: Final Provisions (Articles 89-101) include how and when the Convention comes into force, permitted reservations and declarations, and the application of the Convention to international sales where both States concerned have the same or similar law on the subject.

The CISG applies to contracts of the sale of goods between parties whose places of business are in different States, when the States are Contracting States (Article 1 (1) (a)). Given the significant number of Contracting States, this is the usual path to the CISG's applicability.

《公约》的目标

《公约》的适用范围。根据《公约》规定，适用本公约的合同，其主体必须是具备以下条件：a.双方当事人的营业地必须处在不同的国家；b.双方当事人的营业地所在国必须是缔约国[第一条第1款（a）项]，或者虽然不是缔约国，但如果根据国际私法规则导致适用某一缔约国的法律，也可以适用本公约[第一条第1款（b）项]。比如，

一个由德国贸易商和泰国贸易商签订的合同中规定，仲裁地点在悉尼，适用澳大利亚法律。根据第一条第1款（b）项的规定，就会导致公约的适用，因此很多国家加入公约时会做出保留。

1986年12月11日，中国交存核准书，在提交核准书时，提出了两项保留意见：(1)不同意扩大《公约》的适用范围，只同意《公约》适用于缔约国的当事人之间签订的合同。(2)不同意用书面以外的其他形式订立、修改和终止合同。2013年1月，中国政府正式通知联合国秘书长，撤回对《联合国国际货物销售合同公约》所作"不受公约第十一条及与第十一条内容有关的规定的约束"的声明，该撤回已正式生效。

The CISG also applies if the parties are situated in different countries (which need not be Contracting States) and the conflict of law rules lead to the application of the law of a Contracting State. For example, a contract between a German trader and a Thailand trader may contain a clause that arbitration will be in Sydney under Australian law with the consequence that the CISG would apply. A number of States have declared they will not be bound by this condition.

The CISG is intended to apply to commercial goods and products only. With some limited exceptions, the CISG does not apply to personal, family, or household goods, nor does it apply to auctions, ships, aircraft, or intangibles and services. The position of computer software is "controversial" and will depend upon various conditions and situations.

China acceded to the CISG in 1986. But China excluded two stipulations of the CISG when submitting the instruments of ratification and accession, i.e. article 11 and (b) of (1) of article 1. The Chinese government formally notified the UN secretary general to withdraw a declaration of the United Nations Convention on Contracts for the international sale of goods in January 2013, which is not subject to the provisions of article 11 and the provisions relating to the provisions of article eleventh. The withdrawal has officially entered into force.

(2) The Two Hague Convention on the Unification of the International Sale of Goods
海牙两个关于国际货物买卖合同的公约

The 1964 Hague Conventions include the Uniform Law on the International Sale of Goods (ULIS) and the Uniform Law on the Formation of Contracts for International Sale of Goods (ULFIS), developed by UNIDROIT. Adopted on April 25, 1964, and effective from August 18, 1972, these conventions aimed to standardize international sales laws. However, only nine countries, including Belgium, Germany, Italy, and the UK, have ratified or acceded to them, limiting their global impact.

(3) Convention on the Limitation Period of 1974 and 1980
关于合同的时效期限的两个公约

The Convention on the Limitation Period in the International Sale of Goods (the "Limitation Convention"), prepared by UNCITRAL, establishes uniform rules for the time limits on legal actions related to international sales contracts due to the passage of time. Adopted in 1974 and amended in 1980 to align with the United Nations Convention on Contracts for the International Sale of Goods (CISG), it aims to harmonize limitation periods globally. The 1980 Protocol updated the Convention, which entered into force on August 1, 1988. As of February 2016, 30 states have ratified or acceded to it, while others, like Brazil and Russia, have signed but not ratified. The Convention applies only to international transactions, excluding domestic sales, which remain governed by national laws. China has not joined either the 1974 or 1980 Limitation Convention.

1.2.2.2 Conventions Relating to International Payment
有关国际支付方面的公约

(1) Geneva Convention on the Unification of laws Relating to Bills of Exchange and Promissory Notes
日内瓦统一汇票和本票公约

Convention on the Unification of the Law Relating to Bills of Exchange and Promissory Notes is also known as Convention Providing a Uniform of Law for Bills of Ex-change and Promissory Notes 1930 (ULB), was made and approved by the International Union on June 7, 1930 at the first uniform meeting of the negotiable instruments law in Geneva, which came into effect from January 1, 1934.

Geneva unified law system only solves the two-bill law systems conflict between France and Germany, and many European countries, Japan and some Latin American countries have adopted Geneva Conventions on the laws of negotiable instruments. Because of the provisions of the Geneva Convention are in conflict with the traditions and practices of the notes, the Anglo-American law system countries refused to accede to these conventions. Therefore, two major legal systems in the international law of negotiable instruments have been formed, common law system and Geneva unified bill law system.

(2) Convention on International Bill of Exchange and International Promissory Note of the United Nations
联合国国际汇票和国际本票公约

The United Nations Convention on International Bills of Exchange and International Promissory Notes was adopted by the United Nations General Assembly, forty-third session in 1988, and open for signature. In accordance with the relevant provisions of the Convention, the Convention shall come into force upon approval or accession by at least 10 states, but till now, there are only 5 countries which have ratified this convention, the Convention has not yet entered into force.

(3) Convention on International Factoring (Ottawa, 1988)
国际保付代理公约

Convention on International Factoring was approved by UNIDROIT in 1988 at Ottawa and came into force in 1995. And till now, more than 130 countries have acceded to it.

1.2.2.3 International Conventions Relating to the Carriage of Goods
有关货物运输的国际公约

(1) Conventions Relating to International Marine Transport
有关海洋运输的国际公约

There are four international conventions which play an important role in the unification of the relevant laws and regulations of the bill of lading, such as **International Convention for the Unification of Certain Rules of Law Relating to Bill of Lading** (Hague Rules for short) 统一提单若干法律规定的国际公约（海牙规则）, Protocol to Amend the International Convention for the Unification of Certain Rules of Law Relating to Bill of Lading (Hague-Visby Rules for short), United Nations Convention of the Carriage of

Goods by Sea,1978（Hamburg Rules for short）, and United Nations Convention on Contracts for the International Carriage of Goods Wholly or Partly by Sea（Rotterdam Rules for short）.

·Hague Rules 海牙规则

The Hague Rules of 1924 is an international convention to impose minimum standards upon commercial carriers of goods by sea. Previously, only the common law provided protection to cargo-owners; but the Hague Rules should not be seen as a "consumers' charter" for shippers because the 1924 Convention actually favored carriers and reduced some of their obligations to shippers.

The Hague Rules represented the first attempt by the international community to find a workable and uniform means of dealing with the problem of ship owners regularly excluding themselves from all liability for loss or damage to cargo.

The Hague Rules form the basis of national legislation in almost all of the world's major trading nations, and probably cover more than 90 percent of world trade. The Hague Rules have been updated by two protocols, but neither addressed the basic liability provisions, which remain unchanged.

·Hague-Visby Rules 维斯比规则

The Hague-Visby Rules, an updated version of the 1924 Hague Rules, govern international sea carriage of goods. Amended in 1968 and 1979（SDR Protocol）, they aim to balance carrier and shipper interests by imposing minimum obligations on carriers. While some countries adopted the Hague-Visby Rules, others retained the 1924 Hague Rules or did not adopt the 1979 amendments. The Rules provide less cargo-owner protection than pre-1924 English common law.

·Hamburg Rules 汉堡规则

The Hamburg Rules, adopted in 1978, govern the international goods shipment by sea, aiming to create uniform legal standards and address developing countries' concerns. Effective from November 1, 1992, they were ratified by 34 countries by October 2014. Some nations, like China, drafted their own maritime laws referencing the Hague, Hague–Visby, and Hamburg Rules, while others lack clear regulations. This inconsistency complicates international trade, increasing costs and hindering goods transfer, prompting calls for unified global maritime transport rules.

· Rotterdam Rules 鹿特丹规则

The Rotterdam Rules, a treaty updating maritime carriage laws, aim to modernize and unify international trade regulations, replacing aspects of the Hague, Hague–Visby, and Hamburg Rules. They establish a comprehensive legal framework for door-to-door shipments involving sea transport. As of October 2015, only three states have ratified the Rules, which require 20 ratifications to take effect. While 24 countries, including Spain and Sweden, have signed, major shipping nations like China, Japan, and the UK have not.

(2) Conventions Relating to International Land Transport
有关陆路运输的国际公约

国际铁路货物联运协定（国际货协）

国际铁路运输公约（国际货约）

Conventions governing international land transport include the **Berne Convention concerning International Carriage by Rail (COTIF)** and the **Agreement concerning International Carriage of Goods by Rail (CMIC)**. COTIF consolidates the International Carriage of Goods by Rail (CIM) and Carriage of Passengers and Luggage by Rail (CIV). CIM, signed in 1961 and effective from 1975, has 28 member states, including France, Germany, and Iran. CMIC, established in 1951 and revised in 1974, includes 12 members, such as China, North Korea, and former Soviet Union countries. China joined CMIC in 1953, and its rail transport follows CMIC provisions. The overlapping membership between CIM and CMIC facilitates cross-border rail transport, enhancing international goods movement.

(3) Conventions Relating to International Air Transport
有关航空运输的国际公约

统一国际航空运输某些规则的公约（华沙公约）

The **Warsaw Convention**, signed in 1929, regulates liability for international air carriage of passengers, luggage, and goods. China joined in 1957, and it entered into force there in 1958. The Convention was amended by the **Hague Protocol** in 1955 (effective in 1963, China acceded in 1975) and the **Guadalajara Convention** in 1960 (China has not joined). The Hague Protocol, ratified by 137 of 152 Warsaw parties, is binding in French, with English and Spanish versions. The **Montreal Convention**, adopted in 1999, modernized the Warsaw regime, addressing compensation for air disasters and unifying rules for international air carriage. As of 2024, 137 of 193 ICAO members, including China, the EU, the US, and others, have ratified it. Both conventions aim to standardize and update international air transport regulations.

海牙议定书

瓜达拉哈拉公约

统一国际航空运输某些规则的公约（蒙特利尔公约）

(4) Conventions Relating to International Multimodal Transport
有关国际多式联运的公约

The **United Nations Convention on international multimodal transport of goods** was adopted by the 84 members of UNCTAD unanimously at the second meeting of the United Nations Conference on international multimodal transport in Geneva on May 24, 1980. The Convention consists of 40 articles and an annex. The structure is divided into eight parts, such as general, documents, multimodal transport operator liability, shipper's liability, claims and litigation, supplement regulations, customs matters and final provisions and so on. China has signed it. But it did not attract the necessary number of ratifications and thus has not entered into force.

联合国国际多式联运公约

1.2.2.4　International Convention on the Harmonized Commodity Description and Coding System
关于商品分类的国际公约

The Harmonized System (HS) is an internationally standardized classification framework for goods, governed by the World Customs Organization (WCO) under the International Convention on the

Harmonized Commodity Description and Coding System. Adopted in 1988 and ratified by over 160 countries, the HS provides a universal "language" for trade by assigning unique 6-digit codes to products (e.g., 0902.10 for green tea), with national extensions (e.g., 8-10 digits in China).

The key Features are as follows:

· Structure: Covers 5,000+ product groups across 97 chapters, organized by material, function, or industry.

· Global Adoption: Used for customs tariffs, trade policies, and statistical reporting by 98% of world trade.

· Dynamic Updates: Revised every 5 years (e.g., HS 2022 added drones and 3D printers).

The functions including:

· Ensures consistency in duty calculation (e.g., WTO tariff schedules).

· Supports trade agreements (e.g., origin rules under FTAs).

· Facilitates automation in customs clearance.

The HS reduces trade costs and disputes, making it indispensable to modern supply chains. Non-compliance risks shipment delays or penalties.

1.2.3　International Trade Customs and Practices
　　　　国际贸易惯例

The international trade practice, also known as the "international business practice", "international trade regulations", are the widely recognized and accepted habitual practices, rules, and interpretations by both buyers and sellers and others engaged in related international trade activities, and to serve as a dispute resolution regulation if it doesn't breach the laws, public welfare, bone fides or other contract items. Because international trade covers a very wide field, the range of international trade customs and practice is relatively wide. The following are the main types of international trade practices.

1.2.3.1 International Customs and Practices Relating to Trade Terms
有关国际贸易术语的国际惯例

In order to standardize the understanding of the seller and buyer relating to their obligations in international sales agreement, various nomenclatures have been developed that use abbreviations, such as ex-works, FOB, CIF, landed, and so on. While these shorthand abbreviations can be useful, they can also be sources of confusion. The International Chamber has developed the "**Incoterms**", which were revised in 2020. There are also **the Revised American Foreign Trade Definitions 1941** and **the Warsaw-Oxford Rules 1932**. Although these abbreviated terms of sales are similar, they also differ from nomenclature to nomenclature, and it is important to specify in the sales agreement which nomenclature is being used when an abbreviation is utilized. For the details of the above customs and practices, please refer to Chapter 3.

国际贸易术语解释通则

1941年美国对外贸易定义修订本

1932年华沙—牛津规则

1.2.3.2 Customs and Practices Relating to International Settlement
有关国际货款收付的国际惯例

（1）Uniform Customs and Practice for Documentary Credits
跟单信用证统一惯例

The Uniform Customs and Practice for Documentary Credits (UCP), established by the ICC in 1933, standardizes the use of letters of credit in international trade. Regularly updated, the latest version, UCP600, took effect on July 1, 2007. It clarifies the rights, responsibilities, and payment terms for all parties, resolving conflicts and reducing confusion caused by differing national rules. Used in over 175 countries, the UCP governs 11%–15% of global trade, amounting to over a trillion US dollars annually, and is recognized as the international standard for credit operations.

（2）The Uniform Rules for Collection
托收统一规则

In order to unify the collection business practices, to alleviate the contradictions and disputes caused by all parties involved, the ICC (International Chamber of Commerce) made the Uniform Rules for Collection (URC for short) in 1958. And then the URC was revised in 1978 and 1995. Its latest version is URC522 (1995 Revision) (ICC Publication No.522). The URC has been widely used by bankers from many countries since its publication, it has become the international customs in collection business.

1.2.3.3 Customs and Practices Relating to International Transportation Insurance
运输与保险方面的国际惯例

(1) Institute Cargo Clauses

英国伦敦保险协会的货物保险条款

_{伦敦协会货物保险条款}

The **London Institute Cargo Clauses (I.C.C.)**, developed by the Institute of London Underwriters, are widely adopted in international marine insurance. Originating in the 19th century and first established in 1912, they have undergone several revisions, with the latest version effective from January 1, 2009. These standardized clauses, maintained by Lloyd's and London insurers, significantly influence global marine insurance practices and are used by the most countries worldwide.

(2) York-Antwerp Rules

约克·安特卫普规则

The York-Antwerp Rules, first published in 1890 and last amended in 2016, govern general average adjustments in maritime law. Revised versions, such as the 2004 and 2016 editions, coexist with older rules, allowing parties to choose which version to apply. Although not an international convention, these rules are widely adopted in charter contracts and bills of lading, simplifying the adjustment process, reducing disputes, and aligning with modern shipping practices. They are recognized as international customs, widely accepted by the global shipping and insurance industries.

1.2.3.4 Customs and Practices Relating to International Arbitration
国际仲裁方面的惯例

The **UNCITRAL Arbitration Rules**, established in 1976 and revised in 2010, provide a framework for resolving disputes through arbitration. Effective from August 15, 2010, they are widely used in ad hoc arbitration, investor-state disputes, inter-state arbitration, and commercial arbitration. Alongside **the New York Convention (1958)** and the **UNCITRAL Model Law (1985)**, they form the foundation of international commercial arbitration. Recognized as highly successful, these rules are frequently adopted in contracts or after disputes arise, ensuring a standardized approach to arbitration globally.

联合国国际贸易法委员会仲裁规则

关于承认和执行外国仲裁裁决的公约（简称1958年纽约公约）

1.3 Obtaining the International Trade Qualification
获得对外贸易经营者资格

1.3.1 Organizing for Export and Import Operations
开展进出口贸易采取的形式

Exporting and importing require specialized knowledge, with organizational structures varying by company size and trade volume. In small firms, one person may handle all export or import tasks, while larger companies develop specialized roles within dedicated departments.

Export Department: Often originating from sales or marketing, this department manages export orders, interfacing with freight forwarders, banks, insurers, shipping lines, and government agencies. Personnel handle manufacturing, packing, shipping, and collections, with responsibilities expanding as export volumes grow.

出口部门

Import Department: Typically emerging from purchasing, this department procures raw materials or finished goods from abroad. It liaises with foreign freight forwarders, customs brokers, banks, and

进口部门

insurers. Some Chinese manufacturers now import products previously made domestically due to overseas production shifts.

进出口部门

Combined Export and Import: Smaller companies often merge these functions, with one or two personnel managing both. As business grows, departments separate, though some roles（e.g., banking, freight forwarding）may remain consolidated. Larger firms assign personnel exclusively to exports or imports, streamlining operations.

1.3.2　Obtaining the Foreign Trade Dealer Qualification 取得对外贸易经营者资格

In China, conducting international trade requires an import-export license. Companies can engage in self-support export（handling all procedures themselves）or principal-agent export（delegating tasks to an agency）. Foreign trade dealers, as defined by the Foreign Trade Law of the P.R.C.（2004）, include legal entities, organizations, and individuals complying with relevant regulations. China operates a Record and Registration System for foreign trade operators. Under Article 9 of the Foreign Trade Law, dealers must register with the State Council's foreign trade department or its authorized body to import/export goods or technologies. Without registration, Customs will not process import/export declarations. Foreign trade dealers can also act as agents for others. **Establishing a trade company and obtaining international trade qualifications** typically involves several procedural steps.

开办贸易公司及申请进出口经营资格的流程

For New Entrants 新成立公司获取进出口经营权

- Register with the local Industrial and Commercial Administration Bureau for a business license including "Import and Export of Goods."
- Obtain an organization code certificate from the Quality and Technical Supervision Bureau.
- Open a bank account and register with the tax authority.

For Registered Enterprises 已注册企业获取进出口经营权

- Expand business scope to include import/export at the Industrial and Commercial Administration Bureau.
- Register with the Foreign Trade Authority, update tax registration, and register with Customs for declaration rights.
- Register with the General Administration of Quality Supervision for quarantine/inspection rights, and with the State Administration of Foreign Exchange for foreign exchange settlement.
- Complete China E-port registration.

1.3.3 Obtaining the International Trade Quota or License 获得国际贸易配额或许可文件

The import and export licensing system is a key non-tariff trade measure used globally to manage trade. In China, it regulates goods and technologies under three categories: prohibited, restricted, and free. Traders must determine a product's category using its HS code, as classifications are frequently updated based on international trade conditions. Updates can be tracked on websites like the Ministry of Commerce and General Administration of Customs.

Applying for Quota or License: 申请配额或许可证

Online Application: 网上申请

- Access the Ministry of Commerce's online system (http://cgov.mofcom.gov.cn).
- Submit the application form and required documents as per system instructions.
- Deliver printed documents to the nominated authority after online approval.

Written Application: 书面形式申请

- Submit printed forms and documents directly to the relevant authority (e.g., Agriculture Ministry for pesticides, Ministry of

Culture for artwork).

· The authority reviews the application and notifies the result online or via announcement. Once approved, the applicant collects the quota certificate or license. Traders must stay updated on policies to ensure compliance.

Exercises 练习

I. True (T) or False (F)

1. When exploring international markets, initiating with a micro-environmental assessment is essential for informed decision-making. (　)

2. If every country in the world uses the same currency, the world trade would be much tougher. (　)

3. In international trade, direct email marketing is widely utilized because it is convenient and cost-effective in establishing business relations. (　)

4. The free flow of international trade benefits all who participate in. (　)

5. The United States withdrew from the North American Free Trade Agreement (NAFTA) during the Obama administration. (　)

6. China International Import Expo (CIIE), which started in 2018, has greatly boosted imports. (　)

7. Canton Fair is the largest trade fair in China and an important international comprehensive exhibition. (　)

8. We can search for potential customers in a certain country by using domain name suffixes, such as ".cn" for China and ".fr" for France. (　)

9. Yandex is a preferred search engine for Russia, East Europe, and West Asian. (　)

10. When applying for import or export quotas or licenses,

submissions can only be made in written form. ( )

II. Multiple Choice Questions

1. A PEST analysis comprises of ( ) of the target market.

   A. political analysis

   B. economic analysis

   C. social analysis

   D. technological analysis

2. Which of the following contracts is applicable under the United Nations Convention on Contracts for the International Sale of Goods (CISG)? ( )

   A. A sales contract for goods signed between a Chinese company and a foreign merchant for the purpose of exporting products

   B. An international engineering contracting agreement

   C. An international technology licensing agreement

   D. An underwriting agreement for stocks

3. Foreign trade risks include ( ).

   A. commercial and credit risk

   B. political and legal risks

   C. cargo risk

   D. exchange risk

4. Which of the following statements is NOT true about social media marketing? ( )

   A. Social media marketing still relies on broadcasting.

   B. Exporters should identify key influences for brand-building.

   C. Exporters should post engaging contents to audience for brand-building.

   D. Exporters could add connections for establishing business relationships.

5. Generally speaking, a devaluation of RMB tends to ( ).

   A. reduce China's import

B. reduce China's export

C. promote China's import

D. promote China's export

6. Which is NOT an appropriate way of writing the first email to a prospective customer? (　)

A. Drafting an appealing subject line.

B. Being short and concise with your main body.

C. Elaborating on your strengths.

D. Using simple words.

7. Through customs databases, you expect to learn about (　) of a transaction.

A. the shipper

B. the consignee

C. the notify party

D. the details of the merchandise

8. The United Nations Convention on Contracts for the International Sale of Goods (1980, CISG) defines the scope of application for contracts. Which of the following scenarios should be governed by the CISG? (　)

A. The sale of goods between parties whose places of business are in the same Contracting State.

B. The sale of ships between parties whose places of business are in different Contracting States.

C. The sale of stocks between parties from different countries.

D. The sale of goods between parties whose places of business are in different Contracting States.

9. Which of the following are considered international commercial customs/practices? (　)*

A. Warsaw-Oxford Rules

B. York-Antwerp Rules

C. United Nations Convention on Contracts for the International Sale of Goods(CISG)

D. Uniform Rules for Collections(URC)

10. The CISG is applicable to which of the following transactions?(　)

A. Sale of ships

B. Sale of electricity

C. Sale of aircraft parts

D. Sale of stocks and bonds

III. Web Page Clipping

1.Please log onto the B2B platforms mentioned in this chapter, browse and choose one you like and clip one of its web pages. Select one company you like from the platform. Find out its homepage and the web page for the company profile, which for your reference, is mostly under the menu of "About" or "About Us".

2.Search on the Internet and find the top 10 foreign distributors or retailers in a certain country, and clip two of their web pages.

3.Find a product category you are interested in, search on the Internet for any trade fair in the category, find out its homepage and clip a web page.

IV. Group Tasks

1.A watchmaker designed a unique watch tailored for the Middle Eastern market. This watch converts local time to Muslim time, provides automatic prayer time reminders, and features a "compass" that always points to Mecca. Upon its launch, the watch became an instant hit. In contrast, a company exported 200 metric tons of duck meat to Iran, but the shipment was rejected by Iranian customs because the slaughtering method did not comply with Islamic regulations. Discuss in groups the reasons behind one exporter's failure and the other's success, and analyze the lessons from these two cases.

2.Write a market research plan for a certain product for export. Then conduct the research and write a report. The research report should include: the product, the research goal, the research plan, the research methods, and major findings. You should complete all the tasks in a group, including handing in one research report as a group.

V. Case Study

In the Internet era, knowledge of international trade geography may seem less important, as salespeople can simply search for any country online. However, proficiency in trade geography can sometimes help reduce logistics costs, while a lack of basic knowledge may lead to costly mistakes.

Mr. Chen, a seller on AliExpress, once faced a challenge when a buyer requested a set of plastic soap dishes to be shipped to Rota Island, located in the southern Mariana Islands in the Pacific. The order gave Chen a headache because the small island had no postal service and was surrounded by water, accessible only by small 8–10-seater planes.

"However, I noticed that the nearby Saipan Island has a post office, so I shipped it there and asked a local friend to coordinate pickup with the buyer on Rota Island," he explained. Since the soap box weighed only a few dozen grams, the Guangzhou-based seller spent just over 10 yuan on shipping, with delivery taking about six days.

Chen also encountered a buyer who listed their destination as "Menteneigeluo" (a mistranslated Chinese name). "At first, I thought, 'This oddly named little country must be quite advanced—it has great internet!'" But days later, the package was returned by the post office, which stated the country didn't exist. Upon checking the buyer's provided English name, Chen realized the blunder: "The guy had made up a Chinese name for us to ship to," he said, pointing to the word "Montenegro" on his computer. "That's clearly the Republic of Montenegro!" He advised buyers to always use correct country names to avoid failed deliveries. (Case adapted from Online Trade.)

Question: What lessons can be drawn from this case? What essential knowledge is required for conducting international trade?

Chapter 2

Business Negotiation and Signing the Contract

第二章　商务磋商和签订合同

◆ Learning Objectives

- Know the definition of business negotiation
- Understand the contents and the forms of business negotiation
- Master the general procedures of business negotiation
- Master how to sign an international sales contract

Identifying your target customers is just the first step in developing new markets. After that, business negotiations follow. Negotiations deal with major issues for concluding a deal: product, price, quality, quantity, time and place of delivery, terms of payment, resolving disputes, etc. A successful negotiation ends with a contract.

2.1 Contents and Forms of Business Negotiation
　　　商务磋商的内容和形式

Business negotiation refers to the whole process in which the buyer and the seller negotiate and finally reach an **agreement** on the terms of the transaction through certain **procedures** for the purpose of buying

协议

程序

and selling a certain commodity.

The contents of business negotiation for international sale of goods mainly include the quality, quantity, packaging, price, transportation, insurance, payment, commodity inspection, dispute settlement, claim, force majeure, and arbitration, etc. A transaction can only be concluded when the buyer and the seller reach an agreement.

International negotiations can be conducted orally, in writing, or indicated by acts. For example, an oral negotiation can be a face-to-face talk at your place, the importer's place or at a trade fair; or a talk on the phone or a video via conferencing platform. Oral negotiations are normally suitable for complex transactions that involve many issues, such as transactions of large equipment. A negotiation in writing includes **correspondence** through letters, **electronic data interchange (EDI)**, faxes, emails, instant messages, etc. Sometimes, traders also conclude a deal by performing an act, which occurs more at an **auction house** or a **commodity exchange**.

函电
电子数据交换
拍卖行
商品交易所
《联合国国际货物销售合同公约》
截止到
批准

The *United Nations Convention on Contracts for the International Sale of Goods* (CISG) is an important international convention that governs the majority of international sales of goods. **As of** 2020, it has been **ratified** by 94 countries, representing two-thirds of world trade. China is bound by it in our international business of merchandise trade. However, important non-signatories include the United Kingdom, India, most Middle East nations, South Africa, and several African countries.

2.2 General Procedures of Business Negotiations
商务磋商的一般程序

询盘，发盘，还盘和接受
必不可少的

Generally speaking, you go through four stages in a typical business negotiation: **enquiry, offer, counter-offer, and acceptance**, though some stages might be skipped or repeated under certain circumstances. Among the four stages, only "offer" and "acceptance" are **indispensable**.

If your negotiations turn out well, you'll make a deal. According to CISG, a deal is concluded the moment an acceptance of an offer becomes effective. In the following sections, we will examine key considerations for each stage from the exporter's perspective. However, since each stage may be initiated by either party, the rules and suggestions provided for exporters equally apply to importers in reciprocal scenarios.

2.2.1 Enquiry
询盘（询价/邀请发盘）

When you enter a clothing store, you may ask the shop owner, "Do you have jackets?" or "How much is this jacket? This is an enquiry in a domestic context. An enquiry in an international negotiation, also called an invitation to offer, is an action initiated by the importer or exporter, but mostly the importer, to ask the other party about the price and other terms of sale for certain products. Either party, for importing or exporting something, can enquire about one or more terms of sale, such as prices, catalogs, samples, quality and quantity, time and place of delivery, terms of payment, etc. It can be made orally or in writing with no fixed format. It is not binding on either you or the importer. It is not an indispensable stage for a negotiation, either. Regular business partners may skip it and go straight to making offers. An importer's enquiry may read: "Please **quote** the price of CIF London for Chinese **Rosin**, June shipment." An exporter's enquiry may be: "Can supply Chinese cotton, October shipment. If interested, please fax or email." The following Table 2.1 shows some examples of the inquiry.

报价

松香

Table 2.1 Useful Sentence & Example: Inquiry

1) Please quote your lowest/best CIF price for Model A.
2) Please quote FOB GUANGZHOU/CFR SYDNEY price for...
3) Our customer prefers his quotations to be CFR.
4) Please let us have your lowest/best quotation for Model A.
5) Please make us an offer CIF Kobe for/on 20 M/T beans.
6) Please make the best possible firm offer FOB GZ for/on 5 M/T...

2.2.2 Offer
发盘（报盘/报价/要约）

报价

In the above store-shopping example, the shop owner may respond to your enquiry by showing you the jacket and telling you its price— "It's 200 yuan." This makes a **quotation** in a domestic negotiation. A quotation is part of an offer. You may bargain, for sure, but if you like the jacket and accept the price, a deal is concluded and the shop owner must sell you the jacket under this price. Similarly, in an international negotiation, an offer

商业提议

is a **business proposal** made by the exporter or importer to express his/her wish to sell or buy particular goods under stated terms. An exporter can

递盘

make a "selling offer", and an importer a "buying offer", or a **bid**.

法律上有约束力的
发盘人

Offers in international negotiations mostly contain more terms and are more formal (including price, quantity, time of shipment, terms of payment, etc.). An offer, as defined by CISG, is **legally binding** on the **offeror**—who must honor the deal under the proposed terms. According to CISG, not all business proposals can be interpreted as "offers". A business proposal has to meet certain qualifications to be an "offers",

邀请发盘

otherwise, it's just an **invitation to make offers**, or referred to as

虚盘

"**non-firm offers**" or "**indefinite offers**" in practice. Then, what

"缔结一项针对一个或多个特定人的合同的提议，如果足够明确，并表明发盘人在得到接受时承受约束的意志，则构成发盘。"

"非向一个或一个以上特定的人提出的建议，仅应视为邀请发盘，除非提出建议的人明确表示相反的意向。"

kind of business proposals qualify for an "offer"? CISG states in Article 14（1）that "A proposal for concluding a contract addressed to one or more specific persons constitutes an offer if it is sufficiently definite and indicates the intention of the offeror to be bound in case of acceptance", and in Article 14（2）that "A proposal other than one addressed to one or more specific persons is to be considered merely as an invitation to make offers, unless the contrary is clearly indicated by the person making the offer". According to this definition, two criteria can be used to make the judgment: First, does it have a specific audience? You cannot address a general public in your proposal, like in an advertisement or a pamphlet, unless otherwise indicated. You have to address a specific audience by stating the name of the audience such as the name of an individual or a business. Second, your proposal has to be "sufficiently definite and indicate your intention to be bound" in case the offeree accepts your proposal.

But how to interpret "definite"? Unfortunately, traders around the world have different understandings regarding this. CISG states in Article 14（1）that "A proposal is sufficiently definite if it indicates the goods and expressly or implicitly fixes or makes provision for determining the quantity and the price". In other words, it considers a proposal definite as long as it has the name, quantity, and price of goods. However, this interpretation is rarely used in practice due to its difficulties in execution. A better solution remains the two criteria mentioned above—a specific audience and a clear intention and readiness to conclude the deal. Phrases like "subject to our final confirmation" or "for reference only" to indicate finality, if present, may also be used for reference. Without these phrases, however, you have to rely on yourself to figure out when you are bound by your offer and how you interpret offers made to you. You are highly suggested to ask the other party to clarify if you are not sure.

"一项报盘如果写明货物并且明示或暗示地规定数据和价格或规定如何确定梳理和价格，即为十分确定。"

An offer generally has to fix a **period for acceptance**. Please avoid making offers without fixing such a period. An offer takes effect when it reaches the offeree and his/her acceptance within that period is considered effective.

接受的有效期

Sometimes, you may want to **withdraw your offer** after you've made it. This often happens when you find an error in the offer or when the market has changed so much that executing the offer would bring you a great loss. Whether can an offer be withdrawn? It depends on the time it reaches the offeree. Article 15（1）of CISG states that "an offer becomes effective when it reaches the offeree." Therefore, it can be withdrawn "if the **withdrawal** reaches the offeree before or at the same time as the offer."（Article 15（2））. This implies that you need

撤回发盘

"发盘在送达受盘人时生效。"

撤回通知

a faster means of communication to withdraw your offer, which is sort of like you chase a horse by driving a car. But these stipulations don't apply when a means of communication that reaches the offeree **instantly**, such as telephone calls, emails, instant messages, etc., is employed, which means, the offer cannot be withdrawn in these cases.

即刻的

撤销

"在合同签订之前，发盘在受盘人发出接受通知之前可以撤销。"

What if the offer has already become effective? Can we **cancel** it? Article 16（1）of CISG states that "Until a contract is concluded, an offer may be revoked if the revocation reaches the offeree before he has dispatched an acceptance." But it cannot be revoked if the offer has fixed a period of time for acceptance, or has indicated by other means that it is irrevocable. Besides, if it is reasonable for the offeree to **rely on** the offer as being irrevocable and he/she has acted in reliance on the offer, it cannot be revoked, either. What's more, when a **rejection** reaches the offeror, the offer is **terminated**, even if it is **irrevocable**. The following Tabe 2.2 shows some examples of the offer.

信赖

拒绝通知

终止　不可撤销的

Table 2.2　Useful Sentences & Examples: Offer

1）We quote（for）Model A（at）EUR300. 00 per set CFR Hamburg.
2）It is difficult to quote without full details.
3）We are glad to quote as follows: 　Item No.　　Article & Specifications　　Unit Price（FOB G.Z.）   　123　　　　TV set Model A　　　　　　CAD 800   　124　　　　TV set Model B　　　　　　CAD 750
4）We offer subject to your reply here by 15th May our time 100M/T beans（at）JPY25 000 per M/T CFR Kobe, November shipment, payment by sight L/C.
5）We offer subject to our final confirmation/to prior sale/being unsold/to change without notice/to approval of sample 100M/T beans/5 000 sets of TV sets...
6）We offer until 5 May here 100 "Rainbow" TV sets Art. No. 123 and 100 "Panda" cassette recorders Art. No. 456（at）USD250 and USD100 respectively both on FOB basis, September shipment, payment by sight L/C. This is a combined offer; you must accept both or neither.

2.2.3　Counter-Offer
还盘（还价）

Again, in the store-shopping example, you may not like the price or other terms of the deal and offer your desired terms— "Your price is too high. How about 150 yuan?" That is a **bargain** in a domestic negotiation. Counter-offers in an international trade are similar, which are a reply to an offer with additions, limitations or other modifications. Both the exporter and importer can counter-offer the other's offer and be further counter-offered by the other. So, counter-offers can go on and on for several rounds, but they can also be skipped altogether when the offer is accepted straight away. A counter-offer cancels the original offer and constitutes a new one. As a result, if you are counter-offered, your offer shall **lapse** and you will not be bound by that offer. The same is true for the importer. The following Table 2.3 shows some examples of the counter-offer.

讨价还价

失效

Table 2.3 Useful Sentences & Examples: Counter-Offer

1) We were quoted USD500 per set FOB Guangzhou last week. We will accept the offer if you can lower it to...
2) Model A was quoted (at) USD500 per set FOB Guangzhou a few days ago. If the price can go down by 3%, we are happy to fix the order.
3) Your quotation of box fans is rather high. Our client will only agree to accept if it is changed from FOB Tianjin to CIF San Francisco.
4) Regarding your offer of May 4, we counter-offer USD100...

2.2.4 Acceptance
接受

Finally, in the store shopping example, after several rounds of negotiations, you or the shop owner may accept the terms offered by the other. That makes an acceptance in a domestic negotiation. Similarly, in an international negotiation, an acceptance is the final and definite expression of assent to the terms of an offer or a counter-offer, together with previously agreed upon terms. Both exporter and importer can make an acceptance, which should be in statement or indicated by an act, such as the importer's placing an order. **Silence** or **inactivity** does not in itself **constitute** an acceptance. Like an offer, an acceptance should also

沉默 不行动

等于

be addressed to a specific audience—individual（s）or business（es）. If someone else learns about the terms of the negotiation and accepts, it is not considered an **eligible** acceptance.

An acceptance must be delivered before the offer **expires**. If you accept the offer beyond the expiry date, the acceptance is **ineffective**, unless the other party accepts your late "acceptance" by informing you orally or sending you a notice to say so without delay. But in case your means of communication, such as courier, is solely responsible for the delay, your late acceptance is still regarded as effective, unless the other party thinks otherwise and timely informs you of his/her decision. An oral offer must be accepted immediately unless the circumstances indicate otherwise. An acceptance can be withdrawn before or at the same time it reaches the other party, but you need a faster means of communication for sending the withdrawal.

Sometimes, a **tricky** issue regarding acceptance is how to distinguish it from a counter-offer. Inexperienced traders tend to mistake some counter-offers for acceptances. For example, the importer may reply that he/she accepts the offer, but still wants to make minor alterations. You need to be **alert** to this type of reply—it could be an acceptance or a counter-offer, depending on which terms the importer wants to modify. According to *CISG*, if the **modifications** relate, among other things, to the price, payment, quality and quantity of the goods, place and time of delivery, extent of one party's liability to the other, or the settlement of disputes, they are considered to **materially** alter the offer and therefore **constitute** a counter-offer in effect; otherwise, they may be considered non-material alterations and constitute an acceptance, unless the offeror, without **undue** delay, objects orally to the discrepancy or sends a notice to say so. To sum up, an acceptance must be in strict accordance with the offer. Any modification alters an offer, material modifications turn it into a counter-offer, while non-material modifications keep it as an acceptance, unless the offeror objects to them without delay.

2.3 Signing Sales Contract
签订销售合同

Once an acceptance, be it oral or in writing, reaches the other part, a deal is concluded. Different from those in domestic trade, international lawsuits are costly and time-consuming, so no one likes to get involved in any lawsuits. It is thus important that you negotiate with care so that when a deal is made, both of you reach a common understanding of the terms of sale and know exactly and unmistakably what is expected of you.

However, owing to the inconveniences caused by the long distance between exporter and importer, international contracts tend to be more flexible than domestic ones in format, which could be a traditional contract or alternative formats including a sales confirmation, a purchase confirmation, an agreement, or a confirmed **pro forma invoice**. A sales confirmation is normally drafted by the exporter and sent to the importer for confirmation, while a purchase confirmation is the other way round. A proforma invoice, as a "preview" of the final **commercial invoice**, can serve as an offer in negotiations, and a contract was confirmed by both parties. However, for large and complicated sales, a detailed contract is still needed and signed by both parties. The contract can be signed face to face, but this is rare in international businesses. Mostly, you send two signed copies to the importer, asking him/her to sign and send one back for file. This practice is known as **counter-sign**. Faxed contracts are permissible in urgent situations.

形式发票

商业发票

存档　会签

An import or export contract is generally more detailed than a domestic one and may include the following terms (see Figure 2.1) :

Name and address of the exporter and importer

◆ Date and location of signing the contract

◆ The willingness and guarantee of both sides to sign the contract

	✧ Product description: name, model, quality, quantity, packaging and marking, etc. of the goods
总金额	✧ Unit price and **total amount**
	✧ Terms of payment
	✧ Time of shipment
	✧ Port of loading and port of destination
	✧ Insurance
	✧ Inspection
	✧ Documents required by the importer
申诉或索赔	✧ **Complaint or claim**
	✧ Dispute resolution
不可抗力	✧ **Force majeure**
备注	✧ **Remarks**
	✧ Signatures

SALES CONTRACT

NO.: GDHY0739　　　　　　　　　　　　　　　　　　　　DATE: FEB. 15, 2015

THE SELLER: GUANGDONG HUANYA IMPORT & EXPORT CO., LTD.

　　　　　　　　118 XUEYUAN STREET, GUANGZHOU,

　　　　　　　　P.R. CHINA

THE BUYER:　DIM TRADING CO., LTD.

　　　　　　　　16 TOM STREET, DUBAI,

　　　　　　　　U.A.E.

This Contract is made by and between the buyer and seller, whereby the buyer agree to buy and the seller agrees to sell the under-mentioned commodity according to the terms and conditions stipulated below:

Commodity & specification	Quantity	Unit price	Amount
Ladies Jacket (6204320090) Style no. L357 Style no. L358 Shell: woven twill 100% cotton Lining: Woven 100% polyester As per the confirmed sample of Jan. 30, 2008 and Order No.DIM768	 2250pcs 2250pcs	CIF Dubai, U.A.E. USD12.00/pc USD12.00/pc	 USD27000.00 USD27000.00
TOTAL	4500pcs		USD54000.00
TOTAL CONTRACT VALUE: SAY U.S. DOLLARS FIFTY-FOUR THOUSAND ONLY.			

Size/color assortment for Style no. L357: Unit: piece

Size	S	M	L	XL	Total
White	180	360	450	180	1170
Red	180	360	360	180	1080
Total	360	720	810	360	2250

Size/color assortment for Style No. L358: Unit: piece

Size	S	M	L	XL	Total
White	180	360	450	180	1170
Blue	180	360	360	180	1080
Total	360	720	810	360	2250

More or less 5% of the quantity and the amount are allowed.

PACKING:

9 pieces of ladies jackets are packed in one export standard carton, solid color and solid size in the same carton.

MARKS:

The shipping mark includes DIM, S/C No., style No., port of destination and carton No.

Side mark must show the color, the size of carton, and the pieces per carton.

TIME OF SHIPMENT:

Within 60 days upon receipt of the L/C which accords with relevant clauses of this contract.

PORT OF LOADING AND DESTINATION:

From Guangzhou, China to Dubai, U.A.E.

Transshipment is allowed, and partial shipment is prohibited.

INSURANCE:

To be effected by the seller for 110% of the invoice value covering All Risks as per C.I.C. of PICC dated 01/01/1981.

TERMS OF PAYMENT:

By irrevocable Letter of Credit at 30 days after sight, reaching the seller not later than March. 5, 2015, and remaining valid for negotiation in China for further 15 days after the effected shipment. In case of late arrival of the L/C, the seller shall not be liable for any delay in shipment and shall have the right to rescind the contract and /or claim for damages.

DOCUMENTS:

+ Signed Commercial Invoice in triplicate.

+ Full set of clean on board ocean Bill of Lading marked "freight prepaid" made out to order of the shipper blank endorsed notifying the applicant.

+ Insurance Policy in duplicate endorsed in blank.

+ Packing List in triplicate.

+ Certificate of Origin certified by the Chamber of Commerce or CCPIT.

INSPECTION:

The certificate of quality issued by the China Entry–Exit Inspection and Quarantine Bureau shall be taken as the basis of delivery.

CLAIMS:

In case discrepancy on the quality or quantity (weight) of the goods is found by the buyer, after arrival of the goods at the port of destination, the buyer may, within 30 days and 15 days respectively after arrival of the goods at the port of destination, lodge with the seller a claim which should be supported by an Inspection Certificate issued by a public surveyor approved by the seller. The seller shall, on the merits of the claim, either make good the loss sustained by the buyer or reject their claim, it being agreed that the seller shall not be held responsible for any loss or losses due to natural cause failing within the responsibility of Ship-owners of the Underwriters. The seller shall reply to the buyer within 30 days after receipt of the claim.

LATE DELIVERY AND PENALTY:

In case of late delivery, the buyer shall have the right to cancel this contract, reject the goods and lodge a claim against the seller. Except for Force Majeure, if late delivery occurs, the seller must pay a penalty, and the buyer shall have the right to lodge a claim against the seller. The rate of penalty is charged at 0.5% for every 7 days, odd days less than 7 days should be counted as 7 days. The total penalty amount will not exceed 5% of the shipment value. The penalty shall be deducted by the paying bank or the buyer from the payment.

FORCE MAJEURE:

The seller shall not hold responsible if they owing to Force Majeure cause or causes, fail to make delivery within the time stipulated in the contract or cannot deliver the goods. However, in such a case, the seller shall inform the buyer immediately by cable and if it is requested by the buyer, the seller shall also deliver to the buyer by registered letter, a certificate attesting the existence of such a cause or causes.

ARBITRATION:

All disputes in connection with this contract or the execution thereof shall be settled amicably by negotiation. In case no settlement can be reached, the case shall then be submitted to the China International Economic Trade Arbitration Commission for settlement by arbitration in accordance with the Commission's arbitration rules. The award rendered by the commission shall be final and binding on both parties. The fees for arbitration shall be borne by the losing party unless otherwise awarded.

This contract is made in two original copies and becomes valid after signature, one copy to be held by each party.

Signed by:

THE SELLER:	THE BUYER:
GUANGDONG HUANYA IMPORT & EXPORT CO., LTD.	DIM TRADING CO., LTD
张 立	Jack Chang

Figure 2.1

Exercises 练习

I. True (T) or False (F)

1. Business negotiation includes the steps of enquiry, offer, counter-offer and acceptance, each of which is indispensable. (   )

2. A deal is concluded when an offer is accepted within the period of validity. (   )

3. An enquiry in an international business negotiation generally contains as much information as a domestic negotiation. (   )

4. No matter whether or not the importer and exporter are familiar with each other, the enquiry should not be skipped in a business negotiation. (   )

5. According to *CISG*, an invitation to make offers is not an offer. (   )

6. According to *CISG*, an offer containing the commodity name, quantity and price of the goods is a definite offer. (   )

7. An offer usually requires a fixed period for acceptance. (   )

8. Acceptance should be in the form of a statement or an act. Silence does not constitute an acceptance. (   )

9. In international trade, contracts are seldom signed face to face. (   )

10. The functions of a proforma invoice and a commercial invoice are basically the same. (   )

II. Multiple Choice Questions

1. According to *CISG*, (   ) are indispensable elements for an offer.

    A. commodity name, quality, quantity

    B. commodity name, quantity, price

    C. commodity name, quality, price

    D. commodity name, price, payment

2. According to *CISG*, a deal is concluded (   ).

    A. when the buyer receives the offer

    B. by the time of signing the written contract

C. when the buyer accepts the offer

D. when the contract is approved by the superiors

3. Which of the following statements about the relationship between a withdrawal and a cancellation of an offer is TRUE?(　　)

A. Both occur after the offer takes effect.

B. The former occurs before the offer takes effect, while the latter occurs after the offer takes effect.

C. Both occur before the offer takes effect.

D. The former occurs after the offer takes effect, while the latter occurs before the offer takes effect.

4. The amendment to(　　)may not materially alter an offer.

A. means of dispute settlement

B. packaging of the goods

C. quantity and term of payment

D. time and place of delivery

5*. Under what condition(s)can an offer not be revoked?(　　)

A. When it has fixed a period of time for acceptance.

B. When it has indicated by other means that it is irrevocable.

C. If it is reasonable for the offeree to rely on the offer as being irrevocable and he/she has acted in reliance on the offer.

D. When the rejection reaches the offeree so that the offer is terminated, even if it is irrevocable.

6. "We accept, but just prefer you to change the term of payment from D/P at sight to D/A." This is(　　).

A. a counter-offer

B. an indication of concluding a deal

C. a valid acceptance

D. a rejection of the offer

7*. The main reason(s)leading to the termination of offer include:(　　).

A. The offer is expired

B. The offeror has withdrawn the offer

C. The importer refuses the offer

D. A force majeure incident occurs to the exporter after the offer is made

8. Which of the following statements is TRUE about *CISG*? (　　)

A. *CISG* is binding on every exporter or importer in an international transaction.

B. According to *CISG*, an oral offer must be accepted immediately, unless otherwise indicated.

C. *CISG* is an international convention that is not binding unless made reference in the contract.

D. *CISG* governs both merchandise trade and service trade.

9. Which of the following statements is TRUE about the validity of an offer? (　　)

A. An offer cannot be withdrawn once it is sent to the offeree.

B. An offer cannot be canceled once it is sent to the offeree.

C. An offer cannot be withdrawn once it reaches the offeree.

D. An offer cannot be canceled once it reaches the offeree.

10. Which one of the following is NOT a precondition for a business proposal to constitute an offer? (　　)

A. It must have a clear audience.

B. It must be clear about its readiness to conclude the deal.

C. It is for reference only.

D. It must contain the commodity name, quantity and price.

III. Case Study

1. A buyer from ABC Trading Co., Ltd., an Italian importer of furniture, visited the stall of a **Dongguan** based Chinese furniture manufacturer Okart Furniture Co., Ltd. at the Canton Fair and negotiated terms for a set of **wardrobes**. Okart made an offer orally to the buyer, but he did not respond on the spot. However, in the afternoon, the buyer

东莞

衣柜

revisited the stall to express his willingness to accept the morning's offer. But during the day, Okart had learned that the price of this type of wardrobe had been on the rise. How do you think Okart should handle the matter? And why?

2. One of our foreign trade companies (the C company) received an offer from the D company which is in Paris, France on July 16: "500 **MERIICTON TINPLATE** USDOLLARS540 CFR CHINA PORT AUGUST SHIPMENT SIGHT L/C SUBJECT TO YOUR REPLY REACHING US BY JULY 20." We replied on July 17 stating that we accept the offer if the unit price is USD 500.00 CFR CHINA PORT. If there are some disputes, **arbitration** in China. The D company replied by cable that: "The market is firm, the price cannot be reduced, the arbitration can be accepted, please reply as soon as possible." There was an upward tendency in the tinplate's price at the same time. So we replied by cable that: "we accept your offer of the 16th. The L/C has been established through the Bank of China, please confirm." However, the French businessman did not confirm and returned the L/C. Question: Is the contract established? Do we make any mistakes? Explain the reasons.

3. In reply to a French businessman's inquiry, one of our exporters made an offer to sell a kind of goods, subjected to reply reaching us by the 5th of this month. The French businessman cabled to accept the offer on the 4th of this month. Because of the delay of the **Telegraph Office**, we received his cable on the morning of the 6th of this month. At the same time, we cabled to refuse the offer since the marker price increases. However, the French businessman believed that it was not his duty to make the delay of the acceptance notice and insisted that the contract had been established. We didn't agree on it. Therefore, we **prosecuted** to the court. How should you think the judge's judgment is? If we didn't refuse upon receiving the offer, how to make a judgment? Explain the

reasons.

4. As an exporter, we cabled an American businessman to export agricultural products. Besides the necessary items stated in the offer, the clause "Packing in sound-bags" was also added in. During the validity of the offer, the American businessman replied "Refer to your telex first accepted, packing in new bags", When we received the above reply, we were ready for shipment. The international market price for the agricultural products **tumbled** a few days ago. The American 猛跌 businessman replied that the contract was not established because we did not confirm when they changed the packing condition. We insisted that the contract had been established. So the parties occurred this argument. How to handle this case?

Chapter 3
International Trade Terms
第三章　国际贸易术语

◆ **Learning Objectives**

• Understand the nature of international trade terms, and the purposes of using trade terms in international business

• Know the three basic rules of international trade terms

• Know the interpretations of trade terms in Incoterms®2020

• Master the six main trade terms in Incoterms®2020

国际贸易术语

风险、责任和费用

The seller and buyer in international trade, in general, rarely use cash on delivery. Normally, they will use **international trade terms**, such as "FOB", "CFR" or "CIF", to identify where to deliver the goods, what the price is, and how to clarify the **risk, responsibilities and the expenses** between the seller and the buyer. Different trade terms define different delivery places, different rights and obligations of the buyer and seller. When the buyer and seller agree to use certain trade term in the contract, other terms of the contract should keep in line with it, taking "FOB" term as an example, under FOB term, the buyer should take the responsibility of booking and chartering a ship, as well as paying for the ocean freight, in addition, the buyer needs to effect the insurance and pays the premium. Therefore, even for the same batch of goods, the price will be different when adapting different trade terms. Therefore, it is the trade terms that determine the nature of the contract, as well as the rights and obligations of the buyer and seller. This chapter will introduce the trade terms, the special "language" used in international trade, and **illustrate** how these terms in their simplest forms are used to facilitate transactions.

说明

3.1 International Trade Terms and Its Basic Rules
国际贸易术语及其惯例

3.1.1 The Nature of International Trade Terms
国际贸易术语的性质

Trade Terms Are the Terms of Delivery 国际贸易术语表示交货条件

Trade terms define the division of responsibilities, expenses and risks between buyers and sellers during the delivery of goods, which we call terms of delivery, that is the point at which delivery occurs, i.e., the point at which the risk of loss or damage transfers from the seller to the buyer. For example, under the FOB (Free on Board) term and the DDP (Delivered Duty Paid) term, the rights and obligations of both parties are different.

Trade Terms Specify the Component of Commodity Price 国际贸易术语表示价格的构成

Different trade terms contain different **ancillary** expenses, so even the same transaction will be quoted differently under different trade terms. For example, FOB price does not include freight and premium from the port of shipment to the port of destination, while the CIF price does, that is why FOB price is always lower than CIF price. Thus, the final price of a contract determined by which trade term is chosen by both parties.

从属的

3.1.2 The Purpose of Trade Terms
国际贸易术语的作用

Simplify Transaction Procedures and Promote the Business
简化交易手续，促成交易

In international trade, trade terms can significantly simplify the business negotiation, and promote trade transaction. International trade always involves many procedures, which should be completed either by the seller or buyer. For example, who should effect marine cargo insurance? Who should **book shipping space**? Who should apply for the import or export license? And so on. It is very time-consuming for the exporter and importer to negotiate the obligations and the cost is involved in every procedure listed above for the transaction. But so long as the buyers and sellers agree on trade terms by which the transaction goes, it can easily specify the respective responsibilities, expenses, and risks that should be borne by the buyer and seller, in this way the trade terms can simplify trade procedures, help buyers and sellers save time consultation, then make a deal quickly.

Facilitate cost and price calcalations for buyers and sellers
便于买卖双方核算成本和价格

Since trade terms stand for the components of the international price of a commodity, different trade terms include different costs and the price quoted will vary due to different trade terms. While quoting a price, it is necessary for the buyer and the seller to consider the costs that contain in the trade terms, such as freight, insurance, handling charges, and tariffs, which is conducive to both buyers and sellers on price comparisons and cost accounting.

3.1.3 Three Main International Rules on Trade Terms
三个主要国际贸易惯例

International trade rules refer to the **practices** and **interpretations** that are generally recognized and gradually formed with international trade practice. It includes some interpretations or rules that used to explain some aspects of international trade, such as trade terms, payment terms etc. by some international organizations; traditional practices on some of the major international ports and **terminals**; practices from different industries. In addition, the typical cases or judgments awarded by judicial authority or arbitration organization, also regarded as part of international trade practices. There are three main international trade practices relating to trade terms: "*Warsaw-Oxford Rules 1932*", "*Revised American Foreign Trade Definitions 1941)*", "*International Rules for the Interpretation of Trade Terms 2010*".

(火车、汽车或船的)终点站；终端

Warsaw-Oxford Rules 1932《1932年华沙-牛津规则》

This rule is designed by **International Law Association** to explain the CIF (Cost, Insurance and Freight) contract. During the 1928 convention of the International Law Association held in Warsaw, Poland, a set of rules relating to CIF contract were established—"*Warsaw rules, 1928*", which was amended on Oxford Conference in 1932, still in use now. It combined into 21 provisions. The rule mainly describes the characteristics of a CIF contract, and specifies the division of responsibilities and methods of transfer of cargo ownership between buyer and seller, while using CIF trade terms. When the parties conclude a contract based on "*Warsaw-Oxford Rules*", it means that they agree to make a CIF contract, and "*Warsaw Oxford Rules*" will have a binding. However, if these rules conflict with the stipulations of the contract, the contract shall prevail. As the "*Warsaw Oxford Rules*" only provide interpretations and regulations for CIF terms, it is rarely used by traders in practice.

国际法协会

Revised American Foreign Trade Definitions 1941《1941年美国对外贸易定义修订本》

In 1919, 9 business communities in the United States devised "the U.S. Export Quotation and Abbreviations", which was revised in 1941, and then the *"Revised American Foreign Trade Definitions 1941"* was adopted in the same year by the **U.S. Chamber of Commerce**, the **National Council of American Importers** and the **National Foreign Trade Council**. The definitions provide explanations for six trade terms:

Ex point of origin

FOB (Free on Board)

FAS (Free Alongside Ship)

C&F (Cost and Freight)

CIF (Cost, Insurance and Freight)

Ex dock (named port of importation)

美国商会
美国全国进口商委员会
全国对外贸易委员会

The above definitions are most commonly used by the United States, Canada and some other American countries, but they are rarely used internationally due to their contents have great differences from other general interpretations. In recent years, American business communities or trade organizations consider abandoning this "definition", and use "International Incoterms", which was devised by the International Chamber of Commerce. It should be noted that the rule is still used in the Americas, so when these countries in international trade, the parties agree to adopt this rule, it is necessary to specify that the contract is subject to *"Revised American Foreign Trade Definitions* 1941", otherwise it is non-binding.

Incoterms® *2020*《2020年国际贸易术语解释通则》

《通则》

Incoterms rules were made by the International Chamber of Commerce. Nowadays, **Incoterms** as an international trade practice, is more and more universally recognized and applicable by international trade practice, it has become an important rule for both parties to sign and fulfill a contract, as well as to solve business disputes.

The main reason for successive revisions of Incoterms is to adapt them to contemporary commercial practice. "Incoterms" contained 8 trade terms as amended in the year 1953, two other trade terms were added in the 1967 version, that is the "Delivered at Frontier" (DAF) and "Delivered Duty Paid" (DDP); later the "Departure airports delivery "(FOA) was added in the 1976 version; in 1980 the " Free Carrier (FRC) " and" freight, insurance paid to (destination)(CIP)" were added, until then, *Incoterms® 1980* had already contained 14 trade terms. Further, the revision in 1990 was to adapt itself to the increased use of Electronic Data Interchange (EDI) in business transactions, *Incoterms® 1990* had 13 trade terms. Revision in 2000 took account of the spread of customs-free zones in the 1990s. In *Incoterms® 2010*, 11 trade terms were changed, DAF, DES, DEQ, and DDU in group D were deleted, and DAT and DAP were added. In *Incoterms® 2020*, 11 trade terms remain, DAT of group D is deleted and DPU is added. The changes of *Incoterms® 2020* o ver *Incoterms® 2010* pelease refer to Table 3.1.

The latest version, *Incoterms® 2020*, has **come into force** since January 1, 2020. One of the main features of the *Incoterms® 2020* is that they are available for application to both international and domestic sales contracts. The forming of various **trade blocs**, like the European Union, has made it a must for the rules to be applicable for both international and domestic trade.

实施

贸易集团

Needless to say, every revision of Incoterms is to improve all the trade terms to facilitate their practical implementation. It is notable that even though the new Incoterms entered into force, *Incoterms® 2010* can still be used in doing international trade. It is important, however to clearly specify the chosen version *Incoterms® 2020*, Incoterms® 2010, or any earlier version, through such words as, "the chosen *Incoterms* including the ramed place, followed by *Incoterms® 2020*".

Although international rules play a role in the settlement of trade disputes, we should pay attention to the following questions:

- International trade practice is not legal, so it is not binding on both parties, it may be or may not be used.

- If the buyer and seller in the contract agree to adopt certain practice, then the practice will be binding for both parties.
- If the contract specifies that it adopts to certain practice, when which is contrary to the stipulation in the contract, as long as the stipulation does not conflict with the national law, it will be recognized and protected by the relevant laws. In other words, in such case, both parties should be binding by the stipulation of the contract.
- If the contract neither specifies on an issue clearly, nor designates certain practice adopted, when disputes happen and submitted for litigation or arbitration, the court or arbitration commission can make a judgment based on the relevant practices.

> 如果合同中明确采用某种惯例，但又在合同中出现规定与所采用的惯例相抵触的条款，只要这些条款与本国法律不矛盾，就将受到有关国家法律的承认和保护，即以合同条款为准。

While doing import and export business, we need to understand and master some international trade rules, which are essential while negotiating business, signing a contract, fulfilling the contract, as well as resolving the disputes. When disputes arise, we can struggle for our rights based on these rules.

Table 3.1 Changes of *Incoterms® 2020* over *Incoterms® 2010*

- The Incoterms FCA（Free Carrier）now provides the additional option to make an on-board notation on the Bill of Lading prior to loading of the goods on a vessel.
- The costs now appear centralized in A9/B9 of each Incoterms rule.
- CIP now requires at least an insurance with the minimum cover of the Institute Cargo Clause（A）（All risk, subject to itemized exclusions）.
- CIF now requires at least an insurance with the minimum cover of the Institute Cargo Clause（C）（Number of listed risks, subject to itemized exclusions）.
- The rule Delivered at Terminal（DAT）has been changed to Delivered at Place Unloaded（DPU）to clarify that the place of destination could be any place and not only a "terminal".
- The Incoterms rules of Free Carrier（FCA）, Delivered at Place（DAP）, Delivered at Place Unloaded（DPU）and Delivered Duty Paid（DDP）now take into account that the goods may be carried without any third-party carrier being engaged, namely by using its own means of transportation.
- The *Incoterms 2020* now explicitly shifts the responsibility of security-related requirements and ancillary costs to the seller.

3.2 International Rules for the Interpretation of Trade Terms 2020
《2020 年国际贸易术语解释通则》

3.2.1 Classification of Incoterms® 2020
《2020 年国际贸易术语解释通则》中的贸易术语分类

The Incoterms®2020 divides the 11 trade terms into four categories of group E, F, C, and D. The first group is "E"–terms (EXW), the seller only makes the goods available to the buyer at the seller's own **premises**. The second group is "F"–terms (FCA, FAS and FOB), the seller is called upon to **deliver the goods** to a **carrier** appointed by the buyer; contracts under F–terms are shipment contracts. The third group is "C"–terms (CFR, CIF, CPT and CIP), the seller has to contract for major carriage, but without assuming the risk of loss or damage to the goods or additional costs due to events occurring after shipment or dispatch. Contracts under C–terms are shipment contracts as well. The most important feature for group C is that the division of relevant risk and costs are separated. The fourth group is "D"–terms (DAP, DPU and DDP), the seller has to bear all risk and costs needed to bring the goods to the place of destination. Contracts under "D"–terms are arrival contracts.

> 场所
>
> 交货　承运人
>
> 承运人是指与托运人订立合同，并承担运输义务的一方。

Incoterms®2020 grouped 11 three–letter trade terms into two categories according to the mode of transport (maritime vs. any other modes).

Group 1: Incoterms that apply to any mode of transport 适用于任何运输方式的贸易术语

They are EXW (Ex Works), FCA (Free Carrier), CPT (Carriage Paid to), CIP (Carriage and Insurance Paid to), DAP (Delivered at Place), DPU (Delivered at Place Unloaded) and DDP (Delivered Duty Paid).

These seven kinds of trade terms not only apply to any mode of transport, but also apply to where more than one mode of transport. In addition, they can be used when the vessel carries just part of the consignment.

Group 2: Incoterms that apply to sea and inland waterway transport only 适用于海上和内河水上运输方式的贸易术语

They are FAS（Free Alongside Ship）, FOB（Free on Board）, CFR（Cost and Freight）and CIF（Cost, Insurance and Freight）.

Under these trade terms, the sellers should deliver the goods to buyers at the port, therefore, they are classified as "suitable terms of maritime and inland waterway". As for terms FOB, CFR, and CIF in Incoterms®2020, "delivery" means when the goods have been put "on board of vessel".

风险和费用的划分点　Figure 3.1 illustrates the **critical points for the division of relevant risks and costs** under the eleven terms. When using this chart, it needs to be born in mind that all the issues are discussed from the seller's perspective.

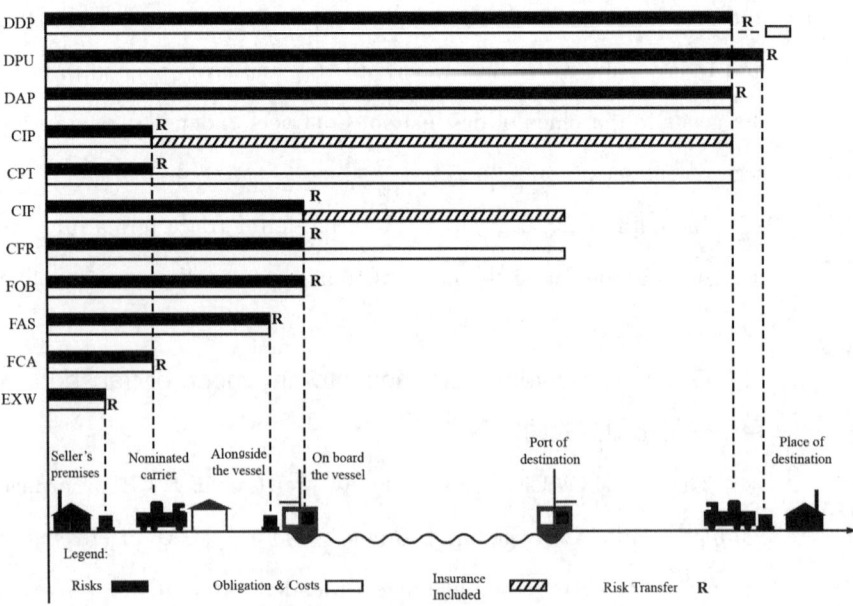

Figure 3.1　Incoterms Chart

3.2.2 Main Trade Terms in *Incoterms*® *2020*
六种主要贸易术语

3.2.2.1 FOB

Free on Board (*... named port of shipment*) 装运港船上交货

(1) Definition

　　定义

FOB is an Abbreviation for "free on board", when using this term, the port of shipment shall be **nominated** behind FOB, for example, if Guangzhou is the port of shipment, said the FOB Guangzhou. FOB means that the seller delivers the goods **on board the vessel** nominated by the buyer at **the named port of shipment** or procures the goods already so delivered. The risks of loss of or damage to the goods passes when the goods are on board the vessel, and the buyer bears all the costs from that moment onwards. This rule is to be used only for sea or inland waterway transport.

被指定

船上
指定装运港

(2) The obligations of buyer and seller

　　买卖双方义务

① The seller's obligations 卖方义务

- The seller must deliver the goods on board the vessel nominated by the buyer at the agreed port of loading within the agreed period, and notify the buyer timely.

- The seller must obtain, at its own risks and expenses, any export license or other official documents and carry out all the **customs formalities** necessary for export.

报关手续
报关是指为了遵守海关条例而需要满足的一些要求，包括了单据、安全、信息或实体检验之义务。

- The seller must bear all the costs and risks of loss of or damage to the goods until they have been loaded on board the vessel.

- The seller must provide the evidence at its own expenses that he has completed the **delivery obligation**. The required documents

交货义务

including commercial invoice, clean on board shipping documents and other documents as contracted, or some electronic information with **equivalent** force.

② The buyer's obligations 买方义务

- The buyer must contract, at its own expense for the **carriage** of the goods from the named port of shipment, take responsibility to charter a ship and booking shipping space, as well as to pay the freight.
- The buyer must give the seller sufficient notice of the delivery time and the vessel name, so as to make the seller ready for shipment.
- The buyer must bear all the costs and the risks of loss of or damage to the goods from the time that the goods have been loaded on board the vessel.
- The buyer must obtain, at its own risks and expenses, any import license or other official documents and carry out all customs formalities for the import of goods and for their transport through any country.
- The buyer must accept the shipping documents provided by the seller, and make the payment accordingly.

(3) Some notable issues under the FOB term
采用FOB术语应注意的问题

① The "delivery point" and "risk-transfer point" 装船概念和风险转移点的问题

The seller must deliver, within the contracted period, the goods either by placing them on board the vessel nominated by the buyer at the loading point, if any, indicated by the buyer at the named port of shipment, or by procuring the goods so delivered. It is the obligation of "delivery" for the seller. The buyer must bear all the risks and costs at the moment when the goods have been delivered. The risk here means the risk of loss of or damage to the goods, and the cost is the cost excluding the normal freight.

② Link-up of vessel and goods 船货衔接问题

Under the FOB term, it is the buyer's duty to arrange shipment of goods, therefore both parties must try to ensure the transfer of goods meet the shipment schedule. On one hand, the buyer should send the ship just in time, on the other hand, the seller should deliver the goods to the nominated port. In order to meet both ends well, the buyer should give the seller prompt notice of the vessel's name, loading berth, and **ETD** after he has contract for the carriage. (Known as "Shipping Instruction").

"Estimated Time of Departure" 的缩写, 预计离港时间。

If the buyer designates the vessel, but fails to notify timely the seller of the vessel's name, loading berth and shipment time; or the vessel nominated by the buyer fails to arrive on time, is unable to take the goods, or closes for cargo earlier than the time notified. Then, the buyer bears all risks of loss or damage to the goods, provided that the goods have been clearly identified as the contract goods. As sending a ship by the buyer is a **precondition** for the seller to fulfill the contract, if the buyer fails to designate a vessel within the stipulated time, the seller may claim damages, or may revoke the contract if serious consequences occur. In contrast, the seller should pay dead freight or demurrage, in case of he did not get ready for the goods within the stipulated time.

前提

The seller shall give the buyer sufficient notice promptly after the goods have been loaded on board the vessel. Under the FOB term, it is the buyer to **effect insurance** and the risks of loss of or damage to the goods are transferred from the seller to the buyer when the goods have been loaded on board the vessel. If the seller does not notify the buyer of the shipment promptly, the buyer may fail to make insurance timely, and the goods may not be insured properly. Therefore, the shipping notice was sent by the buyer can facilitate the seller to take delivery of goods and other matters.

办理保险

Under the FOB term, the seller can provide assistance to the buyer, at the buyer's request, such as chartering a ship or booking shipping space, as well as obtaining the bill of lading or other transport documents, but the buyer should bear all the risks and expenses on his account.

③ Fees for loading the goods on board 关于装船费用的负担问题

Under FOB, the seller bears all the costs until the goods have been loaded on board the vessel, and the buyer bears afterward. However, loading is a continuous process, it is hard to divide all the loading costs between the buyer and the seller. As for liner transport, no disputes will arise, because the liner freight paid by the buyer has already included all the loading charges. But under **voyage charter**, according to the usual practice, the **charter party** will normally stipulate that the ship owner will not bear the loading charges. In this case, both buyer and seller should clarify in their contract who should cover the **loading, trimming, or stowing** charges. To prevent disputes arising between the buyer and seller, **variants of FOB** have been created to specify the division of the loading charges. The five variations of FOB are as follows:

- *FOB Liner Terms*（FOB 班轮条件）This term follows the practice of liner. That is sellers under these terms are not paying the loading, it is the party who contracts for carriage to pay for the loading charges, this party is the buyer.

- *FOB Under Tackle*（FOB 吊钩下交货）This variant allows the seller to cover the cost until the goods are placed somewhere within the reach of the tackle of the vessel nominated by the buyer. Other costs will be borne by the buyer.

- *FOB Stowed*（FOB 包括理舱费）Under this term the seller has to cover the loading charges as well as the stowage charge when the goods are placed inside the hold of the ship.

- *FOB Trimmed*（FOB 包括平舱费）Besides loading the goods on board the vessel, the seller should also trim the goods to make the vessel evenly balanced. The seller pays all the loading and trimming expenses.

• *FOB Stowed and Trimmed*（FOB包括理舱和平舱，或FOBST）

The seller should pay all the loading, stowing and trimming charges.

The above five variants of FOB are usually used by charter transport, there is no need to use the variants by liner transport, since the freight under liner transport includes the loading charges, which are borne by the charterers. Generally speaking, the variants only make the division of cost, the risk-transfer point is still the same that the risk is transferred from the seller to the buyer once the goods are loaded on board the vessel.

3.2.2.2 CFR

Cost and Freight (... named port of destination)成本加运费（指定目的港）

(1) Definition
定义

CFR is an Abbreviation for "cost and freight", the cost here means FOB price. When using this term, the port of destination shall be nominated behind CFR, for example, if Rotterdam is the port of destination, said CFR Rotterdam. CFR means that the seller is responsible for chartering a ship or booking shipping space, delivering the contracted goods on board the vessel at the named port of shipment on schedule. The seller only bears the risks of loss of or damage to the goods before the goods have been loaded on board the vessel, and pays the ocean freight. This rule is to be used only for sea or inland waterway transport.

(2) The obligations of buyer and seller
买卖双方义务

① The seller's obligations 卖方义务

- The seller must contract for the carriage and pay for the freight, as well as deliver the goods on board the vessel at the port of loading within the agreed period, and notify the buyer of the shipment.
- The seller must bear all the costs and risks of loss of or damage to

the goods until the goods have been loaded on board the vessel.
- The seller should effect the export customs clearance.
- The seller must provide the relevant documents, such as transport documents or some electronic information with equivalent force.

② The buyer's obligations 买方义务
- The buyer bears all the costs and risks of loss of or damage to the goods from the time they have been loaded on board the vessel.
- The buyer must take delivery of the goods at the port of destination and carry out all customs formalities for the import of goods.
- The buyer must accept the transport documents provided by the seller, and make the payment as contracted.

(3) Some notable issues under the CFR term
采用CFR术语应注意的问题

① Booking Shipping Space by the Seller 卖方租船订舱问题

Under CFR contract, one basic obligation for the seller is to arrange the shipment from the port of shipment to the port of destination. According to *Incoterms®2020*, the contract of carriage must be made on usual terms at the seller's expense and provide for carriage by the usual route in a vessel of type normally used for the transport of the type of goods sold. Therefore, if the seller fails to arrange the shipment accordingly, and could not deliver the goods on time, which will lead to a breach of contract and may bear the legal responsibility. Usually the buyer has no right to **designate** the vessel or shipping company, however, the seller could accept the buyer's requirements in the case that they are easy to handle and without **additional** expenses, even if these requirements are not **specified** in the contract, such as the nationality of the ship, ship age, ship class, etc. But to the terms specified clearly in the contract, it must be strictly enforced.

② Shipment Notice 装船通知问题

Under CFR contract the buyer is responsible for arranging cargo insurance, when the goods have been loaded on board the vessel, the seller should send shipment notice to the buyer immediately by e-mail, fax, etc. so that the buyer can make the insurance timely. If the seller fails to provide shipment details to the buyer after the shipment is made, the buyer will not be able to obtain insurance against his risk of loss of or damage to the goods during the ocean transport, then the seller should bear the risk himself. Therefore, it is significant for seller to provide shipment notice under CFR term.

③ Unloading Charges Issue 关于卸货费问题

Under CFR contract, it is the seller's obligation to make shipment and pay the ocean freight, while adopting liner transportation, the unloading charges are included in liner freight, thus, it is the seller who takes responsibility for unloading charges in liner transportation. However, for charter transportation, it usually specifies in the charter party that the ship-owner doesn't need to bear the loading and unloading charges. Under CFR terms, the loading charges at the port of shipment will be borne by the seller, but disputes arisen in who should bear the unloading charges at the port of destination. CFR variants aim at settling the **miscellaneous** charges occurred when the vessel arrives at the port 各种各样的 of destination. CIF variants are the same with CFR variants.

- *CFR/CIF Liner Terms*（CFR/CIF班轮条件）This term follows the practice of liners which requires the party contracting for carriage, that is the seller to pay for all the unloading charges.

- *CFR/CIF Landed*（CFR/CIF卸到岸上）This variant requires the seller to cover the necessary **handling** costs until the goods are 操作
  placed upon the **dock**, including the **barge** fees and **wharfage** 码头 驳船 码头
  charges.

- *CFR/CIF Ex Tackle*（CFR/CIF吊钩交货）Under this term, the seller will pay for moving the goods from the vessel to a location within the reach of the crane's tackle. The unloading point can be somewhere at the port or in an incoming lighter. That is when the vessel cannot reach the **quay**, the seller only needs to unload the goods to a lighter, and the charge for renting a lighter should be borne by the buyer.

码头

- *CFR/CIF Ex Ship's Hold*（CFR/CIF 舱底交货）Under this term the buyer should pay the unloading charges moving the goods from ship's hold to the unloading dock.

3.2.2.3　CIF

Cost, Insurance and Freight（... named port of destination）成本、保费加运费（指定目的港）

(1) Definition
定义

CIF is an Abbreviation for "cost, insurance and freight". When using this term, the port of destination shall be nominated behind CIF, for example, if Qingdao is the port of destination, said CIF Qingdao. CIF means that the seller is responsible for chartering a ship or booking shipping space, delivering the contracted goods on board the vessel at the named port of shipment on schedule, as well as effecting the insurance and paying the premium and freight necessary to bring the goods to the named port of destination. The seller only bears the risks of loss of or damage to the goods before the goods have been loaded on board the vessel, which is the same as FOB. This rule is to be used only for sea or inland waterway transport.

(2) The obligations of buyer and seller
买卖双方义务

① The seller's obligations 卖方义务

- The seller is responsible for chartering a ship and booking shipping space, delivering the goods on board the vessel at the named port of loading within the agreed period, paying the freight necessary to bring the goods to the named port of destination, and

notifying the buyer of the shipment.
- The seller must bear all the costs and risks of loss of or damage to the goods until they have been loaded on board the vessel.
- The seller should effect insurance and pay the premium.
- The seller should make all the customs formalities necessary for export.
- The seller must provide the relevant transport documents, such as commercial invoice, insurance policy, the normal transport documents for transporting the goods to the port of destination, or some electronic information with equivalent force.

② The buyer's obligations 买方义务
- The buyer bears all the costs and risks of loss of or damage to the goods from the time they have been loaded on board the vessel.
- The buyer must accept the transport documents provided by the seller, and make the payment as contracted.
- The buyer must take delivery of the goods at the port of destination and carry out all customs formalities for the import of goods.
- The buyer must pay all of the additional costs while in transit until the goods arrival at the port of destination, excluding the normal freight and premium.

(3) Some notable issues under CIF term
采用 CIF 术语应注意的问题

① Shipment contract CIF 属于装运合同

CIF contracts are shipment contracts. Under CIF term, the seller fulfills his delivery obligation when he has put the goods on board the vessel at the named port of shipment within the agreed period. That is why we define the CIF contract as a **"shipment contract"**, not an **"arrival contract"**. Risk of loss transfers to the buyer when the goods are placed on board. Under CIF term, although the seller is responsible for carriage and insurance, but he does need to guarantee the safety of

装运合同

到达合同

the goods to the port of destination. In whatever case, there should not be any provision or clause guaranteeing the arrival time of the shipment.

② Issues on Insurance Coverage 关于保险险别的规定

Under CIF terms, the seller is responsible for effecting the marine cargo insurance for the goods from port of loading to port of destination, and paying the **premium**. Since the risks after the goods being loaded on board the vessel are borne by the buyer, but the insurance during the transit is effected by the seller, to some extent, the seller procures the insurance on behalf of the buyer. The seller is required to obtain cargo insurance only on minimum cover if there is no other special stipulation in the sales contract. The minimum insurance amount shall cover the price provided in the contract plus 10%, and shall be provided in the currency of the contract. In practice, in order to avoid the disputes arisen between both parties, they usually specify in their contract what risks to cover and how much the insured amount is.

保险费

③ Symbolic Delivery 象征性交货

CIF is a special type of trade terms that documents submissions are more important than goods delivery, thus, it is known as "symbolic delivery" or "**Payment Against Documents**". Symbolic delivery means that once the seller puts the contracted goods on board the vessel at the port of shipment, and submits the relevant shipping documents to the buyer, then, the seller has completed his delivery obligation, he doesn't need to guarantee of the arrival of goods.

凭单付款

Payment against documents means that the buyer once accepts the shipping documents, he must pay the price as provided in the contract, even if at that time the goods had been lost or damaged. He can lodge a claim after making payments, against the relevant party, such as the insurance company, therefore, CIF is also called documents transaction. Under CIF terms, the seller makes delivery against documents, and the buyer makes payment against documents. As long as the seller has submitted the full set of qualified documents stipulated in the contract within the scheduled time, regardless of whether the goods are damaged or lost, the buyer must pay the price. On the contrary, in case the seller's documents are not **in conformity with** what is required in the contract, even if the goods arrived at the port of destination in good condition, the buyer still has the right to dishonor the payment.

与……一致

The above terms FOB, CIF, and CFR are all commonly used trade terms that deliver the goods at the port of shipment, and the risk-transfer points are the same, the risk transfers from the seller to the buyer when the goods have been loaded on board the vessel. However, the expenses and the obligations for the seller and the buyer are different.

3.2.2.4 FCA

Free Carrier (... named place of delivery) 货交承运人

(1) Definition

定义

FCA is an abbreviation for "free carrier". When using this term, FCA shall be followed by a named place, for example, if the named place is Changsha, said FCA Changsha. FCA means that the seller completes delivery when the goods have been handed over to the carrier nominated by the buyer at the agreed time and place, and requires the seller to clear the goods for export. FCA applies to all kinds of modes of transport, including **multimodal transport**, but the seller is only responsible for handing over the goods to the first carrier. This trade term is widely used in international trade and plays a great important role in international practice.

多式联运

(2) The obligations of buyer and seller

买卖双方义务

① The seller's obligations 卖方义务

· The seller must hand over the goods in conformity with the contract to the carrier nominated by the buyer at the named place within the agreed period.

- The seller is responsible for obtaining an export license or other official authorization and carrying out all customs formalities necessary for export of the goods.
- The seller must bear all the costs and risks of loss of or damage to the goods until the goods have been handed over to the carrier.
- The seller must provide a commercial invoice and the usual proof that the goods have been delivered to the nominated carrier, or some electronic information with equivalent force.

② The buyer's obligations 买方义务

- The buyer must contract at its own expense for the carriage of the goods, and notify the seller of the name of carrier, delivery time and place promptly.
- The buyer must bear all the costs and risks of loss of or damage to the goods from the time that the goods have been delivered to the carrier.
- The buyer must obtain the import license and other official authorization on his own expenses and risk, and carry out all the necessary customs formalities for the import of goods, including the transit formalities when necessary.
- The buyer must pay the price of the goods as provided in the contract, take delivery of the goods as contracted, and accept the qualified documents provided by the seller.

(3) Some notable issues under the FCA term
采用FCA术语应注意的问题

① Delivery Place 关于交货地点的问题

Since the FCA applies to all modes of transport, its delivery place varies due to different modes of transport and different places designated for delivery.

Delivery is completed:

- If the named place is the seller's premises, when the goods have been loaded on the means of transport provided by the buyer.

- In any other case, when the goods are placed at the disposal of the carrier or another person nominated by the buyer on the seller's means of transport ready for unloading.

In general, the loading and unloading obligations under FCA are: If delivery occurs at the seller's premises, the seller is responsible for loading. If delivery occurs at any other place, the seller is not responsible for loading and unloading.

② Contract of Carriage 运输合同问题

Under FCA term, it is the buyer's obligation to make a contract of carriage at its own expense, and to notify the seller of the name of the carrier, delivery time and place promptly. However, if it is more convenient for the seller to make carriage stuff, he may help the buyer to do so, but the risks and expenses should be borne by the buyer himself.

③ Risk-Transfer Point 风险转移问题

The seller must bear all the costs and risks of loss of or damage to the goods until the goods are placed at the disposal of the carrier. When using the FCA term, the goods are always grouped together to form a large collection, which is called "group shipping packing", such as containers and pallets are common collective packing. In this case, the seller should take such collection costs into account while pricing under the FCA term.

3.2.2.5 CPT

Carriage Paid to (... named place of destination) 运费付至(……指定目的地)

(1) Definition

定义

"Carriage Paid to..." means that the seller delivers the goods to the carrier or another person nominated by the seller itself, and that the seller must contract for and pay the costs of carriage necessary to bring the goods to the named place of destination, however, the buyer should bear all risks any other costs occurring after the goods have been so delivered. CPT applies to any mode of transport, including multimodal transport.

(2) **The obligations of buyer and seller**

买卖双方义务

① The seller's obligations 卖方义务

- The seller is responsible for carrying out all of the export customs clearances, and contracting for and paying the costs of carriage necessary to bring the goods to the named place of destination, as well as notifying the buyer once the goods have been so delivered.
- The seller must bear all the costs and risks of loss of or damage to the goods until the goods have been delivered to the carrier.
- The seller must provide the relevant agreed documents, or some electronic information with equivalent force.

② The buyer's obligations 买方义务

- The buyer must bear all the costs and risks of loss of or damage to the goods from the time that the goods have been delivered to the carrier.
- The buyer must bear all of the expenses and unloading charges occurring in the transit of goods, except the normal freight paid by the seller.
- The buyer must accept delivery of the goods at the place of dispatch and receive them from the carrier at the place of destination, accept the qualified documents provided by the seller and pay the price of the goods.

(3) **Some notable issues under the CPT term**

采用CPT术语应注意的问题

① Place of delivery and the transfer of risk 风险和费用划分

Under the CPT term, the seller is responsible for making the contract of carriage and paying the normal freight bringing the goods from the place of shipment to the agreed place of destination, but other expenses are borne by the buyer. CPT is similar to CFR in that the seller bears the cost of carriage, but the risk is transferred from the seller to the buyer at the time when the goods have been delivered to the carrier, that is all the risks during the transit of goods are borne by the buyer.

② Shipping notice 关于装运通知

Under the CPT term, the seller should notify the buyer promptly when the goods have been so delivered to the carrier, so as to ensure the buyer can make the insurance in time and take delivery of the goods from the carrier at the named place of destination. If a specific point is not agreed upon or is not determined by practice, the seller may select the point of delivery and the point at the named place of destination that best suit its purpose. Shipment notice is as important as that for FOB and CFR terms. When CPT, CIP, CFR, or CIF are used, the seller fulfills its obligation to deliver when it hands the goods over to the carrier and not when the goods reach the place of destination.

3.2.2.6 CIP

Carriage and Insurance Paid to (... named place of destination) 运费、保险费付至（……指定目的地）

(1) Definition

定义

CIP is an abbreviation for "carriage and insurance paid to". CIP means that the seller delivers the goods to the carrier or another person nominated by the seller at an agreed place (if any such place is agreed between the parties), and that the seller must contract for and pay the costs of carriage necessary to bring the goods to the named place of destination. The seller also contracts for insurance cover against the buyer's risk of loss of or damage to the goods during the carriage. That is while using CIP term, the seller should carry out both the carriage contract and the insurance contract, pay for the carriage cost and the premium. However, the buyer should note that under CIP, the seller is required to obtain insurance only on minimum cover, the buyer should undertake all the risks and additional expenses occurring after the goods have been so delivered. CIP applies to any mode of transport, including multimodal transport, which is the same as CPT.

(2) *The obligations of buyer and seller*

买卖双方义务

① The seller's obligations 卖方义务

- The seller is responsible for carrying out all of the export customs clearances, making the carriage contract and insurance contract at its own expense, delivering the goods to the carrier, as well as notifying the buyer once the goods have been so delivered.
- The seller must bear all the costs and risks of loss or damage to the goods until the goods have been delivered to the carrier.
- The seller must provide the relevant agreed documents, or some electronic information with equivalent force.

② The buyer's obligations 买方义务

- The buyer must bear all the costs and risks of loss or damage to the goods from the time that the goods have been delivered to the carrier.
- The buyer must bear all of the expenses and unloading charges occurring in the transit of goods, except the normal freight that has been paid by the seller.
- The buyer must take delivery of the goods at the place of destination, accept the qualified documents provided by the seller and pay the price of the goods.

(3) *Some notable issues under the CIP term*

采用CIP术语应注意的问题

Under the CIP term, the seller is responsible for contracting for insurance cover against the buyer's risk of loss of or damage to the goods during the carriage, which is the same as the CIF term, the seller makes the insurance on behalf of the buyer due to the premium contained in the CIP price. Generally speaking, the seller should only cover the agreed coverage against the goods. Otherwise, the insurance shall cover, at a minimum, the price provided in the contract plus 10% (i.e., 110%) and shall be in the currency of the contract. For a CIP contract, the seller has no obligation to cover additional risks, such as **war risk, strike risk, and SRCC risk**, however when required by the buyer, the seller shall provide, but the additional insurance costs of such insurance should be borne by the buyer.

战争、罢工、暴乱及民变险

3.2.3 FOB, CFR, CIF VS. FCA, CPT, CIP
装运港船上交货术语（FOB、CFR、CIF）与货交承运人术语（FCA、CPT、CIP）的异同

Points in common 共同点：

- They are all symbolic delivery and shipment contracts.
- The export clearances are borne by the exporters, and the import clearances are borne by the importers.
- The relationship among the trade terms in each group is the same: the seller is responsible for arranging carriage under terms FOB and FCA; while the buyer is responsible for arranging carriage under terms CFR and CPT; for terms CIF and CIP, the seller undertakes the obligations of arranging carriage and insurance. Other respective notable issues are the same.

The differences 不同点：

- Applicable modes of transport are different

FOB, CFR, CIF apply to water transport (including sea and inland waterway transport), the carrier generally is a shipping company. FCA, CPT, CIP apply to any mode of transport, such as water transport, land transport, and air transport, etc. In addition, they can be used **irrespective of** whether one or more than one mode of transport is employed, the carrier can be a shipping company, railway company, airlines, and multimodal transport operators.

不考虑

· Delivery point and risk-transfer point are different

For terms FOB, CFR, and CIF, the delivery point and risk-transfer point are that when the goods have been loaded on board the vessel. While for terms FCA, CPT, and CIP are that when the goods are placed at the disposal of the carrier.

· The responsibility of loading and unloading charges are differential.

Under FOB, CFR, and CIF terms, for liner transport, it is the party who is responsible for transport is responsible for loading and unloading charges, while for charter transport, the loading and unloading charges will be specified by terms variants. Under terms FCA, CPT, and CIP, it is generally the carrier who bears the loading and unloading duties, so there are no variants in this group.

· The related transport documents are different

The transport documents under terms FOB, CFR, and CIF are generally clean on board bills of lading, which is also a **document of title to the goods.** While for terms FCA, CPT, and CIP, what kind of transport documents submitted depends on the transport mode selected, but one thing to note is that the air waybill and rail waybill are not documents of title to the goods.

物权凭证

· The types of cargo insurance are different.

When using FOB, CFR, and CIF terms, the goods are covered by Marine Cargo Insurance. When using FCA, CPT, and CIP, terms, what type of transport insurance should be covered depends on what kind of transport mode adopted, it can be Marine Cargo Insurance, Overland Transportation Insurance and Air Transportation Insurance.

3.2.4　Other trade terms in Incoterms®2020
《2020年国际贸易术语解释通则》的其他贸易术语

EXW

Ex works（... named place of delivery）工厂交货（……指定地点）

"Ex Works" means that the seller delivers when it places the goods at the disposal of the buyer at the seller's premises or at another named place (i.e., works, factory, warehouse, etc.). The seller does not need to load the goods on any collecting vehicle, nor does it need to clear the goods for export, where such clearance is applicable. The buyer bears all costs and risks involved in taking the goods from the agreed point, if any, at the named place of delivery. This term thus imposes the minimum obligations on the seller, and imposes the maximum obligation on the buyer.

Under EXW term, export clearance procedure is handled by the buyer instead of the seller, in this case, the buyer needs to be aware of whether the exporting country could accept the person or the representative from another country to handle the export clearance formalities. If the buyer cannot directly or indirectly obtain export clearance, he is advised not to use this term. FCA may be preferable, especially for the counties whose land are neighboring.

FAS

Free alongside ship (... named port of shipment) 装运港船边交货 (……指定装运港)

"Free Alongside Ship" means that the seller delivers when the goods are placed alongside the vessel (e.g., on a quay or a barge) nominated by the buyer at the named port of shipment. The risk of loss of or damage to the goods passes when the goods are alongside the ship, and the buyer bears all costs and risks (including the risks and costs that happen during the barging) from that moment onwards. FAS term requires the seller to clear the goods for export. It can be used only for sea or inland waterway transport.

DAP

Deliver at Place (... named place of destination) 目的地交货 (……指定目的地)

"Delivered at Place" means that the seller delivers when the goods are placed at the disposal of the buyer on the arriving means of transport ready for unloading at the named place of destination. This term is very similar to CPT, that the seller will cover the charges and handle the operations necessary to send the goods to the named place of destination. However, one significant difference from the CPT term is that, DAP requires the seller to bear all risks involved in bringing the goods to the named destination. Under DAP at the time of delivery the risk and cost related to unloading the goods are for the account of the buyer. This term may be used to any mode of transport or multimodal transport.

DPU

Delivered at Place Unloaded (... named place of destination) 目的地卸货后交货（……指定目的地）

"Delivered at Place Unloaded" means that the seller must sign a transportation contract or arrange the transportation of the goods, and deliver the goods to the designated destination within the agreed date or time limit, and then deliver them to the buyer for disposal. The seller shall bear all risks and expenses after unloading the goods at the designated destination and before handing them over to the buyer for disposal. The difference between DPU and DAP lies in the unloading fee. The former is borne by the buyer, while the latter is borne by the seller.

The seller must be at the agreed place at the designated destination to unload the goods from the arriving means of transport and place them at the buyer's disposal, or to deliver the goods by obtaining the goods so delivered is the only Incoterms rule that requires the seller to unload at the destination. Therefore, the seller should ensure that it can organize the unloading at the designated place. However, DPU requires the seller to go through export customs clearance, but the seller is not obliged to go through import customs clearance or transit through a third country after delivery, pay any import duties or go through any import customs procedures. This term may be used to any mode of transport or multimodal transport.

DDP

Delivered duty paid (… named place destination) 完税后交货
(……指定目的地)

"Delivered Duty Paid" means that the seller delivers the goods when the goods are placed at the disposal of the buyer, cleared for import on the arriving means of transport ready for unloading at the named place of destination. The seller bears all the costs and risks involved in bringing the goods to the place of destination and has an obligation to clear the goods not only for export but also for import, to pay any duty for both export and import and to carry out all customs formalities. DDP represents the maximum obligation for the seller.

If the seller cannot directly or indirectly obtain import clearance, he is advised not to use this term. If the parties wish the buyer to bear all risks and costs of import clearance, the DAP should be used. Any VAT or other taxes payable upon import are for the seller's account unless expressly agreed otherwise in the sales contract. For example, if the parties wish the buyer to bear certain kinds of expenses, such as value-added tax, then it should stipulate "delivered duty paid, VAT. unpaid (… named place destination)" in the contract. This term may be used to any mode of transport or multimodal transport.

The following Table 3.2 shows the responsibilities, risks, and expenses between the buyer and seller.

Table 3.2   The Responsibilities, Risks, and Expenses between the Buyer and Seller

Term	Export clearance	Import clearance	Contract of carriage	Contract of insurance	Place of delivery	Point of risk transfer	Mode of transport
EXW	B	B	B	B	S's premise or another named place	Goods at disposal of B	Any mode
FCA	S	B	B	B	Specified place of exporting country	Goods at disposal of carrier or forwarder	Any mode

Table 3.2 (continued)

Term	Export clearance	Import clearance	Contract of carriage	Contract of insurance	Place of delivery	Point of risk transfer	Mode of transport
FAS	S	B	B	B	On wharf / barge that is alongside the ship	Goods are alongside the ship	Sea/inland waterway transport
FOB	S	B	B	B	On the ship	Goods are on board the ship	Sea/inland waterway transport
CFR	S	B	S	B	On the ship	Goods are on board the ship	Sea/inland waterway transport
CIF	S	B	S	<u>S</u>	On the ship	Goods are on board the ship	Sea/inland waterway transport
CPT	S	B	S	B	Specified place of exporting country	Goods at disposal of carrier or forwarder	Any mode
CIP	S	B	S	<u>S</u>	Specified place of exporting country	Goods at disposal of carrier or forwarder	Any mode
DAP	S	B	S	S	Specified place of exporting country	Goods reach specified place, NOT unloaded	Any mode
DPU	S	B	S	S	Specified place of exporting country	Goods reach specified place, unloaded	Any mode
DDP	S	S	S	S	Specified place of exporting country	Goods reach specified place, NOT unloaded	Any mode

NOTE: The underlined letters indicate that the insurance is compulsory for the designated party. (B=Buyer, S=Seller)

3.3 Clauses Commonly Used about the Trade Terms in Contract
合同中使用的贸易术语

You cannot rest assured even if the incoterms rules are in place. Only by observing some important **principles** and using them wisely can you make the best of these rules.

原则

3.3.1 Make Reference of Incoterms Rules in Your Sales Contract
在销售合同中引用贸易术语

If you want the *Incoterms 2020* rules to be **applied to** your contract, please make clear reference in your contract in order to avoid confusions with *Incoterms 2010*, as both are equally valid even though the new rules have been published and **taken effect**. This could be achieved through such words and **syntax**, "[the chosen Incoterms rule] +[named port, place of point] + *Incoterms 2020*." For example:

适用

生效

句法

(1) CIF Shanghai Incoterms® 2020, or

(2) DPU 611 Fifth Avenue New York, NY 10022, US, Incoterms® 2020

3.3.2 Select the Appropriate Incoterms Rule
选择适宜的贸易术语

You need to select an Incoterms rule that is appropriate to the goods, to the means of their transport, and to the methods of payment and generally avoid extreme Incoterms rules. And the convention or practices at the specific port or place should also be considered.

Select an Incoterms rule that suits your goods 选择适合你的货物的贸易术语

Bulk goods, such as coal, wheat, and iron ore, can be moved

散货货物

straight to the ship at specific **wharf**, while containerized goods cannot which are normally landed on container yards before loading. Therefore, FAS, FOB, CFR, and CIF can be used for bulk goods, but not quite satisfying for containerized goods.

码头

Select an Incoterms rule that suits the mode of transport 选择适合运输方式的贸易术语

Selecting an Incoterms rule that suits the mode of transport help you clarify both your and the importer's respective obligations and reduce misunderstandings or disputes. For example, if the final destination is a named place on land, Incoterms rules that are applicable for sea transport, such as FAS, FOB, CFR, and CIF should be avoided. For container transport, Incoterms rules compatible with **door-to-door transport** is mostly preferred, such as DAP or DPU.

门到门运输

Select an Incoterms rule that suits the method of payment 选择适合付款方式的贸易术语

As risk exposure is uneven between exporter and importer under certain methods of payment, selecting an Incoterms rule that suits the method of payment helps you reduce risk. For example, a potential risk of losing both money and goods exists under the payment method of cash on delivery by T/T（Chapter 8）. Taking control of the goods as long as possible by asking to arrange for transport helps to prevent this, in which case, CFR, CIF, CPT, DAP, DPU, etc. are more appropriate.

Avoid the extreme Incoterms rules 避免极端的贸易术语

EXW and DDP are the most imbalanced Incoterms rules in terms of risk exposure, allocation of cost and obligations between importer and exporter. Therefore, they are not recommended except under special circumstances. For example, while EXW may mean the least risk, cost and obligations for you, it imposes difficulties on you in filing for tax refund from the tax bureau. As the importer is to clear the goods even for export, it is not convenient for you to get the needed document for tax refund —the copy of the customs clearance form for tax refund. 出口报关单退税联

Similarly, DDP is not convenient for you to clear the goods for import.

Specify Your Place or Port as Precisely as Possible 尽可能精准地描述地址或港口名称

The chosen Incoterms rule can work only if the parties name a place or port, and will work best if the parties specify the place or port as precisely as possible. A good example of such precision would be: "*FCA 38 Cours Albert ler Paris, France Incoterms 2020.*"

Exercises 练习

I. True (T) or False (F)

1. The exporter is not obliged to cover insurance if the deal is under Incoterms DAP, but he/she is if under CIF. (　)

2. The exporter should cover the insurance under DPU for his/her own benefits. (　)

3. In *Incoterms 2020*, "delivery' means sending the cargo to the importer's premise. (　)

4. Under CIP, the exporter must pay the freight and insurance premium and bear all the risks until the goods reach the destination. (　)

5. The common feature of an FOB contract and an FAS contract is that the exporter must load the goods on a named ship. (　)

6. DPU requires the exporter to unload the cargo, while DAP and DDP do not. (　)

7. EXW, DAP, DPU, and DDP can be used for neighboring countries within a free trade area. (　)

8. Since Incoterms rules are widely known in the trade, an international sales contract is based on *Incoterms 2020* **by default**, without the need to **make reference to** it every time we sign a contract. (　) 默认　提及

9. An international contract is legally binding on the importer and the exporter, while the Incoterms is not. (　　)

10. Now that *Incoterms 2020* takes effect, *Incoterms 2010* is no longer valid. (　　)

II. Multiple Choice Questions

1. Under CIP and CPT, the responsibility of booking shipping space or chartering a vessel should be taken by (　　) respectively.

    A. exporter/exporter　　　　B. exporter/importer

    C. importer/importer　　　　D. importer/exporter

2. Among *Incoterms 2020* rules, which rule represents the biggest obligation for the exporter? (　　)

    A. EXW.　　B. CIF.　　C. DPU.　　D. DDP.

3. What's the major difference between FOB and FAS? (　　)

    A. The boundary of risk division.

    B. The party responsible for space booking or ship chartering.

    C. The party responsible for export clearance.

    D. The party responsible for import clearance.

4. Which one of the following is a shared feature of CPT and CFR?

    A. The exporter takes charge of arranging for carriage from the loading port to the unloading port and paying the sea freight.

    B. The importer assumes all risks when the cargo is in transit.

    C. The risk shifts with the completion of cargo delivery.

    D. The exporter assumes all risks until the cargo reaches destination.

5. Which *Incoterms 2020* rule requires the exporter to be responsible for unloading the goods? (　　)

    A. DPU.　　B. DAP.　　C. DDP.　　D. CIP.

6. Which *Incoterms 2020* rule is more appropriate for goods transported in containers? (　　)

    A. FAS.　　B. FOB.　　C. CIF.　　D. CIP.

7. Which *Incoterms 2020* rule doesn't require the exporter to load

the goods?( )

  A. EXW. B. FCA. C. CPT. D. CIP.

  8. Which *Incoterms 2020* rule requires the exporter to cover the cargo as per Institute Cargo Clause C?( )

  A. CIP. B. CIF. C. CPT. D. CFR.

  9. Which *Incoterms 2020* rule obliges the exporter to cover the goods with insurance?( )

  A. DDP. B. CIP. C. DDU. D. DAP.

  10. Which *Incoterms 2020* rule might pose difficulties for the exporter to clear customs?( )

  A. EWX and DDP. B. FCA and DDP.

  C. EXW and FAS. D. FCA and DPU.

III. Group Task.

  1. With the help of digital technology, create a **mind map** of the 11 trade terms in *Incoterms 2020*, **demonstrating** the similarities and differences in the responsibilities, costs, and risk transfer points borne by the buyer and the seller under different trade terms.

思维导图展示

  2. Role-playing. Each group selects one trade term. Group members respectively assume the roles of the seller, the buyer, the carrier, the insurance company, the commentator, etc. Relevant entities such as banks, customs, and commodity inspection bureaus are involved. Props can include transportation vehicles, goods, etc. All group members must collaborate to complete the entire process from contract signing to execution. During the role-play, it is necessary to clarify the division of responsibilities, risks, and costs between the buyer and seller during the delivery of goods.

角色扮演。每组选择一个贸易术语,组员分别饰演卖方、买方、承运人、保险公司、解说员等角色,部门涉及进出口地银行、海关、商检局等,表演道具可以包含运输工具、货物等,合作完成从合同签订到合同履行的全过程。表演中,需明确货物从卖方送到买方过程中,买卖双方的责任、风险和费用的划分点。

IV. Case Study

  1. An exporter exports a batch of Christmas gifts to an English buyer with CIF London and as the Christmas gifts are seasonal, they stipulate in the contract that the buyer shall open a credit before the end of September and the seller shall ship the goods to Hamburg not

later than 5th December. Or else, the buyer has the right to cancel the contract and get refund from the seller. So is the amended contract still a CIF contract? Why?

2. Our importer imports a batch of goods under FOB term. When the goods are being unloaded, a dozen of packages are found broken and **soaked** by seawater. After investigation, the goods are cast broken on deck and then soaked as the **lift hooks** get loosened. Can our importer **lodge a claim** for the failure of the seller to fulfill the obligation of delivery?

浸泡
吊钩
提出索赔

3. An Indian importer has placed an order of a certain kind of **mother board** under FCA（Guangzhou Airport）. The exporter delivered the goods to the carrier at the airport as scheduled. The airline received the goods and **issued** the air waybill. So, the exporter asked the importer to make payment. However, at this time, the market price of the goods fell. The importer then refused to pay, saying that he hadn't officially **taken delivery** and asked the exporter to have the goods shipped back home. This dispute resulted in a **deadlock** between the importer and exporter. Do you think the importer's statement is justified?

主板

开具

提货
僵局

4. A Russian customer ordered a batch of auto parts from an exporter in Northeast China who transported them to a place in Russia by rail under Incoterm DAP. When the goods arrived at the station and were unloaded, the importer found that the unloading charges were not paid and the quantity of goods was short, so the importer asked for a deduction of the unloading charges and of an amount equal to the shortage from the total amount. The exporter claimed that he had loaded the goods in the right quantity and supported his claim with a series of documents. He suspected that the goods were stolen in transit and therefore refused the importer's request for a deduction and asked him to make a claim against the carrier. The questions are:（1）Is the importer's request for the exporter to pay for unloading charges justified?（2）Who should make a claim against the carrier?

Chapter 4

Terms of Commodity

第四章　合同中的商品条款

◆ Learning Objectives

- Know the different ways of quality stipulation
- Master the quantity measurement units and systems
- Understand the approaches to weight calculation
- Understand the functions and features of different types of export packaging

Commodity is the subject matter of international sales contracts. According to **The United Nations Convention on Contracts for the International Sale of Goods (CISG)**, the seller must deliver goods which are of the quantity, quality, and description required by the contract and which are contained, packaged, and identified as required by the contract. An international trade sales contract is dealing with the transfer of ownership of the subject matter. Consequently, in order to prevent potential disputes between the seller and the buyer in the future, the terms and conditions related to the commodity should be clearly defined in the sales contract.

联合国国际货物销售合同公约（CISG）

4.1 Name of Commodity
商品的名称

The description of commodity is actually a legal definition of the subject matter in the transaction. Therefore, when signing an international sales contract, the name (description) of commodity is the first term to be **stipulated** concerning the quality of commodity. If the goods delivered do not conform to the agreed name of commodity, the buyer is entitled to claim against the seller for compensation, reject the goods or even cancel the contract. Therefore, it is of great importance to specify the name of commodity clearly in the contract. When setting the clause of the name of commodity, the following points should be considered:

规定；约定

Being Clear and Specific 品名必须明确具体

The description of commodity names should be accurate and specific, avoiding **ambiguity**. For example, the name "mask" is too general because there are different types of masks on the market. There are significant differences in hygiene and protection between ordinary protective masks and medical protective masks. Therefore, when naming such products, specific names should be given according to their specifications and relevant implementation standards.

模棱两可；含混不清

Being realistic 品名应该实事求是

The regulations regarding commodity names or descriptions should be based on facts, avoiding any exaggeration of the products. For example, "Wuchang Rice" has been granted protection as a product of origin, and it has been included in the first batch of protection lists for **geographical indications** in the China – EU agreement. If the rice sold by a merchant is not from the original production area, it cannot be named "Wuchang Rice".

五常大米
地理标志

Adopting the name of commodity which is widely accepted internationally 尽可能使用国际通用名称

The names of some commodities may vary from country to country. To

avoid misunderstandings, it is advisable to use internationally recognized terms as much as possible. Take **aspirin**, a common drug, as an example. 阿司匹林
In different countries, it may have different brand names. However, from the perspective of the drug's generic name, "Aspirin" is widely recognized by the global medical community and drug regulatory authorities as the international common name for this drug. Using this international common name can ensure that all parties clearly understand the drug's ingredients, efficacy, and usage specifications, thus avoiding medication errors or trade disputes caused by name differences.

Considering tariffs and transportation costs 需考虑关税和运输成本

In international trade, sometimes a certain commodity has different names, and the tariff rates and freight rates of the same commodity may vary due to different names. Therefore, if the stipulations of the commodity description have little impact on the nature of the subject matter, choosing an appropriate name as the commodity name in the contract is beneficial to both the exporter and the importer.

4.2 Quality of Commodity
商品的品质

4.2.1 Definition of Quality of Goods
商品品质的含义

The quality of a commodity refers to the combination of its inherent qualities and external appearance. Inherent qualities include the natural attributes of the commodity such as physical properties, mechanical properties, chemical composition, and biological characteristics. Taking a mobile phone as an example, its inherent qualities are reflected in aspects such as processor performance, battery life, camera **pixel,** 像素
imaging quality. External appearance refers to the shape, color, style,

smell, etc. of the commodity. For instance, the style, color, and fabric texture of clothing all fall within the category of external appearance.

The quality of a commodity is a crucial factor determining its usability and market price. It is directly related to the interests of both the buyer and the seller. Therefore, both the buyer and the seller attach great importance to the quality of the commodity. The quality of a commodity is not only an important clause in an international goods sales contract, but also a matter on which importers and exporters must first reach an agreement during business negotiations. The seller must deliver the goods in accordance with the quality stipulated in the contract. Any non-compliance may lead to disputes between the buyer and the seller. Therefore, special attention should be paid to the quality of the traded commodity. That is to say, the seller must deliver the goods with the quality specified in the contract. If the goods do not meet the requirements of the contract, the importer will have the right to file a claim.

4.2.2　Methods of Stipulating Quality of Commodity
　　　表示品质的基本方法

There are various types and characteristics of commodities in international trade, so are the methods of stipulating quality of goods. Generally, there are two ways to indicate the quality of goods either by actual commodity or by description.

4.2.2.1　Sale by Actual Commodity
　　　　以实物表示商品品质

(1) Sale by Inspection on the Spot
　　看货买卖

Sale by Inspection on the Spot refers to a sales method in which both the buyer and the seller inspect the goods at the location where the goods are situated, and the results of this inspection serve as the basis for the transaction. Under this sales method, the buyer will conduct on-site inspections of the quality, quantity, specifications, etc. of the goods at the place where the goods are located to determine whether the goods meet the requirements of the contract or the standards agreed upon by both parties. This sales method is commonly seen in some **spot-trading** scenarios. For example, in agricultural product transactions, the buyer may visit the farm or warehouse to inspect **on-site** the maturity, quality, and presence of pests and diseases of the crops, so as to decide whether to purchase and at what price.

现货交易

现场的

(2) *Sale by Sample*

凭样品买卖

Sale by Sample means that the sample is used as the basis for the transaction between the buyer and the seller to determine the quality and other transaction conditions of the goods. The following are its common classifications:

① **Sale by Seller's Sample** 凭卖方样品买卖

The seller provides the sample, and the buyer takes this sample as the basis for inspecting and accepting the goods. The quality of the entire batch of goods delivered by the seller must be consistent with the provided sample. For example, a clothing manufacturer sells a new style of clothing to foreign customers. The manufacturer provides several clothing samples to the customers. After the customers approve, they place an order. Then, the entire batch of goods delivered by the manufacturer should match the samples in terms of style, fabric, color, **workmanship**, etc.

手艺；工艺；技艺

② **Sale by Buyer's Sample** 凭买方样品买卖

The buyer provides the sample, and the seller produces and delivers the goods according to the requirements of the buyer's sample. In this case, the seller needs to pay attention to the technical feasibility and **intellectual property** issues of the sample. For instance, a toy company

知识产权

receives an order from a foreign customer. The customer provides a design sample of a toy and requires the toy company to produce according to this sample. The toy company then needs to produce according to the requirements of the sample, such as size, material, and function, to ensure that the delivered products are consistent with the buyer's sample.

③ Sale by Counter Sample 凭对等样品买卖

回样　确认样

Sometimes it is also called "return sample" or "confirming sample". When the buyer provides a sample, if the seller thinks it is difficult to produce according to the buyer's sample or to avoid potential disputes over quality issues during future delivery, the seller will process a similar sample based on the buyer's sample and submit it to the buyer for confirmation. The sample confirmed by the buyer is the counter sample. Subsequently, the transaction is based on the counter sample. For example, in the furniture trade, the buyer provides a furniture sample. The seller makes a slightly improved sample based on the sample and submits it to the buyer for confirmation. If the buyer agrees, then the subsequent transaction will take this counter sample as the quality basis.

④ Some notable issues 凭样品买卖的注意事项

In the trade of sales by sample, there are many points that need attention. Both the buyer and the seller mainly need to focus on aspects such as sample preparation, contract terms, and intellectual property rights. The details are as follows:

样品制备与提供

（A）Sample Preparation and Provision. Firstly, the samples provided should be fully representative and accurately reflect the quality characteristics of the entire batch of goods. For example, in the clothing trade, if there are significant differences in color and fabric texture between the sample and the bulk goods, it may lead to the buyer's dissatisfaction with the quality of the goods and trigger disputes.

Secondly, keep backups. Both the buyer and the seller should properly retain **backup samples** that are exactly the same as the provided samples, which can be used as a basis for verification and inspection in case of disputes in the future. Finally, clear labeling. Key information about the samples, such as specifications, models, components, and production processes, should be clearly marked on the samples or relevant documents to avoid misunderstandings caused by unclear information.

备份样品

(B) **Clarification of Contract Terms.** Firstly, quality description. In addition to stating that the goods are subject to the sample, the contract should also describe the quality specifications of the goods in as much detail as possible to further clarify the specific requirements of the traded goods and prevent potential ambiguities that may arise from relying solely on the sample. Secondly, inspection standards. Clearly define the **inspection standards** and methods for the goods, as well as the selection method of the **inspection agency**. For example, it can be stipulated that a third-party professional inspection agency recognized by both parties conducts inspections in accordance with specific international standards to ensure the fairness and authority of the inspection results. Finally, **handling of non-compliance.** Clearly define in the contract in advance the handling methods in case the goods do not conform to the sample, including whether the buyer has the right to reject the goods, request a price reduction, exchange the goods, or file a claim, as well as specific claim periods and procedures, etc., to protect the rights and interests of both parties.

合同条款的说明

检验标准
检验机构

不合规情况的处理

(C) **Control of the Production Process.** Firstly, production supervision. For the seller, during the production process, it is necessary to produce strictly in accordance with the standards of the sample, establish a complete quality control system, and strengthen the supervision and management of the production process to ensure

生产过程控制

the consistency between the bulk goods and the sample. Secondly, raw material procurement. Ensure that the raw materials required for production are the same as those used in the sample in terms of quality, specifications, etc., to avoid the **non-conformity** between the goods and the sample caused by differences in raw materials. Finally, production records. Keep good records of all aspects of the production process, including raw material procurement records, production process parameter records, quality inspection records, etc., so that the production situation of the goods can be **traced and proven** when necessary, providing a basis for possible problems.

(D) **Intellectual Property Issues.** Firstly, rights review. The party providing the sample should ensure that the sample provided does not infringe on the intellectual property rights of third parties, such as patents, **trademarks**, and copyrights. After receiving the sample, the buyer should also conduct necessary intellectual property reviews to avoid facing legal risks due to purchasing infringing products. Secondly, **liability agreement.** Clearly define the liability for intellectual property rights in the contract. If the sample causes losses to the other party due to intellectual property issues, the liable party shall bear corresponding compensation liability.

(E) **Transportation and Delivery.** Firstly, packaging protection. Properly package the samples and goods to ensure that they are not damaged, deteriorated, or otherwise affected in quality during transportation. For special goods such as fragile and perishable goods, corresponding special packaging measures and transportation methods should be adopted. Secondly, transportation insurance. According to the value of the goods and transportation risks, reasonably select transportation insurance and clearly define the scope of insurance liability and claim settlement procedures. If the goods are damaged or lost during transportation, compensation can be obtained in a timely manner to reduce the losses of both parties. Finally, delivery time. Deliver the samples and goods strictly in accordance with the time and place specified in the contract to avoid causing losses to the other party or affecting the smooth progress of the transaction due to delayed delivery.

4.2.2.2 Sale by Description
凭文字说明买卖

Sale by Description refers to a trading method in international trade where both the buyer and the seller use written language to describe in detail various elements of the goods being traded, such as quality, specifications, grades, standards, brands, and place of origin. These descriptions serve as the basis for determining the goods in the transaction and for conducting the trade. The classifications are as follows:

（1） Sale by Specification
凭规格买卖

Specifications are the main indicators used to reflect the quality of goods, such as chemical composition, content, **purity**, size, length, **thickness**, etc. For example, in the coal trade, it may be specified that the **calorific value** of the coal is not less than 5,500 kcal/kg, the **ash content** is not higher than 20%, and the **sulfur content** is not higher than 1%. As long as the goods meet these specification requirements, they are considered to meet the contract agreement. This method can accurately describe the quality of goods, making it convenient for both parties to determine the transaction terms. It is widely used in the trade of industrial products and primary products.

纯度
厚度
热值　灰分含量
硫含量

（2） Sale by Grade
凭等级买卖

Grade refers to the classification of similar goods into several different levels according to differences in quality, weight, composition, appearance, etc. Usually, they are represented by symbols or numbers such as one, two, three; A, B, C; or first – class, second – class, third – class. For instance, in the tea trade, tea can be divided into different grades such as **special grade**, first grade, and second grade based on factors like **tenderness, color, aroma, and taste**. Goods of different grades usually have obvious differences in quality and price. By simply clarifying the grade of the goods, both the buyer and the seller can generally determine the quality and price range of the goods. The following Table 4.1 is the grade classification and related characteristics of Longjing tea.

Table 4.1 Examples of Sale by Grade

Tea Grade	Appearance	Taste	Soup Color
Longjing–Special Grade	Flat and smooth, with a tender green and glossy color. The bud tips are prominent, and it is at the initial stage of one bud and one leaf.	Fresh, mellow, and refreshing, with a long-lasting sweet aftertaste.	Tender green and bright.
Longjing–First Grade	Fairly flat and smooth, with a green and lustrous color. There are slightly flat fragments. It is either one bud and one leaf or at the initial stage of one bud and two leaves.	Mellow and refreshing, with an obvious sweet aftertaste.	Green and bright.
Longjing–Second Grade	Less flat and smooth, with fragments. The color is still green, and it is one bud and two leaves.	Mellow, with a sweet aftertaste.	Yellow–green and fairly bright.

(3) Sale by Standard
凭标准买卖

A standard is a set of specifications or grades uniformly formulated and promulgated by government agencies or commercial organizations, which is a standardized requirement for the quality of goods. For example, in the steel trade, international standards (such as ISO standards), **national standards** (such as China's GB standards), or industry standards may be adopted. For some widely – accepted standards, both parties only need to indicate the name and version number of the standard in the contract. However, since some standards may be updated over time, it is necessary to clarify the specific standard version in the transaction to avoid disputes caused by inconsistent understanding of the standard.

(4) Sale by Descriptions and Illustrations
凭说明书和图样买卖

For some complex-structured and high-tech products, such as mechanical equipment and electronic products, it is difficult to fully describe their quality and performance with simple specifications, grades, or standards. Detailed product descriptions, drawings, photos, and other materials are needed to specifically describe **the structure, performance, usage method, installation, and debugging requirements**, etc. of the goods. For example, when purchasing a large-scale CNC machine tool, the seller will provide a detailed product description, including the technical parameters of the machine tool, instructions for the operation interface, maintenance requirements, etc., and may also attach drawings of the appearance and internal structure of the machine tool to help the buyer fully understand the goods.

结构、性能、使用方法、安装及调试要求

(5) Sale by Brand or Trade Mark
凭品牌或商标买卖

A brand or trade mark is a logo used by an enterprise to distinguish its products from those of other enterprises. It often represents a certain product quality and characteristics. Brands or trademarks with a certain reputation and popularity in the market usually have products with relatively stable quality and performance. For example, in the clothing trade, well-known brands like "Nike" and "Adidas" have certain expectations from consumers regarding product style, fabric, and workmanship. In a transaction, as long as both parties clarify the brand or trade mark, the quality and style of the goods can be determined to a certain extent.

(6) Sale by Name of Origin
凭产地名称买卖

For some goods with specific quality, characteristics, or reputation, and where this quality, characteristic, or reputation is mainly attributed to their place of origin, the method of sale by name of origin is often used. For example, "**Bordeaux Wine from France**" and "**Jingdezhen Porcelain** from China". The name of the origin itself represents the specific quality and style of the goods. Consumers purchase these goods largely based on their recognition of the unique quality given by the place of origin. In the transaction, the seller must ensure that the goods provided are from the designated place of origin and meet the quality characteristics that goods from that place should possess.

> 法国波尔多葡萄酒
> 景德镇瓷器

4.2.3　Quality Latitude and Quality Tolerance
　　　　品质机动幅度和品质公差

In international trade, "Quality Latitude" and "Quality Tolerance" are both important concepts related to the quality of goods. The following presents their meanings and examples:

Quality Latitude 品质机动幅度

Quality Latitude refers to a certain range or margin within which the quality of goods can fluctuate without affecting their normal use and value. It allows for a certain degree of flexibility in the quality of goods, indicating that as long as the quality of the goods is within this range, it is considered to comply with the contract requirements.

> 品质机动幅度是指的是商品质量可以在不影响其正常使用和价值的情况下波动的一定范围或幅度。

For example, in the export of wool, the contract may stipulate that the wool content is 90% ± 5%. Here, the "± 5%" is the quality latitude. This means that the actual wool content of the wool products can be between 85% and 95% and still be regarded as meeting the contract specifications.

Quality Tolerance 品质公差

Quality tolerance is the allowable range of deviation in the quality of goods due to factors such as production processes and natural conditions. It is mainly used for some products where it is difficult to

> 品质公差是由于生产过程和自然条件等因素导致商品质量可能出现的允许偏差范围。

achieve absolute consistency in quality. Even if the quality of the goods has a certain deviation within the allowable tolerance range, the buyer cannot reject the goods without justifiable reasons.

For example, in the production of screws, there may be some differences in the diameter and length of the screws. If the contract stipulates that the diameter of the screws is 10mm with a quality tolerance of ± 0.1mm, it means that screws with a diameter between 9.9mm and 10.1mm are considered to be in line with the quality requirements. This is because in the actual production process of screws, it is very difficult to ensure that the diameter of each screw is exactly 10mm, and a certain tolerance range is allowed.

4.3 Quantity of Commodity
商品的数量

The quantity of goods is an indispensable factor in a transaction. According to CISG, it is a fundamental obligation of the seller to deliver the goods in the quantity agreed upon. If the quantity of goods delivered by the seller is greater than the agreed quantity, the buyer has the right to reject the excess quantity. If the quantity of goods delivered by the seller is less than the agreed quantity, the seller shall make up the shortfall before the expiration of the specified delivery period. Even if the seller makes up the shortfall, the buyer still reserves the right to claim damages. In international trade, the quantity of commodity is always shown as a specific amount in weight, length, width, area, volume, etc.

4.3.1 Units of measurement
计量单位

In international trade, the measurement units for the quantity of goods mainly include the following categories:

4.3.1.1 Weight Units
重量单位

克   ***Gram (g)***: The basic unit of mass in the International System of Units, often used to measure precious items or fine chemical products, such as gold, pharmaceuticals, etc.

千克   ***Kilogram (kg)***: One of the most commonly used weight units in daily life and trade, widely applied to various goods, such as grains, fruits, industrial raw materials, etc.

吨   ***Ton (t)***: Suitable for large quantities of bulk goods, such as coal, ore, steel, etc. In the trading of bulk commodities in international trade, the ton is a very common measurement unit.

磅   ***Pound (lb)***: An imperial weight unit, used in some trade with countries like the United States and the United Kingdom, such as for some agricultural products, meat, etc. One pound is approximately equal to 0.4536 kilograms.

盎司   ***Ounce (oz)***: The avoirdupois ounce is used to measure general items, with one ounce being approximately 28.35 grams, often used for precious metals like gold and silver, as well as for some foods and pharmaceuticals; the troy ounce is specifically used to measure precious metals such as gold and silver, with one troy ounce being approximately 31.10 grams.

4.3.1.2 Quantity Units
数量单位

件   ***Piece***: The most common quantity unit, used for goods that can be counted individually, such as clothing, machine parts, furniture, etc.

双   ***Pair***: Used to measure items that must be used in pairs, such as shoes, gloves, socks, etc.

套   ***Set***: Applicable to a whole composed of multiple related items, such as a set of furniture, a set of tools, a set of stationery, etc.

打   ***Dozen***: 12 items make up one dozen, often used for measuring some small items, such as eggs, pencils, socks, etc.

Gross: One gross is equal to 12 dozen, that is, 144 items, and may be used in the trade of some traditional textiles, small hardware, etc. 　罗

Ream: Mainly used to measure paper, with one ream usually being 500 sheets of paper. 　令

4.3.1.3　Length Units
长度单位

Meter (m): An internationally used length unit, in international trade, it is often used to measure goods priced by length, such as textiles, wires and cables, pipes, etc. 　米

Centimeter (cm): Used in the measurement of goods that require high precision in size, such as in the size marking of clothing and the length measurement of small parts. 　厘米

Foot (ft): An imperial length unit, in trade with countries like the United States and the United Kingdom, it is often used in the construction materials, wood, shipping and other industries. One foot is approximately equal to 0.3048 meters. 　英尺

Inch (in): Often used in conjunction with the foot, with one inch being approximately 2.54 centimeters, and frequently appears in the size marking of electronic components, mechanical parts, pipes, etc. 　英寸

4.3.1.4　Area Units
面积单位

Square Meter (m^2): Used to measure goods that need to be calculated by area, such as land, building materials (such as tiles, floor coverings) , textiles (such as carpets, fabrics) , etc. 　平方米

Square Foot (ft^2): Used in the imperial measurement system, often used in the real estate, construction and other fields, especially in trade with countries like the United States and the United Kingdom. One square foot is approximately equal to 0.0929 square meters. 　平方英尺

Hectare (ha): Mainly used to measure large areas of land and 　公顷

is more commonly used in international trade in the agricultural and forestry fields. One hectare is equal to 10,000 square meters.

4.3.1.5　Volume Units
体积单位

立方米　　***Cubic Meter (m³)***：Often used to measure goods priced by volume, such as wood, natural gas, petroleum, etc., as well as for the volume measurement of some large mechanical equipment and containers.

升　　***Liter (L)***：Often used to measure liquid goods, such as beverages, alcoholic beverages, edible oils, chemical raw materials, etc. One liter is equal to 0.001 cubic meters.

毫升　　***Milliliter (mL)***：Generally used to measure small amounts of liquid goods, such as pharmaceuticals, perfumes, etc.

立方英尺　　***Cubic Foot (ft³)***：An imperial volume unit, in some trade with countries like the United States and the United Kingdom, it is used to measure the volume of goods or storage space, etc. One cubic foot is approximately equal to 0.0283 cubic meters.

4.3.1.6　Capacity Units
容积单位

蒲式耳　　***Bushel***：Mainly used to measure the capacity of agricultural products such as grains, fruits, and vegetables. The specific capacity definition of the bushel may vary slightly in different countries. In the United States, one bushel is approximately equal to 35.24 liters.

4.3.2　Calculation of Weight
重量计算方法

In international trade, the commonly used methods for weighing goods mainly include the following:

4.3.2.1　Gross Weight
毛重

Gross weight refers to the weight of the goods themselves plus the weight of the packaging materials, that is, the total weight of the goods together with the packaging. The formula is:

Gross Weight = Weight of the Goods + Weight of the Packaging.

This measurement method is mainly applicable to goods with relatively low value, where the packaging is difficult to separate from the goods themselves, or the packaging cost is relatively high, such as bulk commodities like ores, fertilizers, and cement. For such goods, freight, warehousing fees, and other charges are usually calculated based on the gross weight during transportation and warehousing.

毛重＝商品重量＋包装重量

4.3.2.2 Net Weight

净重

Net weight refers to the actual weight of the goods themselves, that is, the weight obtained by subtracting the weight of the packaging materials from the gross weight. This is the most commonly used method for weighing goods in international trade. The formula is:

Net Weight = Gross Weight − Tare Weight (Weight of the Packaging).

净重＝毛重−皮重（包装重量）

This measurement method is applicable to most goods, especially those with high value and where accurate calculation of the weight of the goods themselves is required, such as electronic products, precision instruments, and precious metals. In sales contracts, if there is no special agreement, it is generally assumed that the weight and price of the goods are calculated based on the net weight.

4.3.2.3 Conditioned Weight

公量

For some goods with **strong hygroscopicity and unstable moisture content**, such as wool, cotton, and raw silk, in order to accurately calculate their weight, a scientific method is usually used to remove the moisture from the goods and then add the internationally recognized standard moisture content to obtain the conditioned weight.

强吸湿性和不稳定的水分含量

公量=商品净重×(1+标准回潮率)

公量=商品实际重量×(1+标准回潮率)/(1+实际回潮率)

The formulas are:

Conditioned Weight = Dry Weight of the Goods × (1 + Standard Regaining rate of Water)

Or

Conditioned Weight = Actual Weight of the Goods × [(1 + Standard Regaining rate of Water) / (1 + Actual Regaining rate of Water)].

This measurement method is mainly used for goods like wool, cotton, and raw silk, whose weight is prone to change due to humidity. In international trade, the transactions of such goods often require the use of conditioned weight to determine their true weight and price, in order to avoid weight differences and price disputes caused by different moisture contents.

Note:

Dried net weight: the weight of the goods when all the water content is abstracted by a scientific method from the goods.

Regain rate: the ratio between the water content and the dry weight of the goods.

Standard regain rate: the ratio between the water content and the dry weight of the goods which is accepted in the world market or agreed upon by the seller and the buyer.

Actual regain rate: the ratio between the actual regaining water content in the goods and the actual dry weight.

Example 1

An exporter is shipping a batch of wool with a dry weight of 1000kg. The internationally recognized standard regain rate is 10%. Calculate the Conditioned Weight of this batch of wool.

Answer:

Conditioned Weight=Dry Weight×（1+Standard Regain Rate）

Conditioned Weight=1000kg×（1+0.10）

=1000kg×1.10

=1100kg

Example 2

An exporter is shipping a batch of cotton with an actual weight of 1200 kg. The standard regain rate for cotton is 8%, and the actual regain rate is 10%. Calculate the Conditioned Weight of this batch of cotton using the actual weight and the standard regain rate.

Answer:

Conditioned Weight = 1200kg × (1+0.08) / (1+0.10)

= 1200kg × 0.9818

≈ 1178.16kg

4.3.2.4 Theoretical Weight

理论重量

For some goods with fixed specifications and dimensions, such as **steel plates, steel pipes, and tinplate**, the weight calculated based on their specifications and dimensions is called the theoretical weight. The formula is:

钢板、钢管和马口铁（镀锡板）

Theoretical Weight = Unit Theoretical Weight of the Goods × Quantity of the Goods.

理论重量=货物的单位理论重量×货物数量

This measurement method is mainly applicable to goods with a fixed shape, dimensions, and density. In transactions, if the specifications and quality of the goods meet the standards and the quantity is large, making it difficult to weigh each item one by one, the theoretical weight can be used to calculate the total weight of the goods as a reference for the transaction. However, when delivering the goods, the actual weight shall prevail.

4.3.2.5 Legal Weight

法定重量

Legal weight refers to the net weight of the goods plus the weight of the packaging materials that are in direct contact with the goods, such as the sales packaging. The weight of the pure goods obtained by removing the weight of this part of the packaging is called the net weight. The formula is:

法定重量=货物净重+与货物直接接触的包装重量

Legal Weight=Net Weight of the Goods+Weight of the Packaging in Direct Contact with the Goods.

This measurement method is of great significance in aspects such as customs duty collection and commodity inspection. When customs levy duties on imported and exported goods, the amount of duty payable is usually calculated based on the legal weight.

4.3.3　Precautions in Quantity of Commodity term 商品数量条款的注意事项

溢短装条款

The More or Less Clause is a contractual provision that allows for a certain degree of flexibility in the quantity of goods delivered. It stipulates that the quantity of goods delivered by the seller can be more or less than the quantity specified in the contract within a certain range or percentage, without being considered a breach of contract. For example, it may be stipulated as "±5% more or less", which means the actual quantity of goods delivered can be 5% more or 5% less than the contracted quantity.

Example:

Suppose the contract states: "1000 units of goods, with a ±5% more or less allowance at the seller's option."

The seller is permitted to deliver between 950 and 1050 units. If the actual delivery is 1030 units, this falls within the contractually allowed range, and the buyer cannot reject the goods or claim compensation based on the quantity difference.

By clearly defining the tolerance range of quantity and related matters in advance, the More or Less Clause can effectively reduce disputes between the two parties caused by quantity differences, making the performance of the contract smoother and more stable. At the same time, this clause enables the seller to better handle some uncertainties in the production process, such as slight differences in raw material consumption and production efficiency, and ensure timely delivery.

4.4 Packing of Commodity
商品包装

According to the definition in the national standard "**General Terms of Packaging**", commodity packaging refers to the general term for the containers, materials and **auxiliary items** used to protect products, facilitate storage, transportation and sales during the process of product circulation, as well as the operational activities carried out to achieve these purposes. It includes two aspects: the physical packaging, such as inner packaging that directly contacts the product and is related to sales, and outer packaging mainly for transportation and storage protection; and packaging operations like design, material selection, and the implementation of packaging techniques.

包装一般条款

辅助材料

4.4.1 Transport Packaging
运输包装

Transport packaging refers to the packaging form primarily utilized to safeguard goods during the processes of transportation, loading and unloading, and storage. It is designed to withstand various external forces and environmental impacts that goods may encounter in the logistics chain, ensuring the integrity and quality of the goods upon arrival at their destination, enables the seller to better handle some uncertainties in the production process, such as slight differences in raw material consumption and production efficiency, and ensure timely delivery. See Table 4-2 Types of Packing Containers.

4.4.1.1 Shipping Marks
运输标志

Shipping Marks, also known as **"marks"**, are essential identifying signs on the packaging of goods in international trade. They are a set of symbols, letters, numbers, and simple words printed or attached to the

标志

Table 4.2 Types of Packing Containers

Packaging Type	Description	Main Materials	Suitable For	Characteristics
Cartons	Boxes made from corrugated fiberboard, lightweight and cost-effective.	Corrugated fiberboard	Small to medium-sized goods	Lightweight, eco-friendly, easy to print and handle
Pallets	Platforms for stacking and moving goods, often used with plastic or metal straps.	Wood, Plastic, Metal	Bulk goods and heavy items	Enhances loading/unloading efficiency, reduces labor costs
Wooden Crates	Sturdy boxes made of wood, suitable for heavy or fragile items.	Wood	Heavy machinery, glass products, etc.	High strength, shock-resistant, good protective performance
Plastic Containers	Rigid containers made of hard plastic, offering high transparency and durability.	Plastic	Liquids, chemicals, food products	Moisture-proof, chemical-resistant, transparent
Metal Drums	Sealed metal containers typically used for storing and transporting liquids or powders.	Steel, Aluminum	Chemical products, petroleum products, food items	High strength, pressure-resistant, leak-proof
Woven Bags	Bags woven from polypropylene or other synthetic fibers, offering good breathability.	Polypropylene, Other Synthetic Fibers	Agricultural products, chemical raw materials	Lightweight, low-cost, reusable
Foam Boxes	Boxes with foam material inside, providing excellent cushioning properties.	Foam Plastics	Fragile items like electronics, ceramics	Excellent cushioning, protects against shocks and impacts
Containers	Standardized large metal boxes used for sea, rail, and road transport.	Steel	Large-scale cargo transport	Efficient, secure, suitable for multiple transport modes, facilitates global logistics operations

outer packaging of goods. These marks play a crucial role in the entire logistics process.

Typically, Shipping Marks consist of several main parts. The **consignee** or shipper code is used to identify the owner of the goods, which can be in the form of **abbreviations**, like "ABC Inc." for the consignee. The destination name clearly states the final location where the goods are headed, for example, "Singapore Port". The reference number, such as an order number or a contract number, helps in tracking and **cross-referencing** the goods throughout the transaction. Additionally, the package number is used to mark the sequence of packages within a batch, like "3/100" indicating the third package out of a total of 100. Let's take an example of a shipping mark. Suppose we have a consignment with the following marks:

相互对照

Example:

    Consignee Code: XYZ Trading

    Destination: Hamburg, Germany

    Contract Number: XYZ – 2025 – 050

    Package Number: 15/250

收货人代码：XYZ贸易公司
目的地：德国汉堡
合同编号：XYZ–2025–050
件号：15/250（第15件，共250件）

This shipping mark shows that the goods are destined for Hamburg, Germany, the consignee is XYZ Trading, the contract under which the goods are shipped is numbered XYZ–2025–050, and this particular package is the 15th one among a total of 250 packages in the shipment.

4.4.1.2 Indicative Marks

指示性标志

Indicative Marks are symbols or words printed on the outer packaging of goods. Throughout the entire logistics process, from the initial shipment, warehousing to final delivery, they provide guidance and warnings regarding handling, storage, and transportation. These marks are crucial for ensuring the safety of both the goods and the personnel involved. In international trade, they bridge language and cultural gaps, ensuring proper handling of goods and minimizing the risk of damage.

Common Indicative Marks are widely used across various industries. The **"Fragile" mark**, depicted as a broken wine glass, alerts handlers to be cautious when moving glassware, precision instruments, etc., to avoid damage from external forces. The **"This Side Up" mark** indicates the

"易碎品"标志

"此端向上"标志

correct orientation for handling and storing liquid products, electronic devices, etc., preventing damage caused by inversion. The **"Keep Dry" mark**, represented by a small umbrella, reminds people to control humidity, applicable to humidity-sensitive goods like food and medicine. The **"Handle with Care" mark**, featuring a pattern of two hands holding an object, requires gentle handling of high - value and fragile items.

The following are some common indicative marks（see Figure 4.1）.

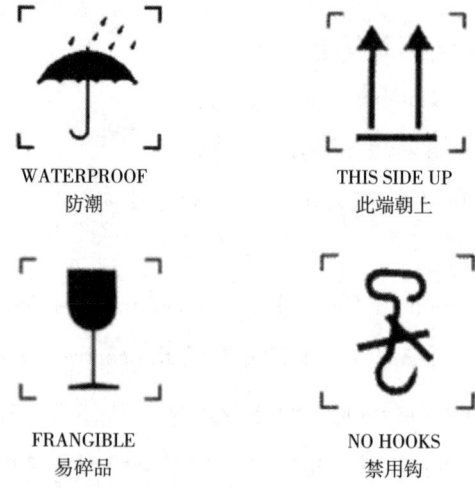

Figure 4.1　Some Indicative Marks

4.4.1.3　Warning Marks
警告性标志

Warning Marks are special combinations of symbols, graphics, or words printed on the outer packaging of goods. They are used to alert potential hazardous properties of the goods, such as **flammability, explosiveness, toxicity, and radioactivity**. Throughout the entire logistics process, from packaging, transportation to storage, Warning Marks play a crucial role in preventing accidents, ensuring the safety of personnel and the environment, and protecting the goods themselves. Their standardized designs can transcend language and cultural barriers, enabling those who come into contact with the goods to quickly identify the dangers, take safety precautions, and reduce safety risks.

Common Warning Marks have specific applications in the transportation of hazardous goods. The **"Flammable" mark** features a flame on a red background, warning that the goods are flammable. Items like fuel and alcohol products, for example, must be kept away from fire sources and heat during transportation and storage. The **"Explosive" mark** consists of a black explosion graphic on an orange-yellow background, reminding that the goods are prone to explosion when subjected to impact, high temperature, etc. Packaging of fireworks, certain compressed gas cylinders, and other such items must be clearly with this mark. The **"Toxic" mark** is a skull-and-crossbones pattern on a black or white background, informing that the goods are toxic and contact may cause serious harm to human health. It is commonly seen on the packaging of pesticides, some chemical reagents, etc. The **"Radioactive" mark** is a trident-shaped pattern with yellow-black warning colors, alerting that the goods are radioactive. Items such as radioactive medical supplies require strict compliance with special protection and operation regulations during transportation and storage.

"易燃"标志

"易爆"标志

"有毒"标志

"放射性"标志

The following are some warning marks printed on the outer package (see Figure 4.2).

EXPLOSIVES　　　　POSION　　　　DANGER OF FIRE
当心爆炸　　　　　当心有毒　　　　　当心火灾

Figure 4.2　Some Warning Marks

4.4.2　Sales Packing
销售包装

Sales packaging, also known as inner packaging or small packaging, is the packaging that comes into direct contact with the goods and is presented to consumers in retail outlets. It plays a crucial role in the sales process of goods, with the following aspects: firstly, it safeguards the product from potential damage during transit, storage, and **on-shelf display**, maintaining its quality and integrity. Secondly, it acts as a powerful marketing tool. Through attractive designs, vivid colors, and unique shapes, it catches consumers' eyes in the crowded marketplace, differentiating the product from competitors and piquing their interest. Moreover, it conveys essential information, including product features, usage instructions, ingredients, and safety warnings, enabling consumers to make informed purchasing decisions. In essence, sales packaging not only protects the product but also promotes it and educates the buyer, playing a pivotal role in the success of product sales.

货架陈列

4.4.3　Neutral Packing
　　　　中性包装

Neutral packing refers to the packaging of goods without indicating the country of origin, place name, manufacturer's name, trademark, or brand on the inner and outer packaging. There are mainly two forms of neutral packing:

Brandless Neutral Packing 无牌中性包装

There is neither the country of origin, place name, manufacturer's name, nor trademark or brand on the packaging. It is completely plain packaging and is often used for some primary products or simply processed products, such as some agricultural and mineral products.

Brand-Designated Neutral Packing 定牌中性包装

There is only the trademark or brand designated by the buyer on the packaging, without indicating the country of origin, place name, and manufacturer's name. This form of packaging is more common in industries such as clothing and toys. Many international brands will entrust factories in other countries to produce products through brand-designated neutral packing and then **affix** their own brands for sale. 粘贴

Neutral packing holds significant importance in international trade. It enables businesses to bypass trade barriers as it conceals the origin of goods, helping them avoid discriminatory tariffs or quotas imposed on certain countries. It also caters to diverse market demands by allowing flexibility in brand promotion and market positioning. In the context of **entrepot trade**, it simplifies the process for middlemen 转口贸易 to resell products. Moreover, it safeguards the intellectual property and business secrets of manufacturers, as the absence of company – related information on the packaging prevents competitors from easily obtaining sensitive details.

Exercises 练习

I. True (T) or False (F)

1. The goods of the best quality shall be chosen as the sample for sale. (   )

2. The breach of the quality clause in the contract is regarded as a fundamental breach of contract. (   )

3. When goods of higher quality than the contract quality are delivered, there will be no dispute. (   )

4. Indication marks are to show the capacity and place of origin of the goods in transit. (   )

5. Warning marks are to warn those who move goods of possible danger. (   )

6. Sale by Grade is a method of stipulating quality where goods are classified into different levels based on their quality, weight, composition, and appearance. (   )

7. Packing is not a competitive force in seeking a new market. (   )

8. Packing is not only designed to protect the goods, but also to preserve the quality of the goods. (   )

9. Net weight refers to the weight of the commodity without any packaging materials. (   )

10. The terms "more or less clause" allow the seller to deliver a quantity slightly different from what is specified in the contract. (   )

II. Multiple Choice Questions

1. Why is it important to use specific names for commodities in a sales contract?

   A. To comply with international trade laws

   B. To ensure the goods are accurately described and avoid ambiguity

   C. To make the contract look more professional

   D. To impress the buyer with detailed information

2. Which of the following is NOT a component of the quality of a commodity?

   A. Physical properties　　　B. Chemical composition

   C. Color and style　　　　　D. Transportation method

3. In a sale by sample, what is the purpose of a counter sample（对等样品）?

   A. To provide a backup in case the original sample is lost

   B. To confirm the quality requirements with the buyer

   C. To serve as a reference for the seller's production process

   D. To replace the original sample if it is damaged

4. Which of the following methods of stipulating quality is most suitable for complex and high-tech products like machinery and electronics?

   A. Sale by Specification

   B. Sale by Grade

   C. Sale by Descriptions and Illustrations

D. Sale by Brand or Trade Mark

5. Which of the following is an example of "Sale by Inspection on the Spot"（看货买卖）?

   A. A buyer orders clothing based on a sample provided by the seller.

   B. A buyer visits a farm to inspect crops before deciding to purchase.

   C. A buyer purchases a product based on its brand reputation.

   D. A buyer orders goods based on a detailed product description

6. Which of the following best describes "Sale by Standard"（凭标准买卖）?

   A. The quality of goods is determined by a sample provided by the seller.

   B. The quality of goods is determined by a well-known brand name.

   C. The quality of goods is determined by a set of specifications or grades defined by a standard.

   D. The quality of goods is determined by the place of origin.

7. Which of the following is NOT a method of stipulating quality in international trade?

   A. Sale by Specification

   B. Sale by Grade

   C. Sale by Color

   D. Sale by Standard

8. What can the buyer do if the goods delivered do not conform to the agreed name of commodity?

   A. Only accept the goods and ask for a price reduction.

   B. Claim against the seller for compensation, reject the goods, or even cancel the contract.

   C. Only ask the seller to replace the goods.

   D. Do nothing but wait for the seller's response.

9. A batch of soybeans is exported from our country, with the contract specifying that the moisture content should be a maximum of 14%, the oil content a minimum of 18%, and impurities a maximum of 1%. The method used to specify the quality in this manner is (   ).

A. sale by specification   B. sale by grade

C. sale by standard   D. sale by sample

10. In the provisions of quality terms, for certain industrial finished products or agricultural products where it is relatively difficult to ascertain their quality, we often stipulate (   ) in the contract.

A. More or less clause

B. Price increase or decrease clause

C. Quality tolerance or quality flexibility margin

D. Net weight of the goods

11. Gross weight of the commodities refers to (   ).

A. the packing weight of the commodities

B. commodity's weight plus the inner packing weight

C. commodity's weight

D. commodity's weight plus the inner and outer packing weight

12. Some foreign importers require that there should be no any origin indications or trade marks on the packing of the goods we provide. This requirement of the foreign importer is (   ).

A. unlicensed neutral packing

B. brand designated packing

C. transportation packing

D. sales packing

13. Which of the following units of measurement is most commonly used for bulk commodities like coal and ore in international trade?

A. Gram (g)   B. Kilogram (kg)

C. Ton (t)   D. Pound (lb)

14. What does "Conditioned Weight" refer to in international trade?

A. The weight of goods after removing moisture

B. The weight of goods with standard moisture content added

C. The theoretical weight based on specifications

D. The net weight of goods without packaging

15. Which type of packaging is primarily used to protect goods during transportation and storage?

  A. Sales packaging   B. Transport packaging

  C. Neutral packaging   D. Inner packaging

III. Web Page Clipping

1. Please visit the Alibaba B2B platform (https://www.alibaba.com), select a product category, and examine the **product descriptions** section. Analyze the following details: product name, quality specifications, quantity, packaging requirements, pricing, **Minimum Order Quantity (MOQ)**.

货物描述

最低起订量

2. Access global customs data platforms (e.g., https://www.trademap.org) or industry B2B platforms (e.g., https://www.globalsources.com), select a product category (e.g., **solar panels, medical masks**), and conduct the following research: Locate sales contract templates from three suppliers based in different regions (e.g., China, Germany, Vietnam). Compare differences in quality clauses, focusing on:

太阳能电池板、医用口罩查找三家不同区域供应商（中国、德国、越南）的销售合同范本，对比其在品质条款中关于检验机构（如SGS vs. TÜV）、索赔期限、处罚条款等方面的设定差异。

  Designated inspection agencies (e.g., SGS vs. TÜV).

  Claims timeframe (e.g., 30 days vs. 90 days after delivery).

  Penalty terms for non-compliance with quality specifications.

IV. Case Study

1. A paper company signed an export contract with a British firm for "**handmade office writing paper**". After receiving the goods, the buyer found that some production processes were **mechanical**, even though all the provided documents indicated the product was handmade. The buyer believed there was "misrepresentation" and demanded a

手工制造办公书写纸

机械化

return. The seller contended that the production was mainly **manual**, particularly the key steps were completely handcrafted, thereby meeting the agreed quality. How do you view this dispute?

手工制作

2. An export company signed an FOB contract with a British firm for 500 cases of canned peaches, specifying "500 cases, 25 cans per case, 425 grams per can." However, the seller shipped 500 cases with 26 cans per case, each can weighing 500 grams. The British firm seeing the discrepancy in quantity and specifications, refused to accept the goods and demanded the contract be canceled. Does the buyer have the right to do so? Why?

3. A tea company signed a contract with an American firm to export a batch of Longjing tea. The quality specification was that the proportion of broken tea by weight should not exceed 6%. Before the deal, our company sent samples to the American side, and after signing the contract, we informed them by telegram that the goods were similar to the samples. After the goods arrived in the US, the American company claimed that although there was an official inspection certificate from the exporting country, the quality of the goods was worse than the samples. They believed the seller should deliver goods identical to the samples and thus demanded a 10% price reduction per ton. The tea company refused, arguing that the contract didn't stipulate delivery by sample. Then the American company had an inspection by a local inspection firm, which issued a certificate stating the proportion of broken tea in the delivered goods was 10%, and they filed a claim based on this. The exporter argued that as an agricultural product, it was impossible to make the goods exactly the same as the sample, and unfortunately, the sample they had retained was lost. How do you view this dispute?

4. Company A signed a sales contract with an overseas Client B to export 1,000 tons of steel. The contract included a More or Less Clause, allowing a 5% fluctuation in the quantity of goods delivered. Company A

actually delivered 1,050 tons, which exceeded the contracted quantity by 5%. Upon receiving the goods, Client B refused to accept the additional 50 tons and demanded that Company A cover the extra transportation costs. Does Client B have the right to refuse the additional 50 tons of steel? Why?

V. Calculation

1. An exporter is shipping a batch of fertilizers with a net weight of 5000 kg and packaging weight of 500 kg. Calculate the gross weight of this shipment.

2. An importer receives a batch of electronic equipment with a gross weight of 1000 kg and packaging weight of 100 kg. Calculate the net weight of the electronic equipment.

3. An exporter is shipping a batch of wool with a dry weight of 1000 kg. The internationally recognized standard regain rate is 10%. Calculate the Conditioned Weight of this batch of wool.

4. There is a batch of raw silk with an actual weight of 800 kg, an actual regain rate of 12%, and a standard regain rate of 11%. What is the conditioned weight of this batch of raw silk?

5. A certain type of steel pipe has a theoretical weight of 20 kg per meter. There is a batch of 150 meters of this kind of steel pipe. What is the theoretical weight of this batch of steel pipes?

6. A batch of imported cosmetics has a net weight of 600 kg, and the weight of the packaging in direct contact with the goods is 50 kg. The customs levies a 5% duty on the legal weight. If the duty per kg is $20, how much duty does this batch of cosmetics need to pay?

Chapter 5

International Cargo Transport and Shipment Clause

第五章　国际货物运输及合同中的装运条款

◆ **Learning Objectives**

- Understand the importance of the characteristics of ocean transportation;
- Know other modes of transportation in terms of their features, suitability and freight calculation;
- Explain applications of ocean bill of lading and its different types;
- Describe a range of other transportation documents;
- Stipulate delivery clause in a sales contract.

In international trade, the seller delivers the goods in exchange for the buyer's payment. It is the seller's basic duty to deliver the goods to the buyer or load the goods on the carrier as nominated at the time, place, and with the mode of transport specified in the contract after signing it.

In common law, according to the cases over the past years, common law countries regard quality clauses, quantity clauses and time of delivery as the fundamentals of the contract. The consequences could be very serious once the rules are broken. In this chapter, time of delivery is the priority of shipment clauses. **Time of shipment and time of delivery** are totally different concepts, but under FOB, CFR, and CIF terms, the seller delivers the documents instead of the goods, which means, once the goods are delivered on board the ship or shipping conveyance at the loading port, the seller's duty to deliver goods is accomplished. The date indicated by the carrier on the shipping documents is the time of delivery and the place of shipment is rightly the place of delivery. That is to say, under the CIF, FOB, and CFR trade terms which indicate symbolic delivery, the shipment just means the delivery, and the time of shipment is rightly the time of delivery.

装运期和交货期

5.1 Means of Transportation
运输方式

In international trade, there are various kinds of modes of transportation: ocean transportation, rail transportation, air transportation, river transportation, postal transportation, road transportation, channel transportation, container transportation, international multimodal transportation, and continental-bridge transportation, etc., of which ocean transportation is the most important, traditional, and time honored means of transport. Currently, as the most preferred mode of transport, ocean transportation accounts for 80% of the total capacity. We'll introduce a few significant means of transportation in international trade hereinafter.

5.1.1 Ocean Transport
海洋运输

Ocean transport, also known as "international marine cargo transportation", is the most important mode of transportation in international logistics. It refers to a method of using ships to transport cargoes between ports in different countries and regions through sea lanes. It is the most widely-used form of international cargo transportation, with over two-thirds of the total international trade volume being transported by sea. Ocean transport plays an important role in the development of international trade and has changed the world tremendously.

Characteristics of ocean transport 海洋运输的特点

Ocean transport is carried out by means of natural waterways, which are not restricted by roads and tracks, and have stronger passing capacity. Its large carrying capacity, long service life, long transportation mileage and low unit transportation cost provide favorable conditions for the transportation of low-value bulk cargo. However, it is the slowest one of all transportation modes, and it is less punctual and riskier as it is easily affected by natural conditions and climates and is likely to encounter other risks during the transit.

Types of ocean transport 海洋运输类型

Different types of cargo vessels are used to meet the needs of shipping different cargoes. According to the operation mode of ships, ocean transport can be divided into liner shipping and charter shipping.

5.1.1.1　Liner shipping

班轮运输

(1) Definition

定义

A liner is a vessel with regular sailings and arrivals and sails on a fixed (regular) sailing route and calls at fixed (regular) base ports. It adopts a comparatively fixed timetable and charges at comparatively fixed rates. Liner transport is suitable for goods in small lots and high frequency, Most goods are transported through liner transport in international trade.

Chapter 5 International Cargo Transport and Shipment Clause

(2) Characteristics
特点

(A) Fixity, namely fixed routes, **fixed ports of call**, fixed dates, and fixed rates. 　　固定的停靠港

(B) Responsibility: Goods are subject to the loading and unloading by the **liners** and **handling charges** are already included in the freight. Liners and the consignor are free from handling charges, **demurrage charges**, and **dispatch money**. 　　班轮公司　装卸费
滞期费
速遣费

(C) Liabilities, obligations, and **exemptions** of liners and the shipper are all on the basis of the **bill of lading** issued by liners. In terms of goods with large transport volume and low value like grains, beans, mines, and coals, the price is negotiated by both parties. 　　豁免
提单

(3) Liner Freight
班轮运费

Freight is the remuneration payable to a carrier for the carriage of goods. Liner freight is usually inclusive of the loading and unloading cost and other costs such as demurrage or dispatch money. Normally, the freight of liner service is made up of two parts: one is **basic freight**; the other is **surcharges and additional fees**. 　　基本运费
附加费

(A) Basic Freight

Basic freight is charged for carriage of goods from the port of shipment to the port of destination. Basic freight constitutes the main cost of liner transportation. The main criteria used in the tariff for calculating basic freight of liners are W, M, W/M, A.V., W/M or A.V., unit/head, minimum rate and open rate.

· W (weight ton) 重量吨: For items marked with "W" in the **tariff**, freight is to be calculated on the basis of weight ton (WT). Internationally, one weight ton equals to one **metric ton** (1,000 kg), or one long ton (1,016 kg) or one short ton (907.18 kg), depending on the measurement system adopted by the shipping company. Freight for heavy cargo is usually charged on this basis. 　　运价表
公吨

・M（measurement ton）尺码吨: For items marked with "M" in the tariff, freight is to be calculated according to the measurement ton（MT）of the goods, i.e., the volume. One measurement ton is one **cubic meter** or 40 **cubic feet**. Freight for light cargo is often charged on this basis. Weight ton and measurement ton both fall under the name of **freight ton**.

・W/M（weight ton/ measurement ton）重量吨或尺码吨: For items marked with "W/M", the freight is to be calculated on the basis of either weight ton or measurement ton, subject to the higher one. When making a comparison between W and M, one has to follow the notion that 1 WT is equal to 1MT.

・A.V.（Ad valorem）从价运费: For items marked with "Ad Val.", the freight is charged according to the value of the cargo. This is normally expressed by a certain percentage（ranging from 1% to 5%）of the FOB price or value of the goods carried. This is more suitable for goods that are of high value such as gold, silver, precious stones, expensive furs and valuable drawings and paintings.

・W/M or A.V. 选择法: For items marked "W/M or Ad Val." the freight is to be calculated on the basis of weight ton, measurement ton, or the value of the goods, subject to the highest one.

・Unit/Head 按件法: For items marked "Unit" in the tariff, freight is calculated according to the number of the cargo carried, e.g. USD60 per Unit of truck, USD15 per Head of live animal.

・Minimum Rate 最低运费法: For the carriage of cargo in extremely small quantities, a minimum freight is adopted for the obtainment of freight.

・Open Rate 议价法: For items marked "Open" in the freight tariff, freight is to be calculated according to the **temporary or special agreement** entered into between the carrier and the consignor. Usually, shipment of cargo in extremely large quantities such as grains, ores, and coal is subject to open rate.

In addition to the basic freight which is calculated on the above basis, payment of surcharges and additional fees may be required on some special occasions or for some cargo that needs special care in handling. There are a great multitude of surcharges and additional charges in freight calculation.

(B) Surcharges

Surcharges refer to various additional fees calculated from basic freight. The common methods for calculating surcharges are to add the basic freight and a certain percentage which is given by the surcharge or additional rate. Commonly used surcharges include **bunker adjustment factor (BAF), currency adjustment factor (CAF), port congestion surcharge, overweight surcharge, overlength surcharge, bulky cargo surcharge, optional unloading surcharge, direct voyage surcharge, transshipment surcharge, port surcharge**, etc. For example, the cargo might be charged overweight surcharge, over length surcharge, and bulky cargo surcharge if it is 5 metric tons per unit, or 9 m per unit, or 6 m³ per unit.

燃油附加费、货币附加费、港口拥挤附加费、超重附加费、超长附加费、重型货物附加费、选港附加费、直航附加费、转运附加费、港口附加费

Total freight can be calculated using the following formula:

Total freight=basic freight rate × (1+ ∑ rate of surcharges) × total freight ton

总运费=基本运费×（1+∑附加费）×总运费吨

Or:

$$F = F_b + \sum S = (f + s_1 + s_2 + \cdots + s_n) Q$$

F stands for total freight

F_b stands for basic freight

S stands for one of the surcharges

f stands for basic freight rate

$s_1, s_2 \ldots s_n$ stands for one of the surcharge rates

Q stands for total freight ton (usually weight ton or measurement ton)

Example:

Suppose: Company A exports 1,000 cases of Commodity Y to London. The volume per case is 40cm × 30cm × 20cm, and the gross weight is 30kg. For Commodity Y, the freight rate basis is W/M, and the Freight Tariff（China—London）is USD230, with a 10% port surcharge. How much is the total freight?

Calculation:

Total weight: 30kg × 1,000 cases=0.03M/T × 1,000 cases = 30M/T

Total measurement: 40cm × 30cm × 20cm × 1,000 cases=0.4m × 0.3m × 0.2m × 1,000 cases=24m³

Weight > Measurement. "W" is the freight calculation basis.

Total freight=basic freight rate ×（1+surcharge）× total weight

=230 ×（1+10%）× 30

=USD 7,590

Answer: The total freight is USD 7,590.

5.1.1.2　Charter shipping

租船运输

不定期船运输

Charter shipping, also called **tramp service**, refers to the way in which the ship owner negotiates with the charterer to lease the ship to the charterer on a bare boat or a time or voyage charter and arranges the transportation of the cargo according to the charter contract. The following are some characteristics of charter shipping: ①The operating arrangements depend on the charter-party, so there are no fixed routes and no schedules; ②It is suitable for the transportation of bulk cargoes like oil, grain, timber, steel, coal, ores, fertilizers, etc.; ③The rental rate or freight rate varies according to the charter market; ④The sharing of loading and unloading fees is divided according to the charter contract.

There are five types of charter shipping: voyage charter, time charter, demise charter, contract of affreightment and time charter on trip basis.

Voyage charter 程租船

Voyage charter, also called trip charter, refers to the kind of charter in which the shipowner is responsible for providing a ship with one or more voyages between designated ports. Generally, in voyage charter, a charterer can charter a ship by **single voyage, round trip voyage, consecutive single voyage, and consecutive round trip voyage.** The vast majority of goods (mainly including liquid bulk and dry bulk) traded on the international spot market are transported by voyage charter. Under voyage charter, the vessel remains under the control of the ship owner who is responsible for the operation and dispatch of the vessel, and the relevant operating fees of the vessel, such as **fuel fee,** material fee, repairing charge, port fee, and freshwater fee, are borne by the ship owner. What's more, the ship owner is also responsible for the employment of the crew and the payment of their wages.

Time charter 期租船

Time charter refers to the method of leasing a vessel by **the ship owner (the ship lessor)** to the charterer for use within a specified period, within which the charterer dispatches and manages the vessel himself. The lease term can be long or short, ranging from a few months to a few years. This chartering method is not based on the number of completed voyages, but limited to the period of use agreed. During the leasing period, the charterer is responsible for the loading, unloading, stowage and trim of cargo. The resulting fuel, port, loading and unloading charges, and stowage materials are borne by the **charterer.** The ship owner shall bear the costs of crew salaries and be responsible for maintaining the seaworthy state of the ship during the leasing period and for the costs incurred. Therefore, time charter generally does not include loading and unloading costs in the charter rate.

Demise charter 光船租船

Demise charter, also called bare boat charter, means that the ship owner leases an empty vessel to the charterer for a certain period of time, which is under the complete control of the charterer. In other words, the charterer is responsible for the hiring of crew, operation management, supplies, and all the operating expenses, while the ship owner no longer bears any responsibility or expense except for the rent collected during the charter period. Therefore, a demise charter is a kind of property lease.

Contract of affreightment 包运租船

Contract of affreightment (COA) refers to the chartering method in which the owner of the vessel completes the entire cargo volume with a certain capacity between certain ports at a predetermined time, voyage, and volume in each voyage. The name and nationality of the ship are not determined in this chartering method, and only the class, age, and technical specifications of the ship are required. So, it is very flexible and convenient for ship owners to dispatch and arrange for ships. The cargoes carried are mainly dry bulk or liquid bulk cargoes, and the charterers are often the largest and most powerful comprehensive industrial and mining enterprises, trading institutions, production and processing groups or large oil companies.

Time charter on trip basis 航次期租合同

Time charter on trip basis is the chartering method aimed at completing a voyage in which the rent is calculated based on the time (days) required for the voyage. This chartering method does not include demurrage and dispatch costs, and the ship owner is not responsible for the operation and management of cargo transportation. In the case of poor loading and unloading ports, or poor sailing conditions on the route, this chartering method is more beneficial to shipowners because it can prevent ship owners from unpredictable conditions and losses.

5.1.2　Air Transport
航空运输

As a modern transportation mode, air transport has developed rapidly with the advantages of being speedy, exact, safe, and convenient. At the same time, the drastic growth of the goods adapted to air transport also pushes the development of the air industry. More and more modern and big airplanes, big airports with perfect facilities and modern telecommunication facilities are produced and constructed to meet the demand of air transportation in international trade. In this way, international trade and the air industry boost each other with the advancement of air technology and air transportation. For the time being, the proportion of air transportation occupied in the whole international transportation is increasing with the growing quantity of cargo transported by air.

The goods which are the most adapted to air transport include urgent cargo, fresh and alive products, precise appliances, valuables, putrescible and seasonal items etc.

Since 1974, China has joined the **International Civil Aviation Organization (ICAO)** .   国际民航组织

5.1.2.1　Classification of Air Transport Modes

航空运输的主要方式

(1) *Scheduled Airline*

班机运输

Scheduled airline refers to the airlines that transport regularly by fixed route, between fixed departure and destination at a fixed time schedule. Usually this kind of flight uses passenger-cargo airplane, some bigger air companies have opened up regular full air cargo flights. With the advantage of its fixed time, route and stop station, the scheduled airline is more suitable for the transport of emergency items, fresh and live produce or seasonal commodities.

(2) *Chartered Carrier*

包机运输

Chartered carrier refers to the airplane that is hired by one consigner or share-hired by several consigners (or air-freight service agency) . Thus, chartered carriers could be divided into two kinds: whole-hired and share-hired. The former kind is suitable for transporting goods in large quantities, and the latter one is suitable for goods to be delivered to the same destination by different consigners.

(3) Consolidation

集中托运

航空货运代理公司　　Consolidation is usually utilized by **air-freight service agencies**,
航空运单　　who combine scattered goods into one batch, with the **airway bills** for each shipment issued respectively for each consignor, then make delivery of the whole batch of goods to the scheduled destination with
总运单　　one set of **chief airway bill**. After the arrival, the goods are cleared,
实际收货人　　sorted out, and dispatched to the **actual consignees** respectively by the local agency of air-freight carrier. The price of consolidation flight is usually 7%—10% lower than that of scheduled airline fixed by
国际航空运输协会　　**International Air Transportation Association**. For this reason, the consignors are more willing to commit the goods to air-freight agency for delivery.

(4) Air Express Service

航空急件传递

Air Express is the fastest one in the current international air transportation modes. Differing from air paravion and air freight, air express service is operated by the organizations specialized in this business field, who are in close cooperation with airline companies,
专人　　with urgent mails transferred by **specially-assigned person**, between consignor, airport, and consignee at the fastest speed. It is most suitable for the delivery of medicine and medical equipment in urgent needs, valuables, blue print documents, and other goods and documents,
桌到桌运输　　therefore it is called **"Desk to Desk Service"**.

5.1.2.2　Air Transportation Freight

航空运费

Air freight varies greatly according to the types and nature of cargo, quantity of cargo, air flight distance and the types of service, and so on. The types of rate available are general cargo rates, minimum charges, class rates, special commodity rates, and so on. Air transportation freight rates are normally based on W, M and W/M. W, the actual gross weight (kilogram), is usually adopted for heavy cargoes, while M, the **measurement weight** (cubic centimeter), is often used for cargoes of large volume. For general cargoes, the usual basis is W/M, the actual gross weight or measurement weight, subject to the higher one. 体积重量

As mentioned before, when W/M is adopted as the freight rate basis for liner freight obtainment, one needs to decide which basis is higher by making a comparison between W and M. In such a case, 1WT is considered to be equal to 1MT, that is, 1M/T= $1m^3$. However, for the comparison between W and M for air freight calculation, 1 unit of weight is 1kg (gross weight) while 1 unit of measurement weight equals to 6,000 cm^3, that is, 1kg=6,000 cm^3, or $1m^3$=167kg ($1m^3 \div 6,000cm^3 \approx 167$ kg).

Example:

Suppose: Company A wants to send the goods to Sydney, Australia. The goods are packed in 50 cartons, each weighing 15kg, with measurement of 50cm × 40cm × 30cm. The air freight rate is quoted at USD 2.00/kg (W/M). How much would the total air freight cost?

Solution:

W: 15kg

M: (50 × 40 × 30)/6,000=10kg, W>M, so W will be adopted for the calculation of air freight.

Total air freight=Total Quantity × Basic Freight Rate
=50 cartons × 15kg × USD 2.00
=USD 1,500

Answer: the total air freight cost is USD 1,500.

5.1.3 Rail Transport

铁路运输

Rail transport is one of the main modes of modern transportation, and it is also one of the two basic transportation modes that constitute land transportation. It occupies an important position in the entire transportation field and plays an increasingly important role.

5.1.3.1 Characteristics of rail transport

铁路运输的特点

Rail transport is less affected by weather and natural conditions and has a high speed and large transportation capacity. It has regular routes and low costs. In addition, it has multiple types of vehicles, enabling it to carry any type of commodities without being limited by weight and volume. However, rail transport is confined to railroads and therefore less flexible.

5.1.3.2 Types of rail transport

铁路运输类型

According to the technical conditions of railways, the current rail transport is divided into three types: full truck load（FTL）, less than full truck load（LTL）and container truck load（CTL）. FTL is suitable for transporting bulk cargoes; LTL is suitable for transporting small quantities of break bulk cargoes; and CTL is suitable for transporting precise, valuable, and vulnerable goods.

5.1.3.3 International Carriage of Goods by Rail

国际铁路货物联运

With one set of uniform transportation documents, the goods are moved through two or more countries by rail as a whole, without the involvement of the consigner and consignee when the goods are delivered from one country to the other country. For the transport mode, the goods are free from the check-in again at the frontier office, and carried over the frontier by train, it benefits international trade and transactions, urging the development of the integrative economy.

5.1.4 Container Transport
集装箱运输

5.1.4.1 Definition
定义

Container, in a literal sense, it is a kind of tremendous holder with a sort of intensity (most containers are made of steel now) for cycling and easy to be mechanically operated.

Container transport is a method of distributing merchandise in unitized form adopting an inter-modal system which provides a possible combination of sea, road, and other modes of transportation.

Types and Specifications of Container 集装箱的种类和规格

The most widely adopted sizes are **twenty-foot equivalent unit (TEU) and forty-foot equivalent unit (FEU)**. But recently, containers are becoming larger and larger. For instance, American President Lines adopt 53-foot container. The generally adopted sizes in China are: 8'×8'×20' twenty-foot equivalent unit (TEU) and 8'×8'×40' forty-foot equivalent unit (FEU).   20英尺和40英尺

5.1.4.2 Goods Handing over of Container Transportation
集装箱运输货物的交接

(1) *Types of Goods*

集装箱货物的分类

Full Container Load (FCL) 整箱货

The FCL consignments are packed into the container as one unit by the consigner for shipment. This means is adopted when the goods are of a container load or many containers load. Except that some consignors have containers, others generally lease a few to send to the production side or the warehouse, and then under the customs official's supervision, the consignor packs the goods into the container, after locking and

场站收据   sealing up the container, getting the **dock receipt（D/R）** in exchange for bills of lading or shipping documents.

Less than Container Load（LCL）拼箱货

LCL stands for less than container load or partial container load as opposed to FCL. LCL consignments are first sent to the container freight station or inland container depot where the carrier can consolidate and pack the goods into containers according to the nature, destination, and weight, and so on, and then send the containers to the container yard for shipment.

（2）Expressions Indicated on the Bills of Lading
在提单上注明集装箱货物运输方式

FCL/FCL—full container load, full container delivery, one consignor, and one consignee.

FCL/LCL—full container load, less than full container received, one consignor, and more than one consignee.

LCL/FCL—less than full container load, full container load, more than one consignor but one consignee.

LCL/LCL—less than full container load, less than full container load and more than one consignor, and consignee.

（3）Container Yard（CY）and Container Freight Station（CFS）
集装箱堆场与集装箱货运站

The FCL and LCL consignments are delivered from different locations. CY is for the delivery of a whole container, while CFS is for the delivery of loose cargo.

So the above FCL/FCL can be expressed as CY/CY and LCL/LCL is CFS/CFS. The former means the FCL received by the carrier is packed at the shipper's or the forwarder's premises, and delivery of that same FCL to the consignee's premises; the latter means the loose cargo first delivered to the carrier's container freight station at the port of origin is packed into the whole container, and that same whole container is emptied at the carrier's container freight station at the port of destination.

5.1.4.3 Calculation of Container Freight

集装箱货运计算

Similar to liner freight, container freight comprises basic charges and additional charges.

(1) Basic Charges

基本运费

There are two general ways to determine basic charges: by freight ton and by box rate. Calculation by freight ton applies to the freight of LCL. The methods are the same as those of liner freight. Box rate applies to the freight of FCL. There are three kinds of box rates:

① Freight for All Kinds (FAK). With this method, the box rate is charged on the basis of the number of containers used, regardless of the classes of the goods.

② Freight for Class (FCS). The box rate is based on the classes of the goods. General cargoes are classified into 20 grades, and freight charged by W/M.

③ Freight for Class of Basis (FCB). The freight is charged by cargo classes or basis such as dry cargo, refrigerated cargo or **hazardous cargo**. 危险货物

(2) Additional Charges

附加费

The additional charges available to liner service are also available to container service. Moreover, there are several other additional fees for container service:

① Inland Transport Charge. This can be covered by either the carrier or the shipper.

② LCL Service Charge. This charge includes the costs of moving containers between the container freight station and the container yard, stowing and keeping the goods at the freight station, stuffing and devanning etc.

③Terminal Handling Charges(THC). Also called port service fee. These include the expenses of receiving FCLs at the shipment container yard, moving and stacking full container sunder the loading bridge, and the similar expenses at the port of destination. Document costs are also included.

5.1.5　International Multimodal Transport
　　　　国际多式联运

Multimodal transportation refers to the container-based process of transporting goods through at least two different modes of transport under a single contract between the shipper and a multimodal transport operator.

5.1.5.1　Constituents of Multimodal Transportation
　　　　　多式联运的组成部分

To conduct multimodal transportation, one must meet the following conditions:

(1)The multimodal transport operator and the shipper must enter into a multimodal transport contract to specify the rights and obligations of both parties. This contract serves as a basis that determines the nature of multimodal transport.

(2)There must be a multimodal transport document(MTD), which is not only a title document but also a negotiable document.

(3)A single freight rate is used for the entire transit. This price comprises transport costs, all overheads, and a reasonable profit.

(4)A single multimodal transport operator takes charge of the entire transit. It is the party that signs the multimodal transport contract with the shipper, that issues the multimodal transport document, and that assumes the responsibility for the entire transit.

(5) There must be two or more means of transport involved.

(6) The transit must be an international carriage that crosses national borders.

5.1.5.2 Features of Multimodal Transportation
多式联运的特点

Multi-modalism represents the trend of international transportation development since it has a number of advantages:

(1) **Simplified procedure.** Although multimodal transport involves more than two different modes of transport, which are to be conducted by different parties, the shipper only deals with one multimodal transport operator under the single contract between the two parties. All other relevant affairs are managed by the operator. Multimodal transport saves the shipper a lot of time, cost, energy and trouble, and it is especially so for inland traders.

(2) **High efficiency and quality.** Containerization features prominently in multimodal transport. Therefore, the advantages of container transport which we discussed earlier are shared by multimodal transport.

(3) **Rationalization of logistics.** Previously there was little cooperation between the carriers of different transport modes with everyone going their own way, but multi-modalism offers great opportunities for carriers to expand their business and work together in a way maximizing facility use and optimizing transport operations.

(4) **Port development.** Multimodal transport serves as a driving force of seaports and airports development, relevant authorities worldwide encourage the upgrading of the existing multi-modal network.

5.1.5.3 Operation Modes of Multimodal Transportation
多式联运的运行模式

Two operation modes are available in multimodal transportation:

(1) **Multimodal Transport Operator (MTO).** The carrier   国际多式联运经营人

that is responsible for the entire carriage is referred to as a multimodal transport operator (MTO). The carrier, however, does not have to be in the possession of all of the means of transport and in practice usually is not. The carriage is often performed by using sub-carriers, in legal language often referred to as actual carriers.

无船承运人　　(2) Non-vessel Operating Common Carrier (NVOCC). It refers to a company that ships goods on behalf of a client, especially internationally, but that does not have its own ships or airplanes. It operates much like any other carrier, issuing its own bills of lading or air waybills. The only difference is that an NVOCC does not own the means of transport.

5.2　Major Transportation Documents
主要运输单据

Transportation documents are the carriage contracts signed between the shipper and the carrier that represent the goods in transit or prove that the goods have been shipped. The main international cargo transportation documents are bill of lading, waybill for either sea, air or rail, and multimodal transport document and the like, with bill of lading being the most frequently adopted documents.

5.2.1　Bill of Lading
提单

A bill of lading, shortened as B/L, is a transportation document issued to the shipper by the carrier or its agent after entering into a contract for the carriage of goods. It plays a vital role in international trade.

5.2.1.1　Functions of bill of lading
提单的作用

A bill of lading is a negotiable instrument functioning as a receipt for the goods, the evidence of contract of carriage and a document of title to the goods.

(1) **Receipt for goods:** The bill of lading acts as a receipt for the goods received. A bill of lading describes the goods put on board a vessel, stating the quantity, and their condition. The form itself is normally filled out in advance by the shipper, then, as the goods are loaded aboard the ship, the carrier will check to see that the goods loaded comply with the goods listed. The carrier, however, is responsible only to check for outward compliance—that is, that the labels comply and that the packages are not damaged. If all appears proper, the appropriate agent of the carrier will sign the bill and return it to the shipper. 货物收据

(2) **Evidence of the contract of carriage:** The bill of lading (B/L) serves as evidence of the contract of carriage between the shipper and the carrier. Upon negotiation with a bona fide third party, the bill becomes **conclusive** evidence of the contract terms. 运输合同的证明 / 确凿的

(3) **Document of title to the goods:** The named consignee or the holder of a bill of lading, provided he has received it in good faith through due negotiation, has a claim to title and, by surrendering the bill, to delivery of the goods. The carrier is under obligation to deliver the cargo only against an original bill of lading. If the carrier delivers goods without the **production** of a bill of lading, he will be liable in contract or **tort** to the bill of lading holder. 货物所有权文件 / 出示, 提供 / 民事侵权

Since possession of the bill of lading is regarded as good as possessing the goods, the buyer can sell the goods on while they are at sea to a third party by simply **endorsing** the bill of lading and delivering it to the third party. The third party, by becoming the holder, can demand delivery of the goods on arrival. Furthermore, as a document of title, the bill of lading also serves a vital function in providing for security, for example, in letter of credit transactions. 背书

It is this function of bill of lading as a document of title that makes the bill of lading a very important document in maritime trade.

Not all bills of lading, however, are transferable. To impart transferability to a bill of lading, it must be drafted as an **order** bill—that is, where the carrier is to deliver the goods to *a named consignee or his order or assigns*. It must be noted that bills of lading made out to **named consignees**, known as **straight bills of lading**, are not transferable.

5.2.1.2 Contents of Bill of Lading

提单的内容

(1) The Face of the Bill

提单正面的内容

① Column 1 on the left is written with the name of the exporting commodity;

② Column 2 is the title of the consignee, or, the owner of the bill;

③ Column 3 is written with the name and address of the buyer. The rest of the bill is written with:

④ Place of receipt or shipment;

⑤ Port of destination or unloading;

⑥ Name of ocean vessel and **Voy. No.**;

⑦ Shipping marks and articles No.;

⑧ Name of commodity and No. of containers or packages;

⑨ Weight and volume;

⑩ Freight prepaid or freight to be collected;

⑪ Copies of original bills of lading;

⑫ Signature of shipping company or its agent;

⑬ Date and place of issue.

(2) The Overleaf of the Bill

提单背面条款

Rights, liabilities, and exemptions of both parties which are main evidence of dealing with disputes are printed on the overleaf.

5.2.1.3　Types of bills of lading

There are a number of different types of bill of lading. The following lists those encountered the most often.

（1）Shipped（on board）B/L（已装船提单）and received for shipment B/L（备运提单）

Shipped B/L is issued by the shipping company after the goods are actually shipped on board the designated vessel. Both the name of the vessel and the date of issue of the B/L are indicated on the shipped B/L. Since the shipping bill of lading provides better guarantee for the consignee to receive the cargo at the destination, the importer will normally require the exporter to produce shipped B/L and most bill of lading forms are preprinted as "Shipped Bill".

Received for shipment B/L arises where the word "shipped" does not appear on the bill of lading. It merely acknowledges that the goods have been received by the carrier for shipment. Therefore, the goods could be in the dock or warehouse.

（2）Clean B/L（清洁提单）and unclean B/L（foul B/L or claused B/L）（不清洁提单）

A clean B/L is a B/L that is free from any **adverse remarks**, 不良批注
made by the shipping company about the condition, packing, or quantity of the goods being shipped. Usually the words "apparent good order and condition", "clean on board", or the like are indicated on the B/L. A clean bill of lading provides proof that up until the time goods were transferred to the carrier, no damage has occurred. This assists in placing responsibility if, in fact goods are eventually delivered in other than undamaged condition.

Unclean B/L, also called foul B/L or claused B/L, is a B/L with adverse remarks or notations（called "clauses"）by the carrier that the goods received for shipping（or their packing）look wet, damaged, or otherwise in doubtful condition, or not of the correct quantity. Importers and their banks normally do not accept foul B/L for payment under a letter of credit.

（3）Straight B/L, blank B/L, and order B/L（记名提单、空白提单及指示提单）

Straight bill of lading has a **designated consignee.** Under this bill, only the consignee at the destination is entitled to take delivery of the cargo. As it is not transferable, it is not commonly used in international trade and normally applies to high value shipments or goods for special purposes.

Blank B/L, also called Open B/L or Bearer B/L, means that there is no definite consignee of the goods. They usually appear in the field of consignee words like "To bearer". Anyone who holds the bill is entitled to the goods the bill represents. No endorsement is needed for the transfer of the blank bill. Due to the exceedingly high risk involved, this bill is rarely used.

Order B/L is widely used in international trade. It means that *the goods are consigned or destined to the order of a named person.* In the field of consignee, "To order", "To order of the shipper", or "To order of the consignee" is marked. This type of bill of lading is a negotiable instrument. That is, it may be used to transfer title to goods being shipped to another party. The transfer may occur at any time during the transit process simply by conveying the order bill to another party. Unless provided otherwise, a consignment that is "to order" means to order of the shipper.

Order B/L can be transferred only after **endorsement** is made. Endorsement here means a signature used to legally transfer the B/L. There are two types of endorsement: **blank endorsement** and **special endorsement.** The blank endorsement is an open endorsement that carries only the signature of the endorser and does not specify in whose favor it is made（who is the new endorsee）. In such instance, whoever bears the B/L after endorsement holds the title to the goods. Special endorsement names the endorsee and requires its endorsement for further negotiation. If the B/L is made out "To order of the consignee", the consignee will endorse the bill to transfer it.

(4) Direct B/L, transshipment B/L and through B/L (直运提单、转运提单及联运提单)

Direct B/L means the B/L, that indicates the goods are shipped from the port of loading directly to the port of destination without involving transshipment.

Transshipment B/L means the B/L that indicates the goods need to be transshipped at an intermediate port as there is no direct service between the shipment port and the destination port.

Through B/L is usually issued for containerized door-to-door shipments that have to use different ships and/or different means of transportation (aircraft, railcars, ships, trucks, etc.) from origin to destination. Unlike in the case of a multimodal Bill of Lading, the principal carrier or the freight-forwarder (who issued the through B/L) is liable under a contract of carriage only for its own phase of the journey, and acts as an agent for the carriers executing the other phases.

(5) Liner B/L, charter-party B/L and container B/L (班轮提单、租船提单及集装箱提单)

Liner B/L is issued by a liner company for shipment on **scheduled port** calls through scheduled routes. 　　停靠港

Charter-party B/L is issued by the carrier (or its agent) based on the **charter-party**. This bill of lading is subject to the clauses of the charter-party. That's why when a charter-party B/L is accepted by the bank or the buyer, the copy charter-party is required. 　　租船合约

Container B/L is issued when the goods are conveyed by container.

(6) Long form B/L and short form B/L (全式提单和简式提单)

Long form B/L is more detailed with the terms and conditions of carriage which are printed on the back of the page. The long form bill of lading is commonly used in international shipping.

Short form B/L (or blank back B/L) is an abbreviated type of document. The terms and conditions of carriage on the reverse (back) of the bill of lading (B/L) are omitted, instead they are listed on a document other than the B/L. Unless otherwise stipulated in the letter of credit (L/C), a short form bill of lading is acceptable. The short form B/L saves the cost of printing (i.e., no printing on the back of the B/L) and if the terms and conditions of carriage change, there is no need to reprint the B/L form.

(7) Miscellaneous B/L (其他提单)

① **On deck B/L:** A B/L contains the notation that the goods have been loaded on the deck of the vessel. It applies to goods like livestock, plants, dangerous cargo, or awkwardly shaped goods that cannot fit into the ship's hold. On deck transit is more dangerous than if cargo is carried in the hold of a ship. Insurance and financing for such transit may be more difficult to obtain or maybe more costly.

② **Stale B/L:** A B/L presented to the consignee or buyer or its bank after the stipulated expiry date of presentation or after the goods are due at the port of destination are described as a "Stale B/L". It is important that the Bill of Lading is available at the port of destination before the goods arrive or, failing this, at the same time. Otherwise, the buyer cannot collect the goods. The late arrival of this important document could bring about undesirable consequences, for instance, incurring additional warehouse rent. Sometimes especially in the case of short sea voyages, it is necessary to add a clause of "Stale B/L is acceptable".

③ **Ante-dated B/L:** This is a B/L, which is dated before the date on which it is issued. When the actual shipment date is later than that stipulated in the L/C, the carrier sometimes, at the shipper's request, issues a B/L with a date of signature that suits the requirement so as to avoid non-acceptance by the bank. Due to the risk of the goods being rejected by the buyer arising from the issuance of such a bill, it is advisable to avoid this **malpractice** even when it seems necessary in certain circumstances. 不法行为

④ **Advanced B/L:** Advanced B/L is the B/L issued in advance when the expiry date of the L/C is due, but the shipment has not yet been effected. The purpose of issuing such a bill is to negotiate payment with the bank in time within the validity of the L/C. The issuance of advanced B/L is also a malpractice and should be avoided. 预借提单

All the above-mentioned bills are not independent of each other. Several types may be combined into one like "Clean on board, to order, blank endorsed B/L". A receipt for the shipment bill may also be a straight and clean bill. B/L are made out in sets, consisting of a number of origins also (usually three) and a number of copies and marked "original" and "copy" respectively. Only the originals signed by the carrier enable the consignee to take delivery of the goods. The copies are just for reference.

The following is sample B/L (see Figure 5.1).

5.2.2 Other shipping documents
其他货运单据

5.2.2.1 Sea Waybill
海运单

Sea waybill is a **non-negotiable document** that constitutes evidence of the contract of the carriage and receipt for the goods by the ocean carrier. It is the evidence that the goods have been taken or loaded on board the vessel that is to be delivered to the designated consignee at the port of destination. 不可转让文件

A sea waybill needs not to be presented for taking delivery of the goods by the consignee, who only needs to prove his identity of being the consignee

Figure 5.1　Bill of Lading

specified in the sea waybill. Therefore, it is not a document of title to the goods and cannot be used to transfer ownership of the goods. The late arrival, loss, theft, etc. the sea waybill will not affect the consignee's delivery of goods, so it can effectively prevent the occurrence of sea shipping fraud and incorrect delivery. Sea waybill is mainly used for the transportation of goods between members of multinational companies and associated companies. And it is a good choice for open account sales and trading between established consignors and consignees.

5.2.2.2　Air Waybill

航空运单

Air waybill, also known as an air consignment note, is the freight document issued by an air carrier or its agent. It is the receipt for the goods received by the air carrier and evidence of the contract of carriage between the consignor and the carrier. As sea waybill, it is not a negotiable document of title to the goods and cannot be used to transfer ownership of the goods. Air waybills are made out in three originals. Original one is to be retained by the carrier for accounting and to serve as documentary evidence. Original two is to accompany the consignment to its final destination and to be presented to the consignee to collect the goods. Original three is given to the consignor as a receipt for receiving the goods by the carrier or its agent.

5.2.2.3　Rail Waybill

铁路运单

Railway waybill is the freight document issued by a railway transport carrier and a contract of carriage between the consignor and the railway companies. It is the most important document for rail transportation and proves the receipt for the goods and the date of acceptance for carriage by the carrier. As sea waybill and air waybill, it is not a negotiable document of title to the goods and cannot be used to transfer ownership of the goods. Rail waybill is in duplicate. The original is to accompany the consignment to its destination and to be presented to the consignee to collect the goods, while the duplicate is given to the shipper as a receipt for receiving the consignment.

5.2.2.4　Multimodal Transport Document
多式联运单据

The multimodal transport document (MTD) is the document that proves the establishment of an international multimodal transport contract, under which the **multimodal transport operator (MTO)** takes over the goods and is responsible for delivering the goods accordingly. It is issued by a multimodal transport operator, and its role is like that of the ocean bill of lading. It is both a receipt for the goods and the evidence of the contract of carriage. It can also be used as a document of title to the goods and can be transferred after endorsement. The multimodal transport document is like a through bill of lading, but they are essentially different. Under a through bill of lading, the principal carrier concluded several separate contracts of carriage for subsequent segments of the transport as agent for the shipper or the on-carriers. It does not normally shoulder responsibility for segments undertaken by the other carriers involved. However, the multimodal transport operator or freight forwarder takes responsibility as principal for the entire carriage. It may, in fact, offer a complete service. Through B/L is issued by the shipping company, covering the entire carriage including ocean transportation, but multimodal transport document is issued by the multimodal transport operator also covering the entire carriage with ocean transportation not being included possibly.

多式联运经营人

5.3　Shipment Clause
装运条款

Shipment clauses in a contract usually cover the time of shipment, port (place) of shipment and port (place) of destination, partial shipment and transshipment. These issues should be negotiated and specified in the contract between the seller and the buyer to ensure the smooth execution of it. The following is an example of shipment clause in the sales contract:

Shipment: To be shipped on and before November 20, 2021 subject to acceptable L/C reaching the Seller by the end of November 5, 2021 with partial shipment prohibited and transshipment allowed.

Port of shipment: Shanghai, China

Port of destination: Hamburg, Germany

5.3.1 Time of Shipment and Time of Delivery
装运时间和交货时间

Time of shipment is the time limit for loading the goods at the port of shipment. Time of delivery is the time limit during which the seller would dispatch the goods to the buyer at the agreed place. For shipment contracts, time of shipment equals time of delivery, and they can be used interchangeably in the contract. However, for arrival contracts, these are two completely different concepts, and the time of delivery should be stipulated in a contract. Time of shipment is a very important condition in the shipment clause in a contract as any delay or advance of delivery constitutes a violation of the contract. There are basically two ways of stipulating time of shipment:

5.3.1.1 Specifying a period of time or a deadline

Examples:

(1) Shipment is to be made during December 2023.

(2) Shipment is to be made on and before December 31, 2023.

5.3.1.2 Setting a time period upon receipt of payment or between the shipment and the deadline by which the relevant L/C must reach the seller.

Examples:

(1) Shipment is to be made within 30 days upon receipt of 60% of

contract value by T/T from the buyer.

(2) Shipment is to be made within 30 days after receipt of the relevant L/C which must reach the seller not later than November 30, 2023.

5.3.2　Port of Shipment and Port of Destination
　　　　装运港和目的港

Port of shipment and port of destination should be clearly specified in the contract when both parties come into agreement. Generally, port of shipment is put forward by the seller for the buyer's confirmation while port of destination is put forward by the buyer for the seller's confirmation.

5.3.2.1　Port of Shipment
　　　　装运港

It is the port where the goods are shipped to and depart from. The points that we should pay attention to when stipulating the port of shipment in an export contract.

(1) The port of shipment shall be close to the origin of the goods.

(2) We should take into consideration the loading and unloading, and specific transportation conditions and the standards of freight and various charges at home and abroad.

(3) Under the FOB terms, the buyer is responsible for chartering a ship. However, when we stipulate the port of shipment, the depth of it shall be suitable to the ship chartered by the buyer.

(4) In export trade, it is the usual practice to designate only one port of shipment in one transaction, but exceptionally, when large amounts of goods are involved and, in particular, the goods are stored at different places, two or more ports of shipment are also specified, such as "Shanghai and Guangzhou", "Dalian/ Qingdao/ Shanghai". Sometimes, as the port of shipment is not yet determined at the time the transaction is being

concluded, a general clause like "China ports" may be used.

5.3.2.2 Port of Destination

目的港

It is the port at which goods are ultimately discharged. The port of destination is usually proposed and determined by the buyer, which shall be convenient for reselling the goods and shall be the one at which the vessel may safely arrive and be always afloat. When we determine the port of destination, we must pay attention to the following points.

(1) We should not accept the port in the country with which our government does not permit to do business.

(2) The stipulation on the port of destination shall be definite and specific. We should not use ambiguous terms, such as "main ports in Europe" or "main ports in Africa".

(3) If we have to choose a port which has no direct liner to stop by or the trips are few, we should stipulate "transshipment to be permitted" in the contract.

(4) The port of destination shall be the one at which the vessel may safely arrive and be always afloat.

(5) As to the business with an inland country, we usually choose a port which is nearest to the country. We usually do not accept an inland city as the place of destination unless through combined transportation for which the combined transport operator will be responsible.

(6) Facilities in the port of loading or unloading are also very important and therefore reasonable attention should be given to issues such as loading and unloading facilities, freight age and additional freight age, etc. The ports of shipment should be, in principle, ports that are close to the source of goods, while the port of destination should be ports that are near the users.

(7) In case the **middleman** abroad has not found a proper buyer when the contract is concluded, in order to make it convenient for the

中间商

"选择港口" seller to sell the cargo afloat, the **"optional port"** may be accepted upon request of the foreign party, the buyer is allowed to choose one from the several ports of destination provided.

(8) Pay attention to the names of foreign ports. Many ports have the same names. For example, there are 12 "Victoria" ports around the world.

5.3.3 Partial Shipment and Transshipment
分批装运和转运

5.3.3.1 Partial shipment
分批装运

Partial shipment, or shipment by installments, means that the goods in one contract are to be delivered in more than one lot. Partial shipment is made because of the large quantity of the transaction, the lack of means of conveyance or shipping space available, the limitation of loading and unloading facilities, the restriction of production ability or market capacity, etc. In view of the different stipulations in international rules, it is advisable to make it clear in the contract as to whether partial shipment is allowed or not. There are two ways of stipulation:

(1) Simply state that partial shipment is allowed. The exact time of delivery, the quantity of each lot and the total lots are not stipulated in the contract. This way of stipulation is favorable to the seller since the seller has an option on the quantity and the time of delivery of each lot in light of the supplies available and the transportation conditions.

(2) State the specific time of delivery and quantity of each lot. For example, a shipment from June to August in three equal monthly lots. This way is usually adopted when the buyer needs to resell the goods or has some special requirements in use.

It should be noted that a shipment is not considered as a partial shipment if it is effected in the same means of conveyance for the same journey to the same destination, even if the dates of shipment, ports of loading, places of taking in charge, or dispatch are different.

5.3.3.2 Transshipment

转运

Transshipment means that the transfer and reloading of goods from one conveyance or vessel to another conveyance or vessel is allowed during carriage from the port/place of shipment to the port/place of destination. Usually, transshipment is effected due to the lack of direct sailing to the port of destination, the lack of shipment at the stipulated period, or not enough amount of cargo to attract liner service. In view of the different stipulations in international rules, it is also advisable to make it clear in the contract as to whether transshipment is allowed or not. In addition, it should also be indicated who bears the cost of transshipment.

Exercises 练习

I. True (T) or False (F)

1. Partial shipment means shipping the cargoes in different lots with different conveyances to the same port/place of the importing country. (　)

2. Containerization refers to a transport mode of distributing cargoes by using unitized containers to allow merchandized handling and a possible combination of rail, road, air and ocean transport. (　)

3. In case of international shipping, CY is Container Yard and CFS is Container Freight Station. CFS is a place where containers are stored before loading on to the vessel or after unloading from the vessel/ship after it arrives at the port, while CY is primarily used for less than container load shipments. (　)

4. Scheduled airlines have fixed schedules, fixed air routes and fixed dock airports. The airplanes are generally combination carriers for carrying both passengers and cargoes. So, an airline waybill is a

document of ownership. (   )

5. Ocean bill of lading has three main functions-receipt: cargo, evidence of a contract of carriage, and document of title. (   )

6. For goods marked "A.V." in the freight tariff, the freight is calculated based on the EXW price of the goods concerned. (   )

7. If the importer takes delivery of the goods with a sea waybill, the original of the document must be presented to the carrier. (   )

8. Liner freight includes basic freight and some surcharges. (   )

9. An ante-dated B/L is usually used when the shipping date stipulated in the letter of credit is due, but the shipper has not gotten the goods ready for shipment. (   )

10. Sometimes when the buyer cannot determine a specific port of discharge during negotiation, he may require two or three ports to be written on the contract as optional ports. (   )

II. Multiple Choice Questions

1. In international cargo transportation, the most widely adopted bill of lading is _____.

A. straight bill of lading

B. unclean bill of lading

C. bearer bill of lading

D. order bill of lading

2. A bill of lading which allows the holder of the B/L to release the cargo regardless of his identity is a (n) _____ B/L.

A. open   B. straight   C. order   D. clean

3. A bill of lading is _____ when its date of shipment is indicated earlier than the actual time of shipment.

A. stale B/L   B. confirmed B/L

C. ante-dated B/L   D. straight B/L

4. A (An) _____ represents title to the cargo.

A. CTD   B. air waybill

C. road waybill   D. bill of lading

5. In the import and export business, _____ can be made out to negotiable document.

A. a rail way bill   B. an ocean B/L

C. an air waybill   D. a parcel post receipt

6. The bill of lading presented to the consignee or buyer or his bank after the stipulated expiry date of presentation or after the goods are due at the port of destination is a _____.

A. stale B/L   B. confirmed B/L

C. ante-dated B/L   D. straight B/L

7. A "freight to be collected" B/L is acceptable to the buyer when the contract is based on _____.

A. FOB   B. CFR   C. CIF   D. CPT

8. Which of the following description does NOT indicate partial shipment?

A. Goods under one contract are shipped by two different vessels.

B. Goods under one contract are unloaded at different ports of destination.

C. Goods under one contract are loaded from different ports onto the same vessel for the same destination on the same trip.

D. Shipment is to be made in April, May and June, in three monthly lots.

9. An order B/L with blank endorsement is a B/L showing _____.

A. neither the name of consignee nor the name of transferor

B. neither the name of consignee nor the name of transferee

C. both the name of consignee and the name of transferor

D. both the name of consignee and the name of transferee

10. A (n) B/L refers to one that is made out to a designated consignee.

A. Straight   B. order

C. specific order   D. bearer

11. The condition for a "door-to-door" service by container transport is_____.

    A. FCL/FCL   B. FCL/LCL

    C. LCL/FCL   D. LCL/LCL

12. Which one of the following is NOT a type of charter transport?

    A. Time charter.   B. Voyage charter.

    C. Bare boat charter.   D. Container charter.

13. Liner freight is charged against a variety of standards, depending on the category of the cargo. _____is the standard that determines the freight rate against the weight, measurement, or value of a cargo, whichever is the highest.

    A. W/M   B. W/M OR AD VAL

    C. AD VAL   D. OPEN RATE

14. Following the Belt and Road Initiative, _____ has been given a spur.

    A. ocean transport

    B. air transport

    C. international railway transport

    D. international multi-modal transport

15. Which of the following commodities does not need air-shipping?

    A. Avocado（牛油果）

    B. Cherry（车厘子）

    C. Blue berry（蓝莓）

    D. Pistachio（开心果）

Ⅲ. Web Page Clipping

Log onto COSCO Shipping Lines Co., Ltd. （https://lines.coscoshipping.com/home/）and Shipping China （http://www.shippingchina.com/）, and search for the following information:

中国远洋运输公司

中国国际海运网

1. Basic information about major shipping routes in China, shipping companies, ship specifications, types of containers, etc.

2. Search for liner routes from China to different countries or regions such as North America, Europe, East Asia, and Southeast Asia （choose any one destination）, look for the latest shipping schedule, clarify the ports available for export on this route, the earliest export time （ETA, ETD, etc.）, and describe the transportation route of this liner.

（1）关于中国海运的主要航线、船公司、船舶规格、集装箱种类等基础信息。

（2）查找中国到北美、欧洲、东亚和东南亚等不同国家或地区（任选一个目的地）的班轮航线，搜索最新船期表，明确该航线可供出口的港口、最早出口时间（ETA、ETD等），描述该班轮的运输轨迹。

IV. Calculation

1. The price quoted by an exporter was "USD38 per case FOB Shanghai". The importer requested a revised CFR Liverpool price. If the size of each case was 50cm × 40cm × 30cm, gross weight per case was 40kg, freight basis was W/M and the quotation for Liverpool was USD100 per ton of carriage, plus 20% bunker adjustment factor（BAF）and 10% currency adjustment factor（CAF）, what would be the CFR price?

2. There is one consignment of 10 cartons of leather shoes. The measurement of each carton is 50cm × 50cm × 50cm, and the gross weight of each carton is 15kg. The air freight rate quoted for the flight required is USD1.3/kg. How much air freight should be paid to the carrier?

3. Company A is to ship their art ware to Turkey and the total quantity is 80 cartons（total weight:4,500kgs/ total measurement: 3.00cbm）. The ocean freight rate is: USD45/freight ton, LCL from Guangzhou, China to Istanbul, Turkey. How much is the total LCL freight?

4. Company B is to export their goods by three 1 × 20' FCL Containers from Guangzhou, China to Felixstowe, UK. The quotation for FCL ocean freight rate is as follows:

O/F（Ocean freight）rate: USD750.00/20';

BAF: USD500.00/20';

CAF:12% of the basic freight

ISPS (International ship and port facility security) USD10.00/20'

How much is the total freight?

IV. Case Study.

1. Sichuan Imp. & Exp. Co. Ltd exported 3000 M/T of soybeans in sacks of 100 kg each to Samson Organic Food Co. Ltd, Singapore. The contract provided that the shipment was not later than March 22, 2023 and the terms of payment was an irrevocable letter of credit. When Sichuan Imp. & Exp. Co. Ltd. booked the vessel, it found that the shipping space was not available for the whole goods, so it made the shipment in March and April 1,500 metric tons respectively.

Questions:

1) Is it necessary for Sichuan Imp. & Exp. Co. Ltd to ask Samson Company to amend the L/C to allow partial shipment?

2) If you were the exporter, how would you deal with it?

2. Shanghai Cinderella Trading Co. Ltd contracted with a U.S. importer to export 2,000 pairs of sneakers in CFR Houston. The time of shipment is between July to August in the contract and letters of credit, 1,000 pairs of sneakers each month, and transshipment is allowed. Our exporter loaded 1,000 pairs of sneakers aboard the ship "Qianjin" on July 31 and got the bill of lading for July, and loaded the rest of sneakers aboard the ship "Elizabeth" on August 10 and got the bill of lading for August.

Both ships were transshipped in Hong Kong and both lots of goods were transported to the final destination by "Nobel" of Maersk INC.

Questions:

1) Was it transshipment? Why?

2) Could the seller get financed safely? Why?

Chapter 6

Cargo Transportation Insurance and Insurance Clause

第六章　国际货物运输保险及合同中的保险条款

◆ Learning Objectives

• Understand the fundamental principles of international cargo transportation insurance

• Know about the risks and losses in marine transportation

• Master the scope of Marine Cargo Clauses 2009 of China Insurance Clause

• Know how to stipulate insurance clauses in international trade contracts

---

In international trade, goods usually travel a long distance to another country. At any stage of the transit, it is possible for the goods to suffer from all kinds of material losses, expenses or liabilities caused by risks such as natural disasters or fortuitous accidents. Therefore, it is extremely important for the traders to buy **cargo transportation insurance** in advance to hedge against the risk of a contingent, uncertain loss with the limited cost.

货物运输保险
以事先的有限费用规
避未来不确定风险

The basic categories of international cargo transportation insurance mainly include marine insurance, land cargo transportation insurance, air transportation cargo insurance, and parcel cargo transportation insurance. Ocean Marine Insurance is the oldest form of insurance, probably dating to the Middle Ages. And it is the most extensive use of insurance in human history. Other cargo insurance is developed based on marine insurance. Therefore, this chapter will focus on the marine cargo insurance.

6.1 Fundamental Principles of Cargo Insurance 保险的基本原则

> 所谓保险，就是指这样一种合同，当事人一方以收取的保费为代价，承担赔偿另一方当事人的保险标的物可能遭受某些危险或风险导致的损失。
> 投保人和保险人
> 保费
>
> 保险承销商 被保险人投保人或保单持有人

Insurance is a contract whereby one party, in consideration of a premium paid, undertakes to indemnify the other party against loss from certain perils or risks to which the subject matter insured may be exposed to. There are two basic parties in involved in a cargo insurance contract: **the insurer and the insured.** The amount of money to be charged for a certain amount of insurance coverage is called **the premium.**

An insurer, or insurance carrier, is selling the insurance, which usually refers to the insurance company. Another name for the insurer is **the underwriter. The insured,** also referred to as **the insurant or policy holder,** is the person or entity buying the insurance policy. In cargo insurance practice, the insurant can be either the seller or the buyer, depending largely on the incoterms adopted for transaction and on which party is subject to main risks in transit. For example, under a CIF contract, the seller must obtain insurance contract even though he is not the party subject to marine risks in transit. Once damage or loss within the insurance coverage occurs, the party suffers will **lodge a claim** against the insurer. This party is referred to as **the claimant.** In cargo insurance, the insured and the claimant may not necessary be the same

> 提出索赔
> 索赔方

party. This is mostly decided by who has **the insurable interest** in the goods damaged or lost. There may also be other parties involving in the insurance such as insurance agents, insurance brokers, insurance notary, etc.

保险利益

In the law, the insured and the insurer must follow the following general principles in signing and performing the contract.

6.1.1 Principle of Insurable Interest
保险利益原则

Can everything be insured? Must be capable of financial measurement. There must be a large number of similar risks. The person applying for insurance must be having insurable interest in the insurance contract.

Insurable interest refers to the legal right to insure arising out of a financial relationship (recognized under law), between the insured and **the subject matter of insurance**. There must be certain property, rights, interests, or lives capable of being insured. The property, rights, interests, etc., must be the subject matter of insurance. The insured must benefit from the safety or well-being of the subject matter and would suffer from its loss or damage. The relationship between the insured and the subject matter of insurance must be recognized by law. In accordance with Article 12 of China's Insurance Law, policy holder or the insured shall own insurable interests when the insurance accidents happen, otherwise, the insurance contract shall be invalid. This principle can make the insured be unable to gain additional benefits from the insurance contract if he has no insurable interest, which will avoid the change of insurance contract into a gambling contract.

保险利益指的是投保人与**保险标的**之间基于某种财务关系（法律认可的关系）而产生的合法投保权利。

6.1.2 Principle of Utmost Good Faith
最大诚信原则

According to the Principle of Utmost Good Faith (or **the Bona**

> 最大诚实信用原则（**善意原则**）是指保险合同的当事人应在订立合同时应该完整和准确地告知对方有关保险标的重要事实，不管对方有没有询问。

Fide Principle), both parties have a duty to disclose, accurately and fully, all facts material to the risk being proposed, whether requested or not. This principle is especially applicable to insurance contracts because, in the case of insurance, the product is intangible. When an insurer decides whether to insure, usually far away from the cargo location, it is difficult to survey the subject-matter insured and only rely on the statement of insurance. Only the proposer knows the details of the risk being proposed.

As the underwriter knows nothing, and the man who comes to ask an insurance knows everything, it is the duty of the assured to make a full disclosure to the underwriter of all material circumstances, without being asked.

Of course, the principle of good faith is the reciprocal duty on both parties. Proposer to disclose all material facts relating to the subject matter of the insurance. The insurer fully discloses the product features and benefits. The insurer does not make untrue statement at the time of negotiating the contract.

> 虚假陈述

Breaching of good faith in case of **misrepresentation** may be innocent or fraudulent. If related to material facts, the contract may be avoided by the aggrieved party. **Non-disclosure** which may

> 未披露

be innocent or fraudulent. If fraudulent, it is called concealment. If substantially false and material, then contract may be avoided.

6.1.3 Principle of Proximate Cause
近因原则

> 近因是指对保险财产造成损失的最直接原因，这原因不是以时间最接近的标准来衡量，而应是影响上的最重要的原因。

Principle of Proximate Cause means the most direct cause. When loss is a result of two or more causes, simultaneously or successively, the **proximate cause** becomes relevant. No matter how many causes there are, only the most direct one can be considered. It is the immediate cause, not the remote or distant one, that should be understood in terms of predominance in certain consequential losses. The losses may be suffered by the insured subject as a result of a peril which is not the proximate cause, are customarily paid. For example, the damage of property is caused by water from fire fighter. Other example, A house caught fire due to the air bombing of an enemy aircraft. The loss was due to fire, but the proximate cause is war (which in this case is excluded). Hence no claim is payable.

Although there are no provisions for the principle of proximate cause in China's Insurance Law and Maritime Code of PRC, in the practice of the international cargo insurance, the principle of proximate cause is an important principle which is commonly used to determine whether the insurer is responsible for the loss of the subject matter insured, and is the appropriate insured liability.

6.1.4　Principle of Indemnity
　　损失补偿原则

Principle of Indemnity is a mechanism to provide financial compensation to place insured in the same pecuniary position as enjoyed immediately before the loss. It may be at the option of the insurer in the form of cash payment, repair, or replacement. It is applicable to property, liability, and other non-life insurance.

损失赔偿原则是指在保险事故发生而使被保险人遭受损失时，保险人必须在责任范围内对被保险人所受的实际损失进行补偿的一种机制，它使被保险人大致恢复到与损失发生之前相同的财务状况。

Insurance contract for the international carriage of goods is a compensatory contract of property insurance. Therefore, in the case of excess insurance and double insurance, the insurer only indemnifies the claimant to the actual loss suffered by the insured. The total indemnification shall be limited to **the insurance amount**, for the purpose of insurance is to compensate rather than benefit from the insurance.

保险金额

6.1.5　Principle of Subrogation
　　代位求偿原则

Insurance subrogation, derived from the principle of indemnity,

在财产保险中，保险事故的发生是由第三者造成并负有赔偿责任，则被保险人既可以根据法律的有关规定向第三者要求赔偿损失，也可以根据保险合同要求保险人支付赔款。如果被保险人首先要求保险人给予赔偿，则保险人在支付赔款以后，保险人有权在保险赔偿的范围内向第三者追偿，而被保险人应把向第三者要求赔偿的权利转让给保险人，并协助向第三者要求赔偿。

根据保险补偿原则，在发生重复保险赔付责任时，将保险标的损失赔偿责任在各保险人之间进行分摊，保险人通常言明他们只愿承担的赔偿比例。

applies only to property insurance, not life or personal accident insurance. It allows an insurer, after compensating the insured, to seek recovery from a third party responsible for the loss. For example, if a house insured for RMB.500,000 is destroyed due to a contractor's fault, the insurer pays the owner and then claims from the contractor.

There are several explanations of the subrogation as follows: firstly, whether it is total loss or partial loss, the insurer shall make the indemnify first to the claimant before he can obtain the right of subrogation; secondly, under a valued policy, the compensation from the third party is less amount than that paid by the insurer, he may recover the difference, if more amount than the insured he must pass the surplus proceeds to the insured; thirdly, the insured can obtain interest on the losses prior to the insurer's indemnification, the insurer can obtain interest on the losses after his compensation, but also can comply with the provisions of the contract.

6.1.6　Principle of Contribution
　　　分摊原则

Principle of Contribution is also the derivative product of the principle of indemnity for insured losses. It is applicable in case of two or more insurers on one risk. It means that under the circumstance of double insurance, all the insurers shall share the cost of indemnity. The insurer who has paid the claim has the right to recover a proportionate amount from other insurers. Insurers word their contribution conditions to state that they are only liable for their ratable proportion of the loss. Principle of Contribution avoids the situation where an insured might get more than the actual loss.

6.2　Marine Risks and Losses
　　　海上风险与损失

Risks in cargo transportation are of many kinds. Different risks could result in the loss of or damage to the cargo in transit. The different risks are covered by different insurance clauses and different insurance clauses mean different premiums. So, we need to have a good understanding of the different risks and losses before we know how to effect insurance. This section will explain the major risks involved in the ocean transport, the possible losses resulted in and the expenses incurred.

In marine cargo transportation insurance, risks fall into the perils of the sea and the extraneous risks.

6.2.1 Marine Risks
海上风险

The Marine risks consist of the perils of the sea and extraneous risks.

Perils of the sea 海上危险

In marine insurance, the perils of the sea include both **natural calamities and fortuitous or unexpected accidents.** 自然灾害和意外事故

- Natural calamities refer to disasters caused by force natural events such as heavy weather, lightening, tsunami, earthquake, volcanic eruption, thunderbolt, floods, and so forth. It should be noted that the natural calamities hereby referred to do not actually include all disasters due to natural forces.
- Fortuitous or unexpected accidents neither do not actually include all accidents due to haphazard causes. It generally includes the accidents due to unexpected causes such as fire, explosion, vessel stranding, grounding, sinking or capsizing, collision, missing and so on.

Extraneous risks 外来风险

Extraneous risks refer to risks caused by other reasons other than perils of the sea, and can be divided into two categories: general

extraneous risks and special extraneous risks.
- General extraneous risks refer to the common risks such as theft, breakage, leakage, contamination, sweat and heating, taint of odor, hook damage, shortage, rust, etc.
- Special extraneous risks refer to risks resulting from military affairs, political factors, and government rules, such as war, striking, confiscation, failure to deliver, rejection, and so forth.

6.2.2　Marine Losses
海上损失

损失，海损

In the context of insurance, the term 'average' does not carry its conventional meaning. Instead, it refers to any loss or damage caused by natural disasters or unforeseen accidents, as well as the associated costs incurred during transit. Marine insurance specifies its coverage based on the nature and extent of the loss, which can be categorized as either total loss or partial loss.

6.2.2.1　Total loss
全部损失

Total loss refers to the loss of the entire value of the subject matter to the insured, normally involving the maximum amount for which a policy is liable. Most insurance policies provide for the payment of total loss up to the insurance amount. Total loss is divided into actual total loss and constructive total loss according to the situation of losses.

Actual Total Loss 实际全损

It means the loss that the insured property is totally destroyed or is damaged in such a way that it can be neither recovered nor repaired for further use, or the insured is irretrievably deprived of it. For example, that a batch of tea under a contract was immersed in seawater and could not be used anymore even if the tea arrived at the final destination. When an actual total loss occurs, the insured is not required to give the insurer notice of abandonment (i.e., the surrender of all rights, title, and interest) in the insured property in return for the sum insured.

Constructive Total Loss 推定全损

It refers to the loss where an actual total loss appears to be unavoidable or the cost to be incurred in recovering or reconditioning the goods together with the forwarding cost to the destination named in the Policy would exceed their value on arrival. For example, when a ship or the consignment has to be abandoned because the cost of salvage or recovery would exceed the value of the ship and the consignment in sound condition upon the arrival of the port of destination. They are treated as totally lost. In constructive total loss cases, the insured may abandon the property by giving a "notice of abandonment" to the insurer who then assumes all rights to the property.

6.2.2.2 Partial loss

部分损失

A partial loss is any loss other than a total loss. It is a partial damage to or the total loss of part of the insured cargo. A partial loss may include a particular average loss, a general average loss and particular charges. Thus, there are two distinct types of partial loss.

General average 共同海损

A loss may be by accidental or intentional. A general average loss is caused intentionally and such a loss is beneficial to others, then those who have benefited should share that loss. Thus, a general average loss is a loss resulting from a voluntary sacrifice or expenditure in time of peril, for the safety of hull, cargo, and freight.

A partial loss can be treated as general average if it is **formed upon the following conditions:** firstly, there must be an event which is beyond the ship owner's control, which imperils the entire adventure; secondly, there must be a voluntary sacrifice, thirdly, the action of the ship's master shall be successful, there must be something saved. The

构成共同海损的条件

voluntary sacrifice might be the jettison of certain cargo, the use of tugs, salvors, or damage to the ship, voluntary grounding, knowingly working the engines that will result in damages.

In the event of a general average loss, all parties involved in the maritime venture (such as hull, cargo, freight, and bunkers) are required to contribute to cover the voluntary sacrifice. The expenses are shared proportionally based on the value of their respective interests in the venture. This is known as a **General Average Contribution**. Internationally general average shall be adjusted at any port or place at the Carrier's option according to the **York–Antwerp Rules** 1974, as amended in 2016, and any other amendments thereto. In our country, the general average shall apply to Provisional Rules of the General Average Adjustment of China Council for the promotion of international trade (Beijing G.A. Settlement Rules for short).

Particular Average 单独海损

It is the accidental damage to part of the cargo. The average is not caused by deliberate act of a person for the common benefit and that loss must be borne exclusively by the owner of the property suffering the loss and is termed a particular average. If a loss or damage suffered by the claimant is covered by an insurance policy, it shall be reimbursed by the insurance company.

Although both general average and particular average belong to the category of partial loss, there are still some differences between them:

- **The causes of loss and expenses are different.** General average is caused by intentional and reasonable measures taken for the safety of the ship and the consignments.

- **Loss of composition is different.** Particular average only includes the loss of the goods caused by the perils of the sea itself, and general average includes both the loss of the goods, and fees paid for the lifting of the common dangerous cargo.

- **Different ways to bear the loss.** The party whose cargo is damaged, while general average should be proportionally contributed among all parties benefited from the intentional measures, assumes particular average.

损失的承担方式不同

6.2.3 Expenses Incurred
海上费用

Expenses are often covered by marine cargo insurance which consists of two types of expenses:

Sue or labor expenses 施救费用

When the subject matter suffers the risks within insurance coverage, the insured takes measures to avert or minimize the loss or damage to the subject matter insured. Expenses incurred to limit physical damages, or to take legal action to protect the ship and its cargoes from further loss once a loss has occurred, usually are reimbursed by the insurer to the extent they reduce the loss otherwise payable by the insurer, according to policy terms.

施救费用是指当被保险货物遭受承保范围内的风险时，被保险人或其代理人或保单受让人为了避免或减少损失的发生而采取相应的施救措施时所发生的费用支出。

Salvage charge 救助费用

The term "salvage" refers to the practice of rendering aid to a vessel in distress. A third party other than the insured or his agents, or any person employed for hire by them takes measures to save the subject matter. Such expenses, where properly and effectively incurred, can be recovered as particular charge or as a general average loss, according to the circumstances under which they were incurred. Salvage charges often take the "No-Cure, No-Pay" principle.

救助费用则是指被保险人、或其代理人、或任何他们雇佣的人以外的第三者对遭受海上风险的货物采取救助措施时，由被救助方向施救方支付的酬谢费。

6.3 Cargo Clauses of Marine Cargo Insurance of C.I.C.
中国海上货物运输保险条款

Ocean Marine Cargo Clauses of the People's Insurance Company of

China was constituted in 1972 and revised many times, the latest version of C.I.C. is 2009 version. It is the main basis for Chinese import and export company to apply for the insurance of marine cargo transportation. The main provisions of C.I.C. include the insurance coverage, exclusions, duration and obligation of the insured and the time of validity of a claim etc.

6.3.1 Basic Ocean Cargo Coverage of China Insurance Clauses(C.I.C.)
基本险保险条款

There are mainly two types of insurance coverage: basic coverage and additional coverage. Basic coverage can be taken out independently. But additional coverage must be insured together with a basic coverage. Moreover, basic coverage mainly includes F.P.A., WPA and All Risks. Additional coverage includes general additional coverage and special additional coverage.

6.3.1.1 Basic Coverage
基本险

This insurance is classified into the following three Conditions— Free From Particular Average(F.P.A.), With Average(W.A.) and All Risks.

Free From Particular Average(F.P.A.) 平安险

> 平安险只负责赔偿因海上风险所造成的全部损失和共同海损，一般对于自然灾害引起的单独海损不予赔偿，除非货物在这之前或者之后发生了意外事故引发的部分损失。

F.P.A. is a limited form of cargo insurance cover under which partial loss or damage resulted from natural calamities is not recoverable, unless these natural calamities occur before or after fortuitous accidents. It provides coverage covering the following losses:

- Total or Constructive Total Loss of the whole consignment hereby insured caused in the course of transit by natural calamities: heavy weather, lightning, tsunami, earthquake, and flood. In case a constructive total loss is claimed for the Insured shall abandon to the Company the damaged goods and all his rights and title

pertaining thereto.
- Total or Partial Loss caused by accidents such as the carrying conveyance being grounded, stranded, sunk or in collision with floating ice or other objects as fire or explosion.
- Partial loss of the insured goods attributable to heavy weather, lightning and/or tsunami, where the conveyance has been grounded, stranded, sunk, or burnt. Irrespective of whether the event took place after or before such accidents.
- Partial or total loss is consequent on falling of entire package or packages into the sea during loading, unloading, and transshipment.
- Reasonable cost incurred by the insured on salvaging the goods or averting or minimizing a loss recoverable under the Policy, provided that such cost shall not exceed the sum insured of the consignment so saved.
- Losses attributable to discharge of the insured goods at a port of distress following a sea peril as well as special charges arising from loading, warehousing, and forwarding of the goods at an intermediate port of call or refuge.
- Sacrifice in and contribution to general average and salvage charges.
- Such proportion of losses sustained by the ship owners as is to be reimbursed by the Cargo Owner under the Contract of Affreightment "Both to Blame Collision" clause.

With Particular Average (W. P. A.)水渍险

WPA is a wider cover than F.P.A.. It provides a more extensive cover against all loss or damage due to marine perils throughout the duration of the policy, including partial loss or damage which may be attributed to natural calamities like heavy weather, lightning, tsunami, earthquake and flood. WPA provides coverage covering the following two parts:

- Risks covered under F. P. A. condition
- Partial losses of the insured goods caused directly by nature calamities such as heavy weather, lightning, tsunami, earthquake

水渍险是除了赔偿因海上风险所造成的全部损失和共同海损外，对于单独海损也予以赔偿。

and/or flood.

All Risks (A.R.) 一切险

All Risks is the most comprehensive among the three basic types of coverage. However, even though the name of this coverage implies all risks, this coverage shall not cover all risks of loss or damage. It does not cover loss, damage, or expense caused by delay, inherent vice or nature of the goods, or special external risks of war, strike, etc. The coverage of All Risks is shown as following:

- Risks covered under the F. P. A. and W. A.
- Total or partial loss of or damage to the insured goods caused by general extraneous risks during the course of transit.

> 一切险（All Risks），简称"A.R."，是我国海洋货物运输保险条款中承保范围最大的一种基本险别。它的名字只是保险公司的一种承保险别的称谓，并不意味着承保所有风险。比如由于运输延迟、货物内在缺陷或者战争、罢工等原因引起的损失都不在一切险的承保范围内。

6.3.1.2　Additional Coverage

附加险

（1）General Additional Coverage

一般附加险

General additional risks cannot be covered independently and should go with F.P.A. or WPA. They are included in All Risks coverage.

- ***Theft, Pilferage and Non-delivery (T.P.N.D. for short)***. It covers the loss of or damage to the insured goods on the insured value caused by: ①Theft and/or pilferage, the risk against the possibility of the cargo being stolen in transit during the voyage; ②Non-Delivery of entire package, the risk against loss of complete packages due to improper unloading or for some other unknown reasons.

> 偷窃、提货不着险

- ***Fresh Water and/or Rain Damage.*** This insurance refers to the risk of loss or damage to the goods directly caused by fresh water and/or rain, not seawater.

> 淡水雨淋险

- ***Risk of Shortage in Weight.*** It covers the shortage of weight for the goods during the course of transit due to the breakage of external package. But, normal shortage of weight in transit is not covered.

> 短量险

- *Risk of Intermixture and Contamination.* It covers risk of intermixture and contamination occurring during the course of transit.   混杂，玷污险

- *Risk of Leakage.* It covers the risk of leakage and seepage of the liquid goods caused by the damaged container during the course of transit.   渗漏险

- *Risk of Clash and Breakage.* It covers the breakage of the fragile goods by vibration, clash or pressing during the course of transit.   碰损，破碎险

- *Risk of Odor.* It covers risk of taint of odor of the insured edibles, herbal medicine, cosmetics, or raw materials etc.   串味险

- *Sweating and Heating Risk.* It covers risk of loss of or damage to the goods by sweating, heating and wetting occurring during the course of transit arising from sudden change of temperature or breakdown of ventilation of the carrying vessel.   受潮受热险

- *Hook Damage.* It covers the damage to the goods caused by hooks in the process of loading and unloading, such as the loss of cereals due to the damage of packing bags by hooks.   钩损险

- *Risk of Rust.* It covers the risk of damage to the goods by rust caused by contamination with seawater during the course of transit. However, goods getting rusty by itself or due to its own flaws are not covered.   锈损险

- *Breakage of Packing Damage.* It covers the damage to the goods resulting from rough handling.   包装破裂险

All the general extraneous risks are included in the coverage of All Risks, so the general additional coverage would better not be insured together with All Risks.

(2) Special additional coverage

特殊附加险

Special additional risks cover the damage or losses arising from special additional reasons such as political events, military affairs, national policies and acts, and administrative measures. The special additional risks include:

战争险
- *War Risks.* It covers loss of or damage to the insured goods caused directly by or in consequence of war, warlike operations, conventional weapons, etc. But it does not cover loss, damage or expenses arising from any hostile use of atomic or nuclear weapons of war.

罢工险
- *Strike, Riots & Commotions (SRCC) .* It covers loss of or damage to the insured goods directly caused by acts of strikes, locked-out workmen, etc.

交货不到险
- *Failure to Delivery Risk.* It refers to the insurer shall pay a total loss of the insured goods in case the goods once loaded on board the seagoing ship, fail to be delivered at the destination within 6 months of scheduled date for arrival due to whatever cause it might be.

进口关税险
- *Import Duty Risk.* It covers the loss caused by Import Customs duty at the port of destination on the portion of the goods damaged by a peril insured against.

舱面险
- *On Deck Risk.* It covers the loss of or damage to the goods caused by the special risks when they have been shipped on deck. Usually they are large volume goods, goods of toxic, flammable and explosive or pollution, and must be stored on the deck customarily.

拒收险
- *Rejection Risk.* This insurance is to indemnify the insured for rejection and/or condemnation at the port of entry by the government of the importing country.

黄曲酶素险
- *Aflatoxin Risk.* It covers the loss of the insured goods when the cargo is rejected or confiscated by reason of the existence of aflatoxin, to an extent exceeding the limit sanctioned by the importing country.

出口货物到香港（包括九龙在内）或澳门存仓火险责任扩展条款
- *Fire Risk Extension Clause for Storage of Cargo of Destination Hongkong Including Kowloon, or Macao.* After being discharged at the final destination in Hongkong, including Kowloon or Macao from the carrying conveyance, if the insured cargo

is directed to be stored in a warehouse specifically designated by the bank to whom the interests in the cargo are assigned, this insurance shall extend to cover fire risk at such warehouse from the time the marine coverage eases until the termination of the said bank's interests in the cargo or the expiration of thirty days counted from the day the marine coverage ceases, whichever shall first occur.

These types of additional coverage also cannot be covered independently and are usually taken out together with F.P.A., WPA, and All Risks.

6.3.2 Exclusions
除外责任

Exclusions refer to the risks and losses not covered under either the basic coverage or the additional coverage by the insurer in marine cargo insurance practice. The exclusions of C.I.C. include:

- Loss or damage caused by the intentional act or fault of the insured.
- Loss or damage falling under the liability of the consignor.
- Loss or damage arising from the inferior quality or shortage of the insured goods prior to the attachment of this insurance.
- Loss or damage arising from normal loss, inherent vice or nature of the insured goods, loss of market and/or delay in transit and any expenses arising there from.
- Risks and liabilities covered and excluded by the ocean marine (cargo) war risks clauses and strike, riot, and civil commotion clauses of this Company.

6.3.3 Duration of Marine Cargo Clause of C.I.C.
保险责任的起讫时限

Just as the usual practice in international insurance market, with regard

1. 由于被保险人的故意行为或过失所造成的被保险货物损失。
2. 属于发货人责任所导致的被保险货物的损失。
3. 在保险责任开始前,被保险货物就已经存在品质不良或数量短差。
4. 由于被保险货物的自然损耗、本质缺陷、固有的特性以及市价涨跌、运输延误等所引起的被保险货物的损失或需额外支出的费用。
5. 在战争险和罢工险条款中所规定的责任范围和除外责任。

to the duration of liability of the insurer in ocean marine cargo insurance, C.I.C. adopts "warehouse to warehouse Clause" (W/W clause for short).

W/W clause, which means insurance coverage of risks to a shipment of goods from the time the goods leave the warehouse for commencement of transit and continue during ordinary course of transit until delivered to final warehouse at destination, or until the expiration of 60 days as of the moment of the insured goods are unloaded (if the shipment fails to reach the aforesaid warehouse), but with exception that the goods be transported to other place of destination not indicated on the insurance documents.

If the insured goods are to **be transshipped to** other place of destination not indicated on the insurance policy, the insurance liability shall be terminated on the commencement of transit to such other destination.

If the insured goods are to **be used for allocation or distribution** on delivery to any other warehouse or place of storage, whether prior to or at the destination named herein, the insurance shall terminate on delivery to the warehouse. The period of cover under the War Risk is more limited and does not comply with the W/W clause, from loading on to the oversea vessel until discharge at the final port or place of discharge. If the goods remain unloaded, the duration of insurance terminates on the expiry of 15 days after the midnight of the day when the vessel arrives at the port of destination.

6.3.4　The Time of Validity of A Claim
保险索赔的时限

The time of validity of a claim under this insurance shall not exceed a period of two years counting from the time of completion of discharge of the insured goods from the seagoing vessel at the final port of discharge.

When presenting a claim to the insurer the insured shall submit the documents such as original insurance policy, invoices, bills of lading, packing list, tally sheet, weight memo, certificate of loss or damage, survey report, and/ or statement of claim. If the third party liability is involved, the claimant must also provide the documents, correspondence letter and supporting documents relating to the third party.

6.4 Coverage of Marine Cargo Insurance of ICC 英国伦敦保险协会的海运货物保险条款

In the international insurance market, the widely used "Institute Cargo Clause" (ICC), developed by the London Insurers Association, is a key standard. While Chinese exporters often use "China Insurance Clause" for CIF/CIP terms, they may accept ICC upon foreign customers' request. First published in 1912, ICC underwent significant revisions in 1982, replacing the traditional S.G. policy and revolutionizing marine insurance. To adapt to global trade and transport advancements, the Joint Cargo Committee revised ICC again in 2008, effective January 1, 2009. The current ICC includes: ICC (A), ICC (B), ICC (C), Institute War Clause, and Institute Strike Clause. ICC (A) – (C) can be independently covered, while War and Strike Clauses require insurer agreement for standalone coverage.

英国伦敦协会海运货物保险条款
1. 协会货物条款（A）简称ICC（A）;
2. 协会货物条款（B）简称ICC（B）;
3. 协会货物条款（C）简称ICC（C）;
4. 协会战争险条款（Institute War Clauses Cargo）;
5. 协会罢工险条款（货物）(Institute Strikes Clauses Cargo);
ICC(A)、(B)、(C)款险可以独立承保，协会战争险和罢工险也具有独立的结构，但是需要与保险公司协商之后可以独立投保。

6.4.1 Institute Cargo Clause (A) 协会货物A款险

6.4.1.1 Risks Covered
承保范围

- It covers all risks of loss or damage to the subject-matter insured except as excluded.
- It covers general average and salvage charges, adjusted or determined according to the contract of affreightment and/or the

governing law and practice, incurred to avoid or in connection with the avoidance of loss from any cause except those excluded.

- 双方过失碰撞条款 It indemnifies the Assured against such proportion of liability under the contract of affreightment **"Both to Blame Collision"** Clause as is in respect of a loss recoverable hereunder. In the event of any claim by ship owners under the said Clause the Assured agree to notify the Underwriters who shall have the right, at their own cost and expense, to defend the Assured against such claim.

6.4.1.2 Exclusions
除外责任

This insurance covers all risks of loss of or damage to the subject matter insured except the following exclusions:

(1) General Exclusion Clause
一般除外责任

- 故意的不法行为 Loss, damage, or expense attributable to **willful misconduct** of the Assured.
- Ordinary leakage, ordinary loss in weight or volume, or ordinary wear and tear of the subject-matter insured.
- Loss damage or expense caused by insufficiency or unsuitability of packing or preparation of the subject-matter insured to withstand the ordinary incidents of the insured transit where such packing or preparation is carried out by the Assured or their employees or prior to the attachment of this insurance (for the purpose of this Clause "packing" shall be deemed to include stowage in a container and "employees" shall not include independent contractors).
- 固有瑕疵或本质 Loss damage or expense caused by **inherent vice or nature** of the subject-matter insured.
- Loss damage or expense proximately caused by delay, even though the delay is caused by a risk insured against (except

expenses payable under its covered general average and salvage charges）.

- Loss damage or expense caused by **insolvency or financial default** of the owners managers charterers or operators of the vessel where, at the time of loading the subject matter insured on board the vessel, the Assured are aware, that such insolvency or financial default could prevent the normal prosecution of the voyage. This exclusion shall not apply where the contract of insurance has been assigned to the party claiming hereunder who has bought or agreed to buy the subject matter insured in good faith under a binding contract.

  破产或债务积欠

- Loss damage or expense arising from the use of any weapon of or device employing atomic or nuclear fission and/or fusion or other likes reaction or radioactive force or matter.

（2）*Unseaworthiness and Unfitness Exclusion Clause*

　　不适航、不适货除外责任

- Loss damage or expense arising from unseaworthiness of vessel or craft, unfitness of vessel craft conveyance container or lift van for the safe carriage of the subject-matter insured, where the Assured or their servants are privy to such unseaworthiness or unfitness, at the time the subject-matter insured is loaded therein.

- The Underwriters waive any breach of the implied warranties of seaworthiness of the ship and fitness of the ship to carry the subject-matter insured to destination, unless the Assured or their servants are privy to such unseaworthiness or unfitness.

（3）*War Exclusion Clause*

　　战争险除外责任

- Loss damage or expense caused by war civil war revolution rebellion insurrection, or civil strife arising therefrom, or any hostile act by or against a belligerent power;

- Loss damage or expense caused by capture seizure arrest restraint or detainment (piracy excepted), and the consequences thereof or any attempt thereat;
- Loss damage or expense caused by derelict mines torpedoes bombs or other derelict weapons of war.

(4) Strikes Exclusion Clause
罢工险除外责任

- Loss damage or expense caused by strikers, locked-out workmen, or persons taking part in labor disturbances, riots or civil commotions;
- Loss damage or expense resulting from strikes, lock-outs, labor disturbances, riots or civil commotions;
- Loss damage or expense caused by any terrorist or any person acting from a political motive.

ICC (A) risk is similar to that of All risks under China's insurance clause, a wider scope of its responsibilities, so use of insurance "excluded liability" means outside of all the risks that their insurance coverage.

6.4.2   Institute Cargo Clause (B)
协会货物 B 款险

6.4.2.1   Risks Covered
承保范围

保险标的物的灭失或损失可合理地归因于下列任何之一者，保险人予以赔偿：

Loss of or damage to the subject-matter insured reasonably attributable to

- Fire or explosion
- Vessel or craft being stranded, grounded, sunk, or capsized
- Overturning or derailment of land conveyance
- Collision or contact of vessel, craft, or conveyance with any external object other than water
- Discharge of cargo at a port of distress

- Earthquake, volcano eruption, or lightning

Loss of or damage to the subject-matter insured caused by

- General average sacrifice
- Jettison or washing overboard
- Entry of sea, lake, or river water into vessel, craft hold, conveyance container, lift van, or place of storage

Total loss of any package lost overboard or dropped whilst loading on to, or unloading from vessel or craft.

下列原因所致保险标的物的灭失或者损坏：
共同海损牺牲
抛货或浪击落海

货物在装卸时落海或摔落造成整件的全损

6.4.2.2 Exclusion
除外责任

Except for the exclusions of ICC（A）, ICC（B）shall not cover:

- Deliberate damage to or deliberate destruction of the subject matter insured or any part thereof by the wrongful act of any person or persons（while ICC（A）only excludes loss, damage or expense attributable to willful misconduct of the Assured）
- Actions of pirates
- Any risks that not on the list of the covered risks of this coverage.
- The scope of ICC（B）insurance is similar to that of W.P.A under C.I.C..

对于任何人的非法行为对保险标的或其任何部分造成的故意损坏或故意破坏

海盗行为
任何没有在本险种下被列举出来的承保风险之内的风险
I.C.C.(C)险的除外责任与I.C.C.(B)险完全相同

6.4.3 Institute Cargo Clause（C）
协会货物C款险

6.4.3.1 Risks Covered
承保范围

Loss of or damage to the subject-matter insured reasonably attributable to

- Fire or explosion
- Vessel or craft being stranded, grounded, sunk, or capsized
- Overturning or derailment of land conveyance
- Collision or contact of vessel, craft, or conveyance with any

external object other than water

- Discharge of cargo at a port of distress

Loss of or damage to the subject-matter insured caused by

- General average sacrifice
- Jettison

6.4.3.2　The exclusions of ICC（C）are the same as that of ICC（B）

除外责任

- ICC（B）insurance and ICC（C）insurance have adopted the manner set out in the risk that their insurance coverage.
- The coverage of ICC（C）is similar to that of F.P.A. under C.I.C., but the coverage is smaller.

6.4.4　Institute Strikes Clause（Cargo）
协会货物罢工险

There are the risks covered under Institute Strikes Clauses（Cargo）.

Loss of or damage to the subject-matter insured caused by

- Strikes, locked-out workmen, or persons taking part in labor disturbances, riles or civil commotions.
- Any act of terrorism being an act of any person acting on behalf of, or in connection with, any organization which carries out activities directed towards the overthrowing or influencing, by force or violence, of any government whether or not legally constituted.
- Any person acting from a political, ideological or religious motive.

The coverage of Institute Strikes Clauses（Cargo）is similar to that of Strike Risk under C.I.C..

6.4.5　Institute War Clause（Cargo）
协会货物战争险

There are the risks covered under Institute War Clauses（Cargo）.

Loss of or damage to the subject-matter insured caused by

- War, civil war, revolution, rebellion, insurrection, or civil strife arising therefrom, or any hostile act by or against a belligerent power;
- Capture, seizure, arrest, restraint or detainment, arising from risks covered under the above, and the consequence thereof or any attempt thereat;
- Derelict mines, torpedoes, bombs, or other derelict weapons of war.

The coverage of Institute War Clauses (Cargo) is similar to that of War Risk under C.I.C..

6.5 Insurance Terms in the International Sales Contract 合同中的保险条款

6.5.1 Insurance Clause of the Contract 合同中的保险条款

There aren't unified contents or unified form of insurance clause in the contract of international sales of goods. And it should be clearly stipulated the provisions such as who is **the insured, the insurance coverage, the insured amount**, the insurance clauses, and which party bears the **insurance premiums**, etc.

被保险人，承保险别，保险金额 保险费

There are the examples of insurance clause:

- In the contracts under FOB, CFR, FCA and CPT trade terms, the buyer is to arrange insurance and pay premium. In the contract regarding insurance, it can only stipulate:
- "To be effected by the Buyers."
- In the contracts under DAP, DAT, and DDP trade terms, the seller is to arrange insurance and pay premium. In the contract regarding insurance, it can only stipulate:
- "To be effected by the Sellers."

- In the CIF or CIP contract, the insurance clause can stipulate:

Insurance to be covered by the sellers for 110% of the total invoice value against All Risks and War Risks, as per and subject to the Ocean Marine Cargo Clause 2009 and Ocean Marine Cargo War Risks Clause 2009 of the People's Insurance Company of China.

6.5.2　Procedures of Cargo Insurance　履约过程中的投保手续

In export trade, under CIF or CIP contract, in accordance with international trade practices, it is the seller who arranges insurance with an insurance company. In our country, usually the insured applies to the insurer one transaction by transaction. While Filling in the insurance policy, the contents such as the insurer's name, the name of the subject matter insured, quantity, packing, and insurance coverage, the amount of insurance policy, name of transport, and transport routes should be stated strictly in accordance with the import and export contracts or letters of credit provisions in detail, which can ensure that the insurance policies obtained after the payment of the premium can be successfully used for settlement of export foreign exchange.

The date of insurance policy should not be later than the time of shipment stipulated in the contract or letter of credit. The recommended minimum insured amount is the total CIF or CIP value plus 10% for other fees and normal marginal of profit under letter of credit, according to the **Uniform Customs and Practice for Documentary Credits**, the International Chamber of Commerce, No.600 publication.（UCP600 for short）.

跟单信用证统一惯例

In import trade, under the terms as FCA, FOB, CFR, and CPT, the buyer effects insurance. In our country, sometimes in order to simplify the insurance procedures to avoid missing of insurance or failing to apply for the insurance in time, generally open cover is recommended for the buyer, that is, the general contract between the insured（normally the importer) and the insurer, often used in import transactions in China. Usually the import & export companies enter into a long-term pre-agreement with the insurance companies. It will no longer need to fill the policy in subsequent each batch of imported goods after shipment, only if the shipping advice will be forwarded to the insurance company in time, which can be regarded as completing insurance procedures, the insurance company will automatically cover the goods.

6.5.3 To Calculate the Insurance Amount and the Insurance Premium
保险金额和保险费的确定

Generally speaking, the Insurance amount, also known as the Insured Amount or the Sum Insured, stands for the amount of insurance indicated in the insurance policy and agreed upon by the insurant and the insurer. It is the highest amount of indemnity given by the insurer when the subject matter is subject to a loss or damage and serves as the basis for the calculation of insurance premium. The value to be insured is based on the value of the commercial invoice where the insurance premium is included as that in a CIF or CIP contract.

Usually, the parties use the following calculation formula to determine the insured amount.

Insured amount = CIF (CIP) × (1+markup rate)

Insurance Premium (I) = insurance amount × premium rate (R) = CIF (CIP) × (1+markup rate) × premium rate (R)

6.5.4 Insurance Documents
保险单据

In international transaction practices, an insurance policy is actually a contract, serving as evidence of the agreement between the insurer and the person taking out insurance. It is not only usual for a certificate of insurance, but also the written basis for the claimant to lodge an insurance claim and for the insurance companies to handle the settlement of claims.

· Insurance policy 保险单

Insurance policy is the most commonly used document that contains all the details concerning the goods, coverage, premium and insured amount on the face and the detailed contract terms at the back. All this information must be sufficient enough for the insured party to assess the risk and make insurance decision. Insurance policy is a contract evidencing insurer-insured agreement, used for claims and settlements in international transactions. Under CIF, it's submitted by seller to buyer and used for bank negotiations.

· Insurance certificate 保险凭证

Insurance certificate, also known as a small insurance policy, is a simplified version of insurance contract. The certificate carries the same contents as the insurance policy except for the detailed terms of insurance responsibility, rights and obligations on the back, serving the same functions in the transaction.

· Open policy 预约保单

An open policy, or open cover, suits high-volume traders, offering continuous coverage for all shipments during its term, typically 6-12 months or indefinitely, with pre-agreed terms but no total insurance limit.

· Combined certificate 联合凭证

Combined certificate is the combination of the invoice and insurance policy, much simpler than the insurance certificate. It is not often used now.

▶ Exercises 练习

I. True (T) or False (F)

1. Partial loss or damage is never recoverable with F.P.A.. (   )

2. In Chinese insurance practice, open policy is the same as the

insurance certificate. (   )

3.Three types of risks are covered by ocean marine insurance, namely the perils of the sea, the extraneous risks, and the force majeure. (   )

4.In ocean marine insurance, natural calamities include heavy weather, earthquake, and tsunami. (   )

5.In marine cargo insurance, general average is to be borne by the carrier, who may, upon presentation of evidence of the loss, recover the loss from the insurance underwriter. (   )

6.Special additional coverage such as war risks, strikes, and so on must be taken out together with F.P.A., WPA, or All Risks. (   )

7.Ocean marine insurance covers two types of losses: partial loss and total loss. (   )

8.The claimant is the party who suffers loss of or damage to the subject matter insured by himself. (   )

9.ICC (C) provides the widest cover and is generally summed up as "All Risks" of loss of or damage to the insured cargo with certain specified exceptions. (   )

10.All Risks coverage provides insurance against all risks of loss of or damage to the cargo insured except for those damages or losses which are due to delay or inherent vice. (   )

II. Multiple Choice Questions

1.According to "Ocean Marine Cargo Clause of the People's Insurance Company of China", the coverage which cannot be effected independently is (   ).

    A. F.P.A.   B. WPA   C. War Risk   D. All risks

2.Company A exported 5 metric tons of tea. The tea suffered heavy storm in transit. The seawater in the ship's hold led the deterioration in the quality of part of the tea exported. This kind of loss is (   ).

    A. actual total loss   B. constructive total loss
    C. general average   D. particular average

3.The main documents adopted by the insured to make claims against the insurer is (　　).

　　A. B/L　　　　　　　　　　B. transportation document

　　C. insurance proposal form　　D. insurance document

4.The coverage of ICC(A) is equivalent to that of (　　) of C.I.C..

　　A.F.P.A.　　　B.WPA　　　C. All Risks　　D. Additional Risks

5.Risks such as "failure to delivery risk" or "rejection risk" fall within the category of (　　)

　　A. general extraneous risks　　B. special extraneous risks

　　C. natural calamities　　　　　D. fortuitous accidents

6.According to C.I.C. of the PICC, the basic coverage that is the least extensive is (　　).

　　A.F.P.A.　　　B.WPA　　　C. All Risks　　D. War Risk

7.Under ＿＿coverage of ICC, only major casualties are covered but not natural calamities.

　　A. ICC(A)　　　　　　　　　B. ICC(B)

　　C. ICC(C)　　　　　　　　　D. Institute War Clause Cargo

8. (　　) is the broadest kind of coverage but does not include all risks.

　　A. Free of Particular Average　　B. All Risks

　　C. With Particular Average　　　D.TPND

9.When the seller contracts for insurance, it is a (n)(　　) contract.

　　A.CFR　　　B.FCA　　　C.FAS　　　D.CIF

10.Perils of the sea, such as vessel being stranded or grounded covered in an insurance policy are one kind of (　　).

　　A. natural calamity　　　　B. fortuitous accident

　　C. general extraneous risk　　D. special extraneous risk

III. Calculations

1.The price quoted by an exporter was "USD450 per case FOB

Shanghai". The importer requested a revised quote for CIF Auckland. If the freight was USD50 per case, 110% of the value was to be insured, and the premium rate for insurance was 0.8%, what would be the new price?

2.Company X transacted with Company Y, exporting a batch of light industrial products under CIF. The total amount of the invoice value was USD 10000. The premium rate was 0.4% and the goods were insured against F.P.A. with a markup of 10%. Please calculate the insurance amount and insurance premium respectively.

3. A foreign trade company is exporting a batch of goods with a quantity of 200 metric tons, priced at USD 1,200 per metric ton CIF Rotterdam. The contract stipulates that the seller shall insure the goods for 10% above the invoice value against WPA (With Particular Average) and shortage risks, with premium rates of 0.2% and 0.3% respectively. Calculate the insurance premium the foreign trade company should pay.

IV. Case Study

1. A Company signed a CIF contract to export candies. The cargo was insured for "All Risks". Due to the long voyage, candies absorbed sweating in the ship's hold, and thus softened and degraded. Was the insurance company liable for the damage? Why or why not?

2. A batch of goods was insured F.P.A. for 110% of the invoice value, a seagoing vessel carrying the goods on May 3rd encountered storms at sea, making the goods partially damaged, the loss value was 1000 Yuan; the ship continued sailing again on May 8th ran aground, also making some of the goods damaged, with the loss value of 2000 Yuan.

Based on the information above, please analyze, whether the insurance company is responsible for compensation? How much should be compensated?

3.On a voyage, the cargo ship had an accidental fire. To save the ship, the captain ordered to have water poured into the compartment. The fire was put out.

1) For party X, her goods burnt amounted to 10% of USD0.5 million cargo;

2) For party Y, his goods damaged due to water poured accounted for 20% of USD 1 million cargo;

3) For the carrier, engine damages due to the fire equaled 10% of USD50 million ship;

4) Extra wages for the seamen totaled USD50,000.

Based on the information above, indicate

1) Which is PA?

2) Which is GA?

Chapter 7
The Calculation of Export Price
第七章　出口价格核算

◆ Learning Objectives

- Know the major factors in pricing decision
- Understand the function and calculation of commission and discount
- Know the conversion of the different trade terms
- Master calculating the export price
- Master the skills of negotiating the price terms of sales contract

In international business, **price clause** is the core terms and conditions of a contract. In the last section we have introduced the 11 kinds of trade terms in *Incoterms2020*, the price term of the sales contract is connected with trade terms, the international price varies due to different trade term adopted. In this chapter we will explain how to **calculate** the export price of commodity and how to stipulate the price terms in international sales contract.

价格条款

核算

7.1 Price Components of Export Commodities
出口商品价格构成

7.1.1 Expression of export price
出口价格构成

In international trade, the price term of sales contract includes the unit price and total price. Total price is the total amount of a deal. The price of a commodity usually refers to the unit price. The standard format of a price in international trade has four components: **a code of currency, price per unit, measurement unit, and trade terms.** They typically look like the following expression.

> USD100 per piece CIF New York or
> FOB Guangzhou EUR25 per dozen

It is up to the exporter if they put the trade term at the beginning or the end of the price. But all terms should be followed by the name of an appropriate place as defined by *Incoterms 2020*.

计价货币、单位价格、计量单位和贸易术语

7.1.2 Pricing methods
定价策略

In order to master the pricing, four pricing methods are illustrated here.

Cost-plus pricing 成本加成定价法

In the cost-plus calculation the exporter starts with the domestic manufacturing costs or factory purchasing costs if he is not the manufacturer. Then he adds overhead costs covering administration, research and development, and marketing. In addition, freight charges, distributor margins, customs handling fees, and profit would also be added. Cost-plus pricing is the easiest way of export pricing.

Marginal cost pricing 边际成本定价法

It is one to make the **incremented** cost of unit product for export is

增加的

lower than the earlier average production cost for the domestic market. When using this method, it is important to find out the **break-even point**—the minimum quantity required by which the exporter can sell at a particular price without a loss. The further the sales are above the break-even point, the higher the profits. Sales below the break-even point result in a loss to the seller. 　损益平衡点

Buyer-based approach 买方主导定价法

Prices are set according to the purchasing power of the buyer and the perceived value in the target market. It needs a good understanding of the marketplace if this approach is to be adopted.

Competition-based approach 竞争导向定价法

If competition is fierce, the exporter has to provide prices **benchmarked** to competitors or market average so as to stay in business. In this case **profit margins** could be lowered. 　基准　盈利率

Generally speaking, no matter what techniques are used, the export price must include cost and expected profit. Otherwise, the export does not make sense.

7.1.3 Pricing Considerations
定价因素

Pricing for foreign markets is usually different from that for the domestic market. Without **adequate** research into the build-up of an export price and unforeseen cost components and **contingencies**, transactions that initially appear attractive may prove unprofitable or unexpectedly resource-intensive. The following part will provide you with details of the major components determining the export price. An export price consists of the actual cost, the expenses, and the profits. 　足够的　偶发事件

Purchase Cost 采购成本

The calculation of **actual cost** of producing a product is the core element in pricing. Production cost in a narrow sense normally includes 　实际成本

material cost, labor cost, allocation of fixed and packing cost. Other administrative costs also considered as part of the overall production costs. If the exporter is not a manufacturer, it is then not necessary for him to concern himself with the details. He can simply conclude all these costs into a **"factory price"** or **"purchasing cost"**. Of course, he should consider the overhead costs as well.

It is noteworthy that, in order to promote the development of export trade, China implements the **export rebates system**, it refers to the refund of export products, domestic production and circulation in the actual payment of the product tax, **value added tax**, business tax and special consumption tax. Therefore, if there is export tax refund, it should be deducted when calculating the actual cost of an export commodity. The steps to calculate the **export tax refunds**: firstly, to determine the actual price of export commodities; and then multiplied by the tax rebate rate with the actual price of the commodity. Which is:

The actual price of export commodity = purchase price（including VAT）/（1 + VAT rate）

Export tax refund = actual price of export commodity × export tax rebate rate

Actual cost of export commodity = purchase price（including VAT）−export tax refunds

Expenses 费用

From the factory workshop until the place of destination in the importing country internationally traded products may incur two categories of expenses: domestic expenses and overseas expenses.

Domestics Expenses 国内费用

Domestic expenses include circulation costs, processing fees, packaging fees, custodial fees（warehouse rental and fire insurance）, domestic transportation cost（from warehouse to harbor）, documents fees（inspection fees, **notary fees**, **consular fees**, certificate of origin and licensing fees, **customs declaration** fees, customs fees), freight (loaded container cost, lifting cost and shipping fees), banking charges (discount interest and other charges).

Generally, there are two ways to calculate the expenses: Firstly, the exporter adds each domestic expense and overseas expense one by one, and then allocate to each unit of export commodity, this method is called Cost-plus Pricing. Secondly, set a basic amount, and then multiplied by a certain percentage, which is generally 3% to 8% of the purchase price, this method is called the proportional method.

The following describes the calculation formula for certain expense:

• Customs Tariff 应纳关税

Export Tariff = duty-paid price of export product × export tariff rate

Export Tariff = FOB/ (1+export tariff rate) × export tariff rate

• Bank Interest 银行利息

Bank Interest = purchasing price (purchasing cost) × loan interest rate (annual) × (the number of days loan/ the number of days in one year). For example, the purchasing cost of one commodity is RMB100, the bank's loan interest rate is 9%, and the loan period is two months, then the bank's loan interest for this unit commodity is $100 \times 9\% \times (2/12) = 1.5$ (RMB)

• Bank Charges 银行费用

Which refer to the international **settlement** fees, such as **transfer fees, collection fees, and credit fees**. Usually charge in two ways: pay-per-transaction (to be shared equally on each unit of goods) or by a certain percentage of the amount charged (usually by the offer price).

结算
汇款手续费，托收手续费，信用证使用手续费

Overseas Expenses 国外费用

Overseas cost mainly comprises overseas freight, overseas premiums, and commission.

Anticipated Profit 预期利润

Another essential part of the export price is the anticipated profit. How much an exporter wants to make out of a particular transaction directly impacts the price level of the product. There are two ways to calculate the anticipated profit: one is to calculate by an absolute number, for example, the profit is USD10 per M/T. The other is to calculate by a percentage of a certain amount, for example, the profit is 10% of the "factory price".

7.2 Calculation of Export Price
出口商品价格核算

7.2.1 Calculation for the main trade terms
主要贸易术语的价格核算

We take the cost-plus approach as the basic tool for pricing. The calculation requires one to analyze in detail the cost incurred. Using a worksheet can make the process easier and clear to understand. Table 7.1 provides a sample calculating chart for the nine Incoterms terms if a waterway transport is employed. Here only some typical items are listed. The **actual** application of such a worksheet may be subject to **specific** cost variations among different transactions.

实际的　具体的

After having a general idea about the cost elements responding to Incoterms, the following part will focus on the particulars of the calculation of the most commonly adopted trade terms: FOB, CFR, and CIF, and the price conversion of the three terms.

Components of FOB, CFR and CIF 价格构成

FOB= actual cost + domestic expenses + net profit

CFR= actual cost + domestic expenses + ocean freight + net profit

CIF= actual cost + domestic expenses + ocean freight + insurance premium + net profit

Ocean freight quotations can be provided by shipping lines or **shipping forwarder**. The amount of ocean freight depends on the mode of transport and the calculation method adopted, the details of

货运代理

calculating the ocean freight refer to Chapter 5.

The insurance premium rate for a product can be obtained from any insurance company, the details of calculating the overseas insurance premium refer to Chapter 6.

Table 7.1 Costing Worksheet

Item	Sub-Total	Total
Manufacturing cost		
+Export packing (optional, depending on mode of transport)		
+Profit margin		
+Administration overhead		
−Possible discounts/rebates/sales commission		
=Selling price ex-works (EXW)		
+Local transport cost from plant to place of loading (train/truck)		
+Costs for export clearance		
=Selling price free carrier (FCA)		
+Local transport costs to shipping port		
+Local transport insurance to shipping port if applicable		
=Selling price free alongside ship (FAS)		
+Storage costs, terminal handling charge (THC), loading onto ship		
=Selling price on board (FOB)		
+Main ocean freight to port of destination		
Selling price cost and freight (CFR)		
+Minimum marine cargo insurance premium		
Selling price cost, insurance, freight (CIF)		
+Additional costs for full transport insurance		
+Local transport costs to nominated destination		
Selling price delivered at terminal (DAP)		
+Unloading charges at the nominated destination		
Selling price delivered at place (DPU)		
+Cost of import customs clearance		
+Import duties, any VAT or other taxes payable upon import		
Price delivered duty paid (DDP)		

Price Conversion 价格换算

When the buyer and the seller negotiate about the price, often they will change their trade terms they offered according to the requirement of the other party. This concerns the price conversion. Formulas for price conversion are as follows:

价换算为CFR或CIF价

FOB converts into CFR or CIF FOB

CFR=FOB+F

CIF=（FOB+F）/[1−（1+insurance markup）× Premium Rate]

价换算为FOB或CIF价

CFR converts into FOB or CIF CFR

FOB= CFR − F

CIF=CFR/[1−（1+insurance markup）× Premium Rate]

价换算为FOB或CFR价

CIF converts into FOB or CFR CIF

FOB = CIF × [1−（1+insurance markup）× Premium Rate] − F

CFR = CIF × [1−（1+insurance markup）× Premium Rate]

Note: F=ocean freight

7.2.2 Price Including Commission 佣金

净价

If a price shown in the contract directly comes from the calculation of basic costs and profit, it is called a "**net price**". But occasionally traders have to make some adjustments to the net prices to achieve the goal of promoting sales. These adjustments include commission and discount.

中间商
代理商

Commission is an incentive payment made to the **middlepersons** or **brokers** for their intermediary service. The commission can be paid by the exporter to the sales agent, or paid by the importer to the purchase agent.

Chapter 7 The Calculation of Export Price

Expression 表示方式

Commission is normally expressed by mentioning a percentage as **commission rate** at the end of the price with commission. For example: 　佣金率

USD200 per yard CFR Hongkong including 2.5% commission

A more frequently adopted way of quoting price including commission is to use a capitalized "C" to deducting the commission behind the trade terms. For example:

USD2000 per dozen CIFC 5 Singapore or

USD2000 per dozen CIFC 5% Singapore

Sometimes the commission can be expressed in specific amount, such as:

USD25 commission per M/T

A price which contains a proportion as commission payment is called a "**price including commission**", it can be made openly or 　含佣价 implicitly in the contract.

Calculation 佣金计算

It is internationally customary to calculate commission by some percentage of the amount of transaction. There are two ways introduced for commission calculation:

• Commission calculated based on FOB price or FCA price 　按FOB或FCA价计算佣金

This means that if the deal is finalized by CIF, CIP or any other terms, costs like ocean freight and insurance should be deducted before the commission is calculated. The reason is that the freight and insurance are not sales revenue to the seller, the seller does not need to pay commission for the freight charge, insurance or any costs of the same nature, but only for the value of the goods itself.

For example: the CIF price is USD1000, the ocean freight is USD100, and the premium is USD10, the commission rate is 2.5%. Then, the commission=（1000−100−10）×2.5%＝22.25（USD）. 　按发票价格或成交价格计算佣金

• Commission calculated based on the invoice value or contract value of a transaction

This way is most commonly used for commission calculation. Commission can be calculated based on pricing including commission, and the net price can be obtained by deducted to commission from price including commission.

Commission=contract value × commission rate

For example, if the contract value of a transaction based on CIFC2.5%London is USD1000, the commission rate is 2.5%, then commission value will then be 1000×2.5%＝25（USD）. Sometimes one needs to calculate the price including commission from a net price. The formula will be:

Price including commission=net price/（1-commission rate）

Commission=Price including commission × commission rate

Net price=Price including commission-Commission

Net price refers to the contract price that without commission and discount, such as "USD1000 per M/T net FOB Guangzhou".

For example: If the net CIF price of one export good is 1000 US dollars, the commission rate is 5%, then its

CIF price including commission=net price/（1-commission rate）=1000/（1-5%）＝1052.64（USD）

Commission=Price including commission × commission rate=1052.64×5%＝52.64（USD）,or

Net price=Price including commission-Commission= 1052.64-1000＝52.64（USD）

Payment 支付方法

Commission is usually paid by the exporter when he receives the full payment. However it is better for the involved parties to reach an agreement in advance if the commission is paid in this way, so as to avoid disputes. Otherwise, the middlemen may require the payment of commission once the contract is concluded, in this case, the fulfillment of the contract may be riskier because of the lack of guarantee from the middlemen.

7.2.3 Discount
折扣

Discount is the price deduction allowed by the seller to buyer. What discount is allowed depends on the mutual relationship between the seller and buyer.

Expression 表示方法

The discount is normally expressed in the contract as a percentage of the total value or a fixed amount. For example:

USD200 per dozen CIF New York less 1.5% discount

Or expressed in specific amount, such as:

USD3 discount per dozen

Calculation 折扣计算

The calculation of discount is simple, it is not necessary to consider the FOB value or CIF value, normally it is based on the contract price. The discount rate multiplied by the contract value is the discount amount. That is,

Discount=contract price × discount rate

Then the actual price of the product will be:

Actual price = contract price–discount

= contract price ×（1–discount rate）

In addition, a discount may be calculated based on the quantity of the commodity. For example, if the discount for a commodity is USD 5 per piece, and the total amount is 500 pieces, then the discount=5 × 500 ＝2500（USD）

Payment 支付方法

It is normally deducted by the seller directly during the payment of goods.

Case: Guangdong Xingguang Exp–Imp company purchases one lot of lead ingot（铅锭）from Sunshine Steel factory. The purchasing price including VAT is RMB16000/MT, the VAT rate is 17%, and the export tax rebate rate is 13%, the total export expenses are 6% of purchasing value, the profit is 11% of purchasing value. The ocean freight from Guangzhou to London is USD115/MT, and it covers All Risks for 110% of invoice value, the premium rate is 0.7%. Please calculate the CIF London price. If the customer wants the CIFC5% price, then what price shall Guangdong Xinggang Exp-Imp company quote? Suppose the exchange rate is 1USD=6.42RMB

$$\begin{aligned}
FOB &= [15000-15000 \div (1+17\%) \times 13\% + 15000 \times 6\% \\
&\quad + 15000 \times 11\%] \div 6.42 \\
&= (15000 - 1666.67 + 900 + 1650) \div 6.42 \\
&= USD\ 2474.00
\end{aligned}$$

CFR = FOB + F = 2474.04 + 115 = USD 2589.04

CIF = CFR ÷ (1−1.1×0.7%) = 2589.04 ÷ 0.9923 = USD 2609.13

CIFC5% = CIF ÷ (1−5%) = 2609.13 ÷ (1−5%) = USD 2746.45

7.2.4 Understand the price
出口效益衡量指标

Profit-loss rate for export goods 出口商品盈亏率

Profit-loss rate for export goods is probably the best known and most widely used ratio for measuring the profitability of a company or a particular transaction. It refers to the ratio between export-loss amount and total export cost. The formulas are as follows:

Profit-loss Rate for Export Goods = (Export Net RMB Income (FOB) − Export Total Cost) / Total Export Cost × 100%

Export Profit-Loss Amount = Export Net RMB Income (FOB) − Total Export Cost

NOTE: All the figures normally would be calculated in the exporter's local currency.

出口销售人民币净收入

The export net RMB income refers to FOB price, which is

exchanged into RMB by the current exchange rate. The **total export cost** is the sum of purchasing cost (including Value Added Tax) and domestic charges, excluding the export tax refunds. If the profit-loss rate is greater than zero, there will be benefits, otherwise loss. One thing should be noted that the calculation of both export income and cost must exclude any overseas transportation charge and insurance cost since exporters are not supposed to make profit from the transportation charge and insurance payment.

Exchange cost of export products 出口商品换汇成本

Exchange cost of export products is also an important index to show the profits and losses of the export business. It refers to the ratio between total cost of export goods and the foreign exchange net income. That is to say, how much RMB can be exchanged for 1 US dollar, or the total RMB cost needed for exporting goods worthy of net 1 US dollar. The formula is as follows:

The exchange cost of export products = Total Export Cost (RMB) / Foreign Exchange Net Income (USD) × 100%

Total Export Cost is composed of purchase cost, domestic expenses and export tax, which means the total domestic cost paid by foreign trade enterprises for export commodities.

Foreign Exchange Net Income comprises total export foreign exchange excluding labor cost and other non-trade foreign exchange (freight, insurance premiums, and banking charges).

FOB—Foreign Exchange Net Income;

CIF—Foreign Exchange Net Income excluding freight, insurance premiums and commissions.

If the export exchange cost is greater than the exchange rate quotation when making settlement, there will be losses, conversely, there will be profits. For export company, thus, the lower of the exchange cost of export goods the better.

出口总成本

出口总成本是指出口商品采购价（含增值税）加上定额费用，减去出口退税收入。

出口商品盈亏率大于0为盈利，反之为亏损。

出口商品换汇成本也是用来反映出口商品盈亏的一项重要指标。它以某商品的出口总成本与出口所得的外汇净收入之比，得出用多少人民币换取1美元，即该商品出口净收入1美元需要的人民币总成本。出口商品换汇成本高于银行外汇牌价，则出口亏损；反之，则出口盈利。

按FOB价格术语——就是外汇净收入；
按CIF价格术语，扣除运费、保费、佣金得出外汇净收入。

There is an inner link between the exchange cost and the profit-loss rate, the greater the export loss ratio is, the higher the exchange cost will be. On the contrary, the smaller the loss rate or a little profit is, the lower the exchange cost will be.

Example: A trading company exports 10,000 sports shoes. The purchase price (pre-tax) of each shoe is 70 Yuan, the value-added tax rate is 17%, the tax rebate rate is 11%, fixed cost of the company is 5%, the price of export is 9.68 Dollars per pair CIF New York, ocean freight is 4,350 Dollars, insurance premiums are 1 100 Dollars. The foreign exchange rate of BOC is 1Dollar= 6.57 Yuan. Please calculate the export exchange cost.

Answer:

Total Export Cost=Actual Cost + Domestic Expenses=70−70÷(1+17%)×11%+70×5%=66.92 Yuan

Foreign Exchange Net Income=9.68−4 350÷10 000−1100÷10 000=9.135 Dollars

Export Exchange Cost =66.92 Yuan /9.135 Dollars=7.33 Yuan

7.3 Export Quotation Accounting in Trade Practice
实际业务出口报价核算

7.3.1 Export Quotation Accounting
出口报价核算

Being aware of Export Exchange Cost lays the basis of export price accounting. Quotation can be calculated via the actual cost according to tax refund after negotiating with the suppliers.

Example: A trading company exports a number of umbrellas to the UK, shipped in a **20-feet container**, purchase price (Tax Price) charges: 50 RMB each, value added tax rate: 17%, tax rebate rate: 9%, fixed cost (domestic cost): 5%, expected profit: 10%, container freight:

20英尺的集装箱

2 200 Dollars, 40 umbrellas each carton, carton size: 46 × 38 × 26, G.W.36kg, N.W.20kg. The buyer requires insurance to be covered against all risks, premium rate of 0.6%, and the foreign exchange rate of BOC: 1Dollar = 6.57 Yuan. Commission rate: 3%. Please quote an export price of CIFC3 London.

Calculation provided as follows:

Actual Cost=Purchase Cost−Tax Refund=50−50/（1+17%）× 9%=46.15 Yuan

Domestic Expenses= Purchase Cost × 5% = 50 × 5% = 2.5 Yuan

Ocean Freight: the volume of a 20-feet container is 25 cubic meters, the number of packaged umbrellas:

25/（0.46 × 0.38 × 0.26）=550 cartons, 550 × 40 = 22 000 in total

Freight for each raincoat: 2 200 × 6.57/22 000 = 0.66 Yuan

CIFC3=[Actual Cost+Domestic Expenses + Ocean Freight
     +Expected Profit (Price × 10%)+Commissions (Price × 3%)
     + Premium (Price × 110% × 0.6%)]/6.57

=（46.15+2.5+0.66）/[（1−3%−110% × 0.6%−10%）× 6.57]

= 8.70 Dollars

7.3.2 Export Counter-offer Accounting
出口还价核算

During an international trade negotiation, the buyer usually does not accept the price offered by the seller at the very first time. Instead, it will be negotiated several times, that is what we call Offer, Counter-offer, Re-offer, and Re-counter-offer. The deal will be done until **consensus** is reached. The seller will decide whether to accept the counter offer or not via calculating whether they are profitable or not, how much the profit will be and what the profit rate is. There is an important skill to be grasped to decide whether to accept the counter offer or the re-counter-offer.

一致的意见

利润额=销售收入+退税收入−采购成本−出口运费−保险费−客户佣金−国内费用 又因为，实际成本=采购成本−退税收入

所以也可以表述为：利润额=销售收入−实际成本−出口运费−保险费−客户佣金−国内费用 采购成本=销售收入−公司利润−保险费−客户佣金−国内费用−出口运费+退税收入

The formula is in line with the buyer's counter offer:

Profit=Sales Revenue+Tax Refund−Purchase Cost−Export Freight−Insurance Premium−Commission−Domestic Cost

As, Actual Cost=Purchase Cost−Tax Refund

The formula can also be expressed in another way as follows:

Profit=Sales Revenue−Actual Cost−Export Freight−Insurance Premium−Commission−Domestic Cost

Purchase Cost=Sales Revenue−Company Profit−Premium−Commission−Domestic Cost−Export Freight+Tax Refund

Connected to the previous example（接上例）: the trading company charges USD8.70/PC for each raincoat CIFC3 London, if the buyer offers a counter offer at USD7.98/PC CIFC3 London. The trading company considers the counter offer, if accepting it,

the profit can be calculated as follows:

Profit=Sales Revenue−Actual Cost−Export Freight−Premium−Commission−Domestic Cost

$=7.98 \times 6.57 - 46.15 - 0.66 - 7.98 \times 6.57 \times 110\% \times 0.6\%$

$- 7.98 \times 6.57 \times 3\% - 50 \times 5\%$

$=1.2$ Yuan

Profit Rate=Profit/Sales Revenue × 100%

$=1.2/(7.98 \times 6.57) \times 100\%$

$=2.29\%$

If maintaining the profit rate at 10%, the purchase price that the company can accept is as follows:

Purchase Cost=Sales Revenue−Company Profit−Premium−Commission−Domestic Cost−Export Freight+Tax Refund

$=[7.98 \times 6.57 \times (1-10\%-110\% \times 0.6\%-3\%) - 0.66]/[(1+5\%-9\%/(1+17\%)]$

$=42.64$ Yuan

If the exporter can reduce the profit rate to 8%, the price that the factory can accept is 48 Yuan each, then the count-offer the exporter can provide is:

CIFC3=[Actual Cost + Domestic Expenses + Ocean Freight

+Expected Profit + Commissions +Premium

=（48−48/1.17×9%+48×5%+0.66）/[(1−8%−3%−110%

×0.6%）×6.57]

=8.17 Dollars

If the trading company charges USD8.17/PC CIFC3 London, that means the company can sustain the profit rate at 8% and the manufacturing factory can keep the charge of 48 Yuan.

7.4 Price Terms in Sales Contract
合同中的价格条款

The price term is one of the main terms and conditions of the international sales contract, it is used to determine the contract price, therefore, the price term should be complete, clear, specific, and correct. Generally a price term includes two basic elements, which are **unit price** and **total amount** of goods, and the involved currency should be the same.

单价　总价

7.4.1 Examples for prices terms in the contract
合同中的价格条款举例

Unit price: USD12.00 per M/T FOB stowed and trimmed Singapore.

Total Amount: USD1 200 000.00（SAY US DOLLARS ONE MILLION AND TWO HUNDRED THOUSAND ONLY）

Unit price: JPY3 000 per set CFR Tokyo including 2% discount

Total Amount: JPY5 880 000（SAY JAPANESE YEN FIVE MILLION EIGHT HUNDRED AND EIGHTY THOUSAND ONLY）

7.4.2 Some notable issues while stipulating the price terms
规定价格条款的注意事项

- Select the appropriate trade terms according to transport mode and marketing intent to be adopted.
- Fighting for favorable currency in international settlement and adding hedging terms if necessary.
- Adopt flexible pricing methods, so as to avoid the risks from price fluctuation.
- With reference to the international trade practices, using commissions and discounts reasonably.
- If there are quality latitude and "more or less "clauses stipulated in terms of quality and in terms of quantity, as to the difference in quality or quantity, the pricing of this part should be set forth in the contract in full detail.
- It should clearly stipulate in the contract referring to the measurement unit, involved currency, port of loading, port of destination, etc., so as to execute the contract well.

Exercises 练习

I. Case Study

1. DD Company offered to sell goods at "USD2 000 per M/T CIF Toronto with 'all risks' and 'war risk' for 110% of the value". The importer requested a revised quote for FOB Guangzhou. The freight for Guangzhou–Toronto was USD50 per M/T, and the premium rates for "all risks" and "war risk" were 1% and 0.2% respectively. To get the same export revenue, what FOB price should the exporter offer?

2. A trading company exports a number of commodities abroad, the original price is USD 2 000 per metric ton CIFC3% London, the buyer

requires CFRC5% London. Insurance coverage for the original premiums is against all risks including war risks, the rates were 0.8% and 0.6%, in accordance with 110% CIF price. Please calculate CFRC5%London.

3. The purchase price (without VAT) for an export product is 4500RMB per metric ton, the total local cost is RMB400/MT, and the total tax is RMB60/MT. Its CIFC5% London price was USD750/MT, the ocean freight was USD20/MT, the insurance premium was USD10/MT. Suppose the bank exchange rate was 1USD/6.5RMB, then what would be the profit-loss rate for this transaction? And what about its export cost for foreign exchange?

4. A UK client ordered 10,000 pieces of jeans, requiring CIFC5 LONDON, premiums covering all. Purchase cost is 30 RMB per jean, logistics cost is 15,000 RMB, expected profit rate is 10%, commodity value-added tax rate is 17%, rebate tax rate is 13%. Please calculate the CIFC5 LONDON the company should charge.

(P.S.: 25 jeans each carton, carton size: $45 \times 36 \times 25$, G.W.35kg, N.W.32kg, freight from starting harbor to London: 150 USD per ton, overseas shipping premium is defined as 0.6% by W/M, which covers all insurance. Foreign exchange rate of BOC: 1 USD=7.61/7.64RMB)

Chapter 8
Terms of Payment

第八章　国际贸易支付及合同中的支付条款

◆ **Learning Objectives**

• Understand the payment instruments and methods used in international trade settlements

• Be familiar with the types of Bills of Exchange and understand their key components

• Master the nature, functions, and essential elements of a Letter of Credit(L/C)

• Be well-versed in the payment terms and conditions outlined in international trade contracts

In international trade, the importer is obligated to pay the exporter the agreed amount in the specified currency, within the agreed time frame, and through the agreed payment method. For exporters, the timing and method of receiving payment for goods shipped overseas are critical concerns. While payment in domestic trade is relatively straightforward—often made either in advance or shortly after delivery—international trade introduces complexities. Delays in communication, shipping, and delivery are inevitable, raising questions about liability for such delays. Should the seller wait months for payment, or should the buyer pay months before receiving the goods? Additionally, in cases of non-payment, the seller may face costly legal proceedings and potential total loss. To address these challenges, various **payment methods** have been developed for international trade. Typically, every international sales contract includes a payment clause that outlines four key elements: timing, method, place, and currency of payment. The different export financing methods reflect variations and arrangements of these elements. 支付方式

In international trade, the most commonly used payment instruments are currencies and bills. Currencies are used for accounting, settlement, and payment, while bills are primarily used for settlement and payment. In practice, sellers rarely insist on cash payments and instead accept certain financial instruments, such as **bills of exchange (drafts)**, **promissory notes**, and **checks**, as substitutes. Among these, promissory notes and checks are used less frequently in foreign trade, making the bill of exchange the most prominent instrument. Therefore, the focus here will be on the bill of exchange. 汇票 本票 支票

8.1 International Trade Payment Tools
国际贸易的支付工具

8.1.1 Bill of Exchange
汇票

8.1.1.1 Definition of Bill of Exchange (draft)
汇票的含义

A bill of exchange, also called a draft, is defined as "an unconditional order in writing, addressed by one person to another, signed by the person giving it, requiring the addressee to pay on demand, or at a fixed or determinable future time, a sum certain in money, to or to the order of a specified person or to the bearer." The operation process of a draft includes drawing, presentation, acceptance, payment, endorsement, dishonor, and recourse. Drafts are negotiable instruments and may be sold.

8.1.1.2　Content of Bill of Exchange（draft）

汇票的内容

The following specimens of bill of exchange can help us make clear the content of it.

（Specimen A）

```
No. 1206
$10000                                           New York，8th January, 2025
On demand pay to Tom Smith or bearer the sum of USD Ten Thousand only.


To: Mr. Fox Bryan
London
                                                     （signed）David White
```

（Specimen B）

```
No. 668/96
Exchange for $8 500                      Shanghai, China, 8th August, 2024
At 60 days sight of this First of exchange （the SECOND of the same and date being
unpaid）pay to or to the order of Shanghai T&G Import and Export Corporation the
sum of USD eight thousand five hundred only.
To: BCM Import and Export Co., Ltd.
    58 Linden Street
    Miami, U.S.A.
                                         Shanghai T&G Import and Export Corporation
                                                                          Manager
                                                                       （signed）
```

Based on the definition of a bill of exchange, the two examples can be broken down into the following components:

无条件的书面支付命令

（Ⅰ）**An unconditional order in writing**

出票人

（Ⅱ）Addressed by one person/party（**the drawer**）

In A: David White，New York

In B: Shanghai T&G Import and Export Corporation

受票人/付款人

（Ⅲ）To another（**the drawee**）

In A: Fox Bryan，London

In B: BCM Import and Export Co., Ltd, Miami

(IV) Signed by the person/party (the drawer) giving it

- Requiring the person/party to whom it is addressed (the drawee or the payer)
- **To pay** 支付命令
- **On demand, or at a fixed or determinable future time** 即期或固定日期或在可以确定的将来时间
  - √ In A: on demand
  - √ In B: 60 days after sight (a determinable future time)
- **A sum certain in money** 确定的金额
  - √ In A: $10 000
  - √ In B: $8 500
- To, or to the order of, a specified person/party or to bearer (**the payee**) 收款人（抬头分为某人、指定人、来人）
  - √ In A: Tom Smith (or bearer)
  - √ In B: Shanghai T&G Import and Export Corporation

8.1.1.3 The Parties

当事人

A bill of exchange involves three parties:

Drawer: the person who writes the order and gives directions to the person to make a specific payment of money. He is usually the exporter or his banker in import and export trade; usually, he is also a creditor of the drawee. 出票人

Drawee (or the payer): the person to whom the order is addressed and who is to pay the money. He is usually the importer or **the appointed bank under a letter of credit** in import and export trade. In addition, when **a time bill** has been **accepted** by the drawee, he becomes an **acceptor** who is the same person as the drawee. The drawer and the acceptor must be different persons. 受票人/付款人

信用证项下的指定银行

远期汇票　承兑

承兑人

Payee: the person (individual, firm, corporation, or bank) to whom the payment is ordered to be made. The drawer and payee may be 收款人

often the same person. In this case, the bill may be worded "Pay to our order…". The payee is usually the exporter himself or his appointed bank in import and export trade. The payee may also be **the bearer** of the bill. The payee may be the original payee in the bill, or may be some party to whom the original payee has transferred the instrument. If a bill with such instruction "Pay…Co. or order" or "Pay to the order of … Co.", it means to pay to the payee or to anyone to whom he in turn directs payment to be made. In this way, the bill should be **endorsed** by the payee, now **the endorser**, and can be passed on to a new payee, **the endorsee**, thus making it negotiable. A bill may have many numbers of endorsers.

The relationship among these parties in bill of exchange may be described as a triangle (see Figure 8.1):

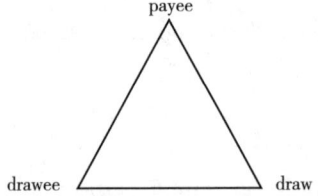

Figure 8.1　The Parties in Bill of Exchange

8.1.1.4　Classification of Bills of Exchange
汇票的分类

Depending on different criteria, bills of exchange can be classified into several categories:

· **Commercial Bill and Banker's Bill**

Bills of exchange can be divided into commercial bills and banker's bills, depending on the drawer. A commercial bill is issued by a business entity and is commonly used in international trade finance. On the other hand, a banker's bill is issued by a bank and is primarily utilized for remittance purposes.

- Clean Bill and Documentary Bill   光票汇票和跟单汇票

A clean bill refers to a draft that is not accompanied by any supporting documents. It is rarely used in commercial transactions and is typically employed to collect items such as commissions, interest, sample fees, or advance payments. In contrast, a documentary bill is a draft that is accompanied by shipping documents, such as a bill of lading, insurance policy, or commercial invoice. This type of bill is commonly used to secure payment for the import or export of goods.

- Sight (or Demand) Bill and Time (or Usance) Bill   即期汇票和远期汇票

Bills of exchange can be categorized into sight (or demand) bills and time (or usance) bills, based on their payment terms. A sight bill requires the drawee to make payment immediately upon presentation or "at sight." In contrast, a time bill requires the drawee to accept the bill first and pay it at a specified or determinable future date. In other words, acceptance is a prerequisite for payment. The future payment date may be set as a specific number of days after acceptance.   见票即付

√ At.... days after sight, such as "30 days sight" or "60 days after sight";   见票后×××天付款

√ At.... days after the date of the draft, such as "90 days after date of this draft";   出票后×××天付款

√ At a fixed date in the future, such as "On July 18, 2025".   将来某一指定日期付款

- Commercial Acceptance Bill and Banker's Acceptance Bill

In the case of time or usance commercial bills, if the drawer is a commercial entity and the drawee is also a commercial entity, the bill, once accepted by the drawee, is referred to as a commercial acceptance bill. On the other hand, if the drawer is either a commercial firm or a bank, and the drawee is a bank, the bill, once accepted by the bank (drawee), is known as a banker's acceptance bill.

8.1.1.5 Use of Bill of Exchange in Foreign Trade
汇票在贸易中的运用

A bill of exchange (or draft) is a payment order issued by an exporter and presented to an importer, typically through a bank. It can be made payable either immediately upon presentation (known as a sight draft or demand draft) or after a specified period following presentation (known as a time draft or usance draft). In the case of a time draft, the drawee must first write "Accepted" on the document and sign it. The exporter can then obtain immediate payment by discounting the draft with a bank, supported by a letter of hypothecation.

If a time draft is not honored (paid) at maturity, it will be formally recorded and protested by a Notary Public, and then re-presented to the drawee. Such drafts, along with the corresponding payment terms like "Documents against Acceptance" (D/A), inherently carry risks for the exporter or their bank.

Sight drafts involve less risk since the title to the goods is only transferred upon payment. However, even in this case, the exporter may face the risk of the draft being dishonored, leaving them with the goods still in transit or unsold. When drafts are presented under a letter of credit (L/C), the exporter is fully protected, and only the issuing and confirming banks assume the associated risks.

8.1.2 Promissory Note
本票

无条件支付承诺

制票人

A promissory note is **an unconditional promise** in writing made by one person to another signed by **the maker**, engaging to pay, on demand or at a fixed or determinable future time, a sum certain in money, to, or to the order, of a specified person or to the bearer.

The main difference between a promissory note and a draft lies in that there are three parties, namely drawer, drawee and payee involved in a draft but only two, **drawer and payee in a promissory note**. The payer of promissory note is the drawer himself.

本票只有制票人和收款人两个当事人

Promissory notes can be made by commercial firms, called commercial promissory notes, or bankers, called bank promissory notes. Commercial promissory notes can be sight promissory notes or time promissory notes, while bank promissory notes can only be sight. In international trade, most promissory notes are drawn by bankers which are mostly not negotiable.Figure 8.2 shows the sample of promissory note.

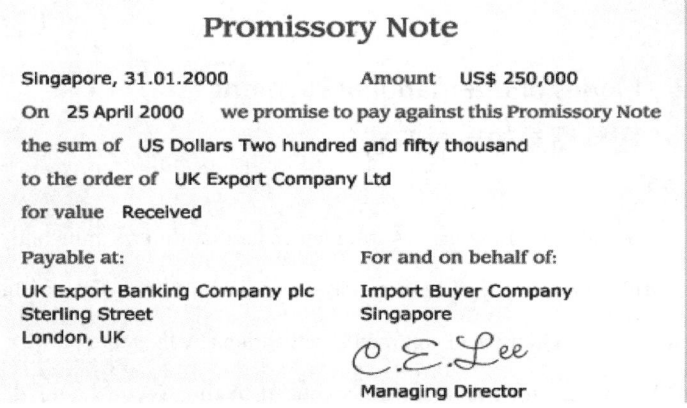

Figure 8.2 Promissory Note Sample

8.1.3 Cheque (Check) 支票

A cheque is **an unconditional order in writing** drawn on a banker and signed by the drawer, requiring the banker to pay on demand a sum certain in money to or to the order of a specified person or to bearer.

无条件书面支付命令

In international trade, a cheque issued by an overseas bank is not easily negotiable by the exporter. If the exporter's bank is willing to negotiate the cheque on their behalf, the exporter can receive payment immediately, albeit at the cost of a discount. However, if the bank is unwilling to negotiate, the exporter would need to request their bank to collect the cheque, a process that is both time-consuming and relatively costly.Figure 8.3 shows the cheque sample.

Figure 8.3   Cheque Sample

8.2   Modes of International Payment
国际贸易的支付方式

International trade carries inherent risks that differ significantly from domestic transactions, as both exporters and importers face uncertainties regarding the fulfillment of contractual obligations by the other party.

Exporters, for instance, are exposed to the risk of buyer default, where importers may fail to make full payment for the goods. This can occur for various reasons, such as the importer's bankruptcy, the outbreak of war, or the imposition of trade embargoes by the importer's government on either the exporting country or specific commodities. Additionally, importers might encounter difficulties in securing the necessary foreign exchange to complete the payment, or they may simply prove unreliable and refuse to honor the agreed-upon payment terms.

On the other hand, importers face the risk of delayed shipment, where goods may arrive long after payment has been made. Such delays can stem from port congestion, labor strikes, or slow order processing by exporters. Furthermore, complications in customs clearance within the importing country can lead to business losses. There is also the possibility of receiving incorrect or mismatched goods.

To mitigate these risks, various payment methods have been developed specifically for international trade. These payment methods can generally be categorized into three main types, as outlined below.(see Table 8.1) :

Table 8.1 Modes of Payment in International Trade

Modes of Payment in International Trade	Remittance	M/T （mail transfer）	
		T/T （telegraphic transfer）	
		D/D （demand draft）	
	Collection	D/P （documents against payment）	D/P at sight
			D/P after sight
		D/A （documents against acceptance）	
	Letter of Credit		

Remittance and collection fall under **commercial credit**, whereas a letter of credit operates under **banker's credit**. In international trade, "credit" determines which party assumes the responsibility for making payment and transferring the shipping documents, which represent ownership of the goods. In remittance or collection transactions, the buyer is responsible for payment, and the seller is responsible for delivering the documents. In contrast, in a letter of credit transaction, the bank acts on behalf of both parties, handling the payment and the exchange of documents.

商业信用
银行信用

8.2.1 Remittance
汇付

In the context of remittance, the payer instructs their bank or another financial institution to transfer a payment to the payee. The remittance process involves four parties: **the remitter, the payee, the remitting bank, and the paying bank.** In international trade, remittance is commonly used in transactions under terms such as cash in advance, cash with order, cash on delivery, or open account. There are three main types of remittance.

汇款人、收款人、汇出行和汇入行

8.2.1.1 Types of Remittance

(1) Mail Transfer (M/T)

信汇

Mail transfer is the most common method of remittance. The buyer gives money to the remitting bank (his local bank), which then issues a trust deed for payment and sends it to the paying bank (his branch or correspondent bank) in the seller's place by mail instructing him to pay the specific amount to the seller. This method costs less, but slower.

(2) Telegraphic Transfer (T/T)

电汇

The procedure under T/T is similar to that of M/T except that the instructions from the buyer's bank to its branch or correspondent bank at the seller's end are made by cable instead of by mail. The payment can be processed more quickly, allowing the seller to receive the funds promptly. But the buyer has to be charged more for it.

(3) Demand Draft (D/D)

票汇

Under demand draft, the remitting bank, at the request of the buyer, draws a demand draft on its branch or correspondent bank instructing it to make a certain amount of payment to the seller on behalf of the buyer.

8.2.1.2 Advantages and Disadvantages of Remittance

汇付的利与弊

In international trade, most transactions involving remittance are conducted through mail transfer (M/T) or telegraphic transfer (T/T). T/T is advantageous for the seller as it allows for prompt receipt of funds, accelerates cash flow, increases interest income, and mitigates the risk of exchange rate fluctuations. However, it is less favorable for the buyer, who must bear higher cable fees and bank charges. In practice, if T/T is not explicitly stipulated in the transaction, the buyer is generally advised to use M/T for payment. When the payment amount is relatively large, the money market is highly volatile, or the settlement currency is at risk of devaluation, it is prudent for the buyer to opt for T/T. In short, the choice between T/T and M/T should be clearly specified in the contract based on the specific circumstances. As for demand draft (D/D), it is transferable, which distinguishes it from M/T and T/T.

8.2.2 Collection
托收

When immediate funds are not required, or when bills are not attractive enough to a bank for negotiation, an exporter may submit them to their bank for collection. The exporter instructs their bank to arrange for the acceptance or payment of the bill overseas, and the bank executes this task through its overseas branch or a correspondent bank.

In a collection arrangement, the exporter draws a draft, attaches the shipping documents, and submits the draft to a local bank (**the remitting bank**) to apply for collection. The remitting bank is then 汇出行 entrusted to collect the payment from the buyer through its overseas correspondent bank (**the collecting bank**). Throughout the collection 代收行 process, banks merely act as intermediaries for collecting and remitting funds and assume no liability for the importer's failure to pay.

The procedure of collecting payment is illustrated as follows (see Figure 8.4):

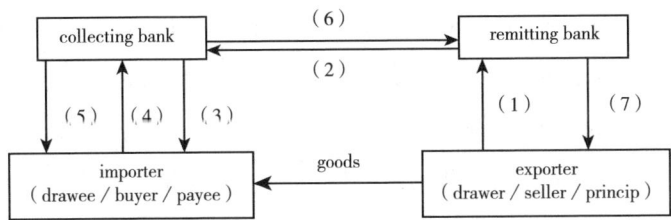

Figure 8.4 Procedure of Collecting Payment

Remarks:
(1) The exporter dispatches the goods and draws a draft, then sends the draft

together with shipping documents to the remitting bank to make an application for collecting money on his behalf.

(2) The remitting bank sends the draft and shipping documents to a correspondent bank overseas (the collecting bank).

(3) The collecting bank presents the draft and documents to the importer for acceptance (D/A) and payment (D/P).

(4) The importer makes payment (D/P) or endorses the bill for acceptance.

(5) The collecting bank hands over the documents to the importer.

(6) The collecting bank notifies the remitting bank of crediting the money to their account.

(7) The remitting bank makes payment to the exporter.

光票托收和跟单托收

Collection means the handing by banks, on instructions received, of documents (financial documents and/or commercial documents), in order to: a. obtain acceptance and/or, as the case may be, payment, or b. deliver commercial documents against acceptance and/or as the case may be, against payment, or c. deliver documents on other terms and conditions. Collection is of two types: **clean collection and documentary collection.** The parties to a collection financial document not accompanied by commercial documents (financial documents means bill of exchange, promissory notes, checks, payment receipts or other similar instruments used for obtaining the payment of money; commercial documents mean invoices, shipping documents, documents of tittle or other similar documents whatsoever, not being financial documents).

Documentary collection means the collection of: a. financial documents accompanied by commercial documents; b. commercial documents not accompanied by financial documents. The documentary collection is widely used in international trade. Documentary collection falls into two kinds: documents against payment (D/P) and documents against acceptance (D/A).

8.2.2.1 Documents Against Payment (D/P)

付款交单

Under this payment term, the exporter must ship the ordered

goods and deliver the relevant shipping documents to the buyer abroad through the remitting bank and the collecting bank, with instructions not to release the documents to the buyer until full payment is received. According to the timing of payment, the document against payment can be further divided into D/P at sight and D/P after sight.

(1) D/P at Sight
即期付款交单

Under this payment term, the seller draws a sight draft and sends it along with the shipping documents to the collecting bank. Then, the collecting bank presents the sight draft and shipping documents to the buyer. When the buyer receives them, he must make the payment immediately to obtain the shipping documents. This method is also called "Cash against Documents," and its procedure is illustrated below.

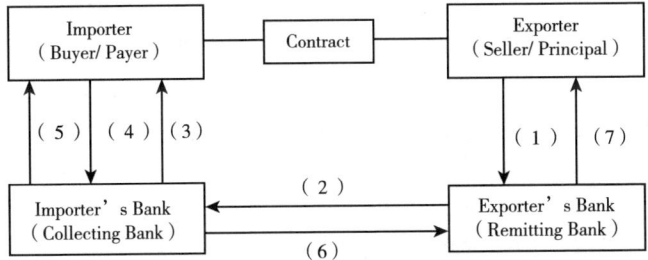

Figure 8.5   Procedure of D/P at Sight

Note:

(1) According to the contract, the exporter loads the goods and draws a sight draft, then sends the draft together with shipping documents to his bank for collecting a documentary bill on his behalf.

(2) The remitting bank sends the documentary bill to a correspondent bank overseas the collecting bank for collecting money.

(3) The collecting bank presents the bill and documents to the importer for payment.

(4) The importer makes payment.

(5) The collecting bank hands over the documents to the importer.

(6) The collecting bank notifies the remitting bank of crediting the money to their account.

(7) The remitting bank makes payment to the exporter.

(2) D/P After Sight

远期付款交单

Under this term, the seller draws a time (or usance) draft. The collecting bank presents the time draft and shipping documents to the buyer. When the buyer sees them he just accepts the time bill and then effects payment at the maturity of the draft. When receiving the money from the buyer, the collecting bank hands over the shipping documents to him. The procedure of D/P after sight is shown in the following diagram (see Figure 8.6)

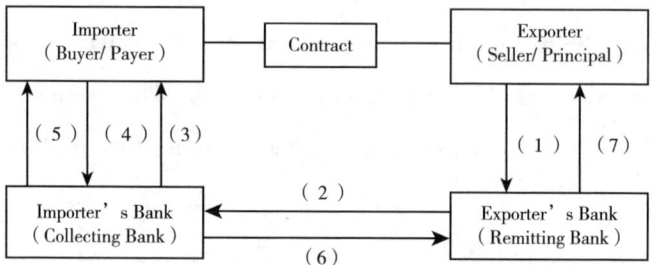

Figure 8.6　Procedure of D/P after Sight

Note:

(1) According to the contract, the exporter loads the goods and draws a time draft, then sends the draft together with shipping documents to his bank for collecting a documentary bill on his behalf.

(2) The remitting bank sends the documentary bill to a correspondent bank overseas–the collecting bank.

(3) The collecting bank presents the bill and documents to the importer for acceptance. After the importer accepts the draft, the collecting bank takes back the draft and documents.

(4) The importer makes payment when the time falls due.

(5) The collecting bank hands over the documents to the importer.

(6) The collecting bank notifies the remitting bank of crediting the money to their account.

(7) The remitting bank makes payment to the exporter.

8.2.2.2　Document Against Acceptance

承兑交单

This term of payment is applicable only to a time bill that is used in documentary collection. In which the collecting bank will release the shipping documents to the buyer without any payment but merely against the acceptance of the bill by the buyer to honor the draft at a certain future date agreed upon between the seller and the buyer. D/A is always after sight (see Figure 8.7).

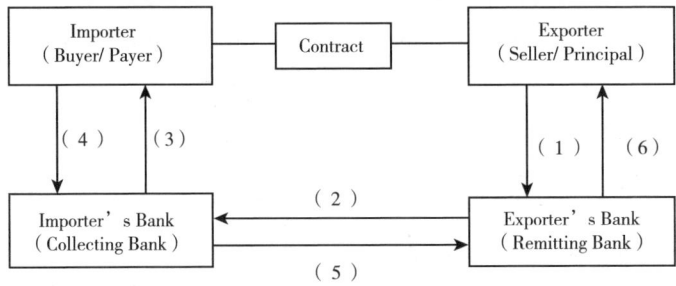

Figure 8.7　Procedure of D/A

Note:

(1) According to the contract, the exporter loads the goods and draws a time draft, then sends the draft together with shipping documents to his bank for collecting a documentary bill on his behalf.

(2) The remitting bank sends the documentary bill to a correspondent bank overseas-the collecting bank.

(3) The collecting bank presents the bill and documents to the importer for acceptance, after that, the collecting bank takes back the draft and gives the shipping documents to the importer.

(4) The importer makes payment when time falls due.

(5) The collecting bank notifies the remitting bank of crediting the money to their account.

(6) The remitting bank makes payment to the exporter.

8.2.2.3　Advantages and Disadvantages of Collection
托收的利与弊

There are some advantages for the exporter under the mode of collection. Since the remitting bank instructs the collecting bank not to hand over the shipping documents to the buyer until the draft is accepted or paid, thus, a lot of risks in "shipment earlier, settlement later" can be avoided. What is more, the buyer's lack of commercial integrity can also be prevented. For example, under D/P, without making payment, the buyer cannot obtain the documents of title to the goods and take delivery of the goods. The ownership of the goods still belongs to the seller. If the buyer dishonors the draft, the seller can sell the goods to others. When facing a market with fierce competition, the exporter can use collection to win customers and promote its sales. On the other hand, the importer may also get advantages from collection. Firstly, it can facilitate the importer to obtain financing. Under D/P after sight, capital tie-up of the importer can be avoided or reduced. Secondly, the expenses are low. Under collection, the importer does not need to pay the service fee as required for the opening of L/C.

However, problems still exist. Under D/P, there is the possibility of the buyer or his bank refusing to honor the draft and take up the shipping documents, especially at a time when the market is falling. In such a case, the seller may face the risk of non-payment or late payment by the buyer, although he is still the owner of the goods.

As for D/A, the most striking disadvantage is that after the buyer accepts the draft, the documents of title will be surrendered to him. So, if the buyer goes bankrupt or become insolvent before the payment of the draft, the seller will bear the losses of all the payment. Therefore, D/A is more risky than D/P for the exporter.

In international trade, payment through collection is accepted only when the financial standing of the importer is sound or where a previous course of business has inspired the exporter with confidence that the importer will be good for payment. As far as the seller's benefit is concerned, D/P at sight is better than D/P after sight, and D/P is better than D/A.

In order to prevent the various disadvantages of collection, a much better mode of payment in international trade has been developed, that is, letter of credit.

8.2.3 Letter of Credit (L/C)
信用证

The payment methods mentioned above are typically used when a buyer and seller have established a certain level of trust. However, trading partners have other options. If an importer's bank is confident in its customer's creditworthiness, it can issue a letter of credit in favor of the exporter. This letter guarantees payment to the exporter, provided the goods are shipped in compliance with the terms specified in the letter of credit—terms that are based on the contract between the buyer and seller. In this way, the bank provides financial backing for the transaction between the importer and exporter. As a result, the letter of credit has become a safer and more efficient method of securing payment in international trade.

8.2.3.1 Definition of Letter of Credit (L/C)
信用证的含义

A letter of credit, often abbreviated as L/C or simply called a credit, is a document issued by a bank on behalf of the buyer and addressed to the seller. In this document, the bank commits to paying or accepting drafts drawn on itself, **provided the seller strictly complies with the terms and conditions outlined in the letter of credit.** The bank will only honor the exporter's draft if the submitted documentation precisely matches the specified requirements. By issuing a letter of credit, **the bank essentially replaces the buyer's payment obligation with its own commitment.** While a letter of credit is not technically a guarantee, it functions similarly by assuring the seller of payment as long as all stipulated conditions are met.

只有在提交的单据和规定相一致时,银行才保证付款给卖方。
通过信用证,银行就取代了它的客户(即买方)的付款保证。

8.2.3.2 Circulation of Letter of Credit
信用证流程

After signing a contract with the exporter that stipulates payment

开证申请人	by letter of credit（L/C）, **the importer** requests their bank to issue an L/C **in favor of the exporter.** If the bank accepts the importer's application, **the issuing bank** prepares the letter of credit and notifies its overseas branch or correspondent bank to advise **the beneficiary**（the exporter）. The exporter then **reviews** the L/C to ensure it aligns with the terms of the sales contract. If discrepancies are found, the exporter may request amendments. However, if the L/C is irrevocable—as is typically the case—it cannot be modified unless all parties agree to the changes.
以出口商为受益人	
开证行	
受益人	
审核信用证	
提单	After confirming the letter of credit, the exporter delivers the goods to the shipper, who then issues **a bill of lading.** Other documents, such as invoices and insurance documents, are prepared by the exporter.
开立以开证行为付款人的汇票	The next step occurs when the exporter **draws a draft on the opening bank** and present it, with the letter of credit plus documents to his or her own bank. Usually, this bank will investigate the documents and, if they are in order, it will pay the draft. The letter of credit and documents are sent to the opening bank. It is the bank's responsibility to examine the documents in relation to the letter of credit issued. If discrepancies exist, they will have to be corrected, either by a new letter of credit, by new documents, or by amendments. **Discrepancies** include any one of the following: the letter of credit expired; the draft was not properly drawn; there was no indication on the bill of lading that goods were received on board; there was insufficient insurance; or an invoice description did not match that of the letter of credit. If no discrepancies are found after careful checking, the opening bank will reimburse the money to the exporter's bank（negotiating bank）in accordance with the terms of the credit. The opening bank then presents the documents to the buyer for payment or acceptance. Documents will be released to the buyer upon his payment of the amount due or acceptance of the draft. With the documents, the buyer can take delivery of the goods.
单证不符点	

The circulation of letter of credit can be illustrated as follows（see

Figure 8.8):

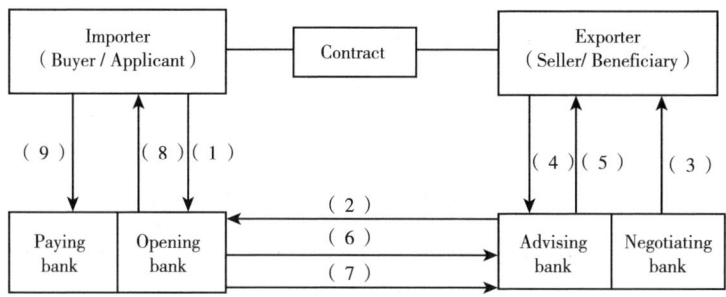

Figure 8.8 Circulation of Letter of Credit

Note:

(1) The buyer makes application for a letter of credit with his bank and signs the opening bank's agreement form. The opening bank approves the application and issues the actual letter of credit document.

(2) The opening bank forwards the letter of credit to the advising bank.

(3) The advising bank delivers the letter of credit to the beneficiary.

(4) Having examined the letter of credit, the beneficiary (seller) ships the goods to the buyer. After that, the beneficiary prepares documents, draws a draft, and presents them to his bank.

(5) The beneficiary's bank negotiates the documents and pays funds to the beneficiary in accordance with the letter of credit.

(6) The negotiating bank forwards the documents to the opening bank.

(7) The opening bank receives the documents and checks them. If the documents are in order and comply with the letter of credit, the opening bank credits the negotiating bank's account.

(8) The opening bank notifies the buyer to make payment for documents.

(9) After making payment, the buyer receives the documents and takes delivery of the goods.

8.2.3.3 Major Parties Involved in a Letter of Credit

信用证主要当事人

- The **applicant**, who is usually the importer who applies to the bank for the letter of credit. 开证申请人

- The **opening bank**, or **issuing bank**, which opens the letter of credit upon the request of the importer. It holds itself responsible for the payment of the goods. 开证行

- The **advising bank**, or notifying bank, which is authorized by the 通知行

issuing bank to transfer the letter of credit to the exporter's bank. It is in the exporter's country and usually the correspondent bank of the issuing hank. It is only responsible for the authenticity of the letter of credit.

受益人
- The **beneficiary**, who is usually the exporter and is entitled to use the letter of credit for the payment of the goods.

议付行
- The **negotiating bank**, which is willing to buy on discount the documentary draft drawn by the beneficiary. It can either or not be designated in the letter of credit. In the transfer of the bill of exchange, the negotiating bank can be taken as the bona fide bearer of the bill of exchange. The negotiating bank and the advising bank can be the same bank, as is to be decided by the letter of credit.

付款行
- The **paying bank** is designated by the letter of credit to pay the draft. In most cases, it is the issuing bank. It might also be some other bank, for example, if the currency used in the letter of credit is that of a third country, the paying bank may be a bank in that country. Once the paying bank has made the payment, it cannot reclaim it through recourse.

保兑行
- The **confirming bank** is requested by the opening bank to confirm the letter of credit. If a bank has confirmed the L/C, it holds itself responsible for the negotiation or payment of the L/C. Mostly, the confirming bank is advising bank, but it can also be some other bank in the country of the exporter.

8.2.3.4 Advantages and Disadvantages of Letter of Credit
信用证的利与弊

Under the letter of credit payment method, both the exporter and the importer benefit from protection. The importer is assured that the goods will comply with the agreed terms, while the exporter is guaranteed payment for the goods. Additionally, the importer may secure more favorable trade terms by utilizing the letter of credit system, although this advantage may be partially offset by the bank's fees.

When an importer needs to open a letter of credit for an overseas purchase, they can apply to their bank for an L/C of any amount. Typically, the bank will not require the importer to pay the full amount of the L/C upfront but will only request a deposit. This arrangement prevents the importer's capital from being tied up. In essence, the bank finances or guarantees the remaining balance of the purchase price.

For the exporter, the letter of credit provides confidence that payment will be made by the importer's bank, even if the exporter is unfamiliar with the creditworthiness of the foreign bank. The confirming bank honors drafts drawn under the letter of credit and has no recourse to seek reimbursement from the exporter, even if the issuing bank fails to reimburse the confirming bank.

From the above discussion, it is clear that a banker's letter of credit is a highly desirable method for ensuring payment in international trade.

However, a letter of credit does not entirely eliminate all risks that businesses may face. Since the issuing bank makes payment based on the submission of relevant documents rather than the actual goods, importers may still be vulnerable to fraudulent activities. For example, the beneficiary (exporter) might receive payment by presenting falsified documents that do not match the physical goods or even documents for non-existent goods. Beyond fraud, errors by personnel, improper procedures, ambiguous language, or negligence can also lead to losses for the parties involved.

8.2.3.5　Illustration of Letter of Credit

信用证的内容

The chief contents of the L/C can be seen as a combination of the chief contents of the sales contract, the required documents and the bank assurance. It might be further broken into the following provisions

（Details for L/C please refer to Figure 8.1）：

信用证当事人
- The **parties involved**, including the applicant, the issuing bank, the negotiating bank, and the paying bank.

信用证相关信息
- **Remarks about the L/C**: such as the No. of the L/C, its type, the issuing date, the amount of the L/C, the expiry date and place, etc.

汇票条款
- The **clauses of the bill of exchange**, such as the amount of the bill, the drawer and drawee, the paying date, etc.

运输相关条款
- The **clauses about shipping**, such as the port of shipment, the port of destination, partial shipment and transshipment, and the latest date of shipment.

有关商品的条款
- The **clauses about the description of the goods**, such as the name of goods, specifications, quantity, packing, unit price, total amount, and so on.

所需单据条款
- The **clauses about the documents**, include what kinds of documents are required, the required number of copies of the documents, the content of the specific document, etc.

交单期限 所有单据都应在装船日期后21内提交，并同时要在信用证有效期内。
- The **period for presentation**. The documents should be presented within 21days after the date of shipment indicated on transport document but within the credit validity. Otherwise, the banks will not accept the presentation.

开证行保证付款条款
- **Guarantee clauses of the opening bank**, which testifies that the opening bank will hold itself responsible for the payment to the beneficiary or the holder of the draft.

特别条款
- **Particular clause**, such as the special provisions about the deal in accordance with the particular business or political situations of the importing country.

Letters of credit（L/C）come in different forms. Although the International Chamber of Commerce has recommended several standard forms, issuing banks rarely use them. Most issuing banks use their own forms, which are based on or adapted from the standard forms. The legal framework governing the use of letters of credit is the Uniform Customs and Practice for Commercial Documentary Credits (UCP).

8.2.3.6 Types of Letter of Credits

信用证类型

In international trade, various types of letters of credit are used to fulfill different trade and payment needs. Based on different criteria, letters of credit can be broadly categorized into the following types.

- **Irrevocable and Revocable Letter of Credit** 不可撤销与可撤销信用证

An irrevocable letter of credit cannot be modified, amended, or withdrawn by either the issuing bank or the buyer before the expiry date of the credit validity without the consent of the beneficiary. As long as the shipping documents submitted by the exporter comply with the terms of the L/C, the issuing bank is obligated to make the payment. Therefore, it is widely used in international trade.

As the name suggests, a revocable letter of credit can be canceled or amended at any time during the credit validity period without prior notice to the beneficiary. This type of L/C is generally unacceptable to exporters and rarely used in international trade because it offers no guarantee to them.

- **Confirmed and Unconfirmed Letters of Credit** 保兑与不保兑的信用证

A confirmed letter of credit is guaranteed by another bank (usually the advising bank) on behalf of the issuing bank. The exporter then holds a confirmed irrevocable L/C, which provides double payment guarantees from both the confirming bank and the issuing bank. The confirming bank is primarily responsible to the beneficiary.

An unconfirmed letter of credit is advised by the advising bank, but the bank does not assume responsibility for the documents. It merely notifies the beneficiary that the credit has been opened.

- **Transferable Letters of Credits** 可转让的信用证

In the case of a transferable letter of credit, the beneficiary authorizes the advising bank or negotiating bank to transfer the right to issue a draft in full to another party (the second beneficiary). The second beneficiary is the one who draws the bill of exchange, presents the shipping documents, and receives payment. However, the first beneficiary remains responsible for fulfilling the seller's obligations as stipulated in the sales contract. A transferable letter of credit can only be transferred once. The second beneficiary cannot transfer it further.

即期与远期信用证

· Sight and Usance Letters of Credit

A sight letter of credit is also referred to as "L/C available by draft at sight" or "L/C by sight draft." Under a sight letter of credit, the negotiating bank makes payment immediately upon the seller's presentation of the sight draft and shipping documents as specified in the L/C. Similarly, when the negotiating bank submits the sight draft and documents to the issuing bank, the latter also reimburses the payment immediately.

When the seller presents a time draft along with the shipping documents specified in the L/C to the negotiating bank, the bank does not make payment immediately. The negotiating bank forwards the draft and documents to the issuing bank. The issuing bank also does not make payment immediately. It simply accepts the draft and returns it to the seller. Payment is made when the time draft matures. This type of letter of credit is known as a usance letter of credit.

可循环的信用证

· Revolving Letter of Credit

If a contract is concluded for the long term and allows partial shipments, or if the parties wish the contract to proceed without interruption, the buyer often requests the establishment of a revolving letter of credit. It notifies the seller that once a shipment has been made, documents presented, and payment made, the credit automatically becomes available again in its original form, allowing another shipment to be made, and so on. The L/C can be reused under the same terms without the need for issuing another L/C until the stipulated number of uses or the stipulated total amount has been reached. It also simplifies procedures and reduces costs.

• **Back-to-Back Letter of Credit** 背对背信用证

In a back-to-back letter of credit, two letters of credit are involved. One is issued in favor of the exporter, who is not the actual supplier of the goods; the other is issued by the exporter in favor of the actual supplier. It is typically used when the supplier wishes to keep their identity confidential. The back-to-back credit will show a lower amount for the value of the goods, with the difference representing the exporter's profit. The tenor is often shortened by a few days to allow for the substitution of invoices.

• **Red Clause Credit** 红条款信用证

A red clause credit is similar to a normal letter of credit, except that it contains a clause (originally typed or printed in red) authorizing the negotiating bank to make an advance to the exporter. Through this clause, the beneficiary may take advantage of the importer's credit standing. Nowadays, red clause credits are mainly used in situations where the buying company (importer) has an agent in the exporting country whose role is to purchase merchandise for export. To finance these purchases, the importer may arrange to open a red clause letter of credit.

8.3 Other Methods of Payment
其他支付方式

L/C offers a safe way for settling payment for goods in international trade. However, in certain situations, L/C cannot be used, such as when the deal covers a long period of time or when the business involves non-trade transactions. In such cases, a letter of guarantee and a standby L/C can be used.

With the development of international trade, other methods have been developed for payment settlement, among which factoring is increasingly being used.

Additionally, various payment methods can be combined for payment settlement for various reasons and in various situations, including L/C with collection, L/C with remittance, documentary collection with a down payment, and documentary collection with a standby L/C.

8.3.1　Letter of Guarantee
保函

A letter of guarantee (L/G) is a document issued by a bank, where the bank promises the beneficiary to assume responsibility for debts or losses caused by a third party's fault or breach of contract. It is used in various situations, with two common types being tender guarantees and performance guarantees.

投标保函　　**A tender guarantee** is issued by a bank at the bidder's request. It assures the beneficiary (the tender inviter) that the bank will compensate for losses if the bidder withdraws or amends their bid before the bidding begins, or refuses to sign or pay the margin after winning the bid.

履约保函　　**A performance guarantee** ensures that the issuing bank will pay a specified amount or take remedial measures if the principal fails to fulfill their obligations. In international trade, it can be provided by either the importer or exporter. If issued by the importer's bank, it guarantees payment to the seller if the importer defaults. If issued by the exporter's bank, it compensates the buyer if the exporter fails to deliver goods on time.

保函与信用证的不同之处　　An L/G differs from a letter of credit (L/C). Under an L/C, the issuing bank guarantees payment for goods, while under an L/G, the bank only assumes responsibility if the principal fails to meet their obligations. Additionally, under an L/C, the seller can receive payment through negotiation, but this is not possible under an L/G. The issuing bank of an L/C handles only documents and is not involved in the sales contract. In contrast, under an L/G, the bank must investigate claims of non-performance, potentially involving it in disputes.

In some countries, such as the USA and Japan, banks are prohibited from engaging in commercial disputes. Therefore, they issue standby letters of credit instead of L/Gs to serve similar purposes.

8.3.2 Standby L/C
备用信用证

A standby letter of credit (standby L/C), also known as a commercial paper L/C, guarantee L/C, or performance L/C, is a type of **clean L/C**. It serves as a promise by the issuing bank to the beneficiary that it will assume liabilities if the applicant fails to fulfill contractual obligations. If the applicant performs as required, the standby L/C remains unused. However, if the applicant defaults, the beneficiary must submit a written statement to the bank requesting compensation.

光票信用证

Standby L/Cs are similar to letters of guarantee (L/G) in that both rely on bank credit and promise compensation if the principal fails to meet obligations. However, under an L/G, the bank only acts if the applicant defaults and may become involved in disputes between the parties. In contrast, under a standby L/C, the bank pays upon receiving the beneficiary's statement, remaining independent of the underlying contract.

Both standby L/Cs and L/Gs enable progress payment or deferred payment. Progress payment is used for installment-based sales, where the buyer pays an initial deposit and the balance in installments as goods are delivered. Deferred payment involves an initial earnest payment, with the balance paid in installments over a longer period, effectively functioning as a credit sale using foreign funds. Deferred payment includes interest, which must be specified in the contract. These methods can also be combined, where installment payments under progress payment are delayed until after each delivery.

8.3.3 Combined Use of Different Method of Payment 不同支付方式的结合使用

In international trade, usually only one method is used for a single transaction. However, sometimes more than one method is used for payment. The common combined methods include L/C with collection, L/C with remittance, documentary collection with down payment, and documentary collection with standby L/C.

Combination of L/C and Collection 信用证和托收的结合

Payment made in this way will be partially by L/C and partially by collection. This requires the buyer to open an L/C for a certain percentage of the total payment for the goods, with the balance collected. In the sales contract, it should also be clearly stated that the amount payable under the L/C will be available against a clean draft, while the balance will be available against a documentary draft through collection. The shipping documents will not be released to the buyer unless full payment has been made.

Combination of L/C and Remittance 信用证和汇付的结合

Payment made in this way is partially through L/C and partially through remittance. If the remittance is made before the shipment of the goods, it is treated as an advance payment. If the remittance is made after the shipment of the goods, it is typically used for the balance of the payment for the consignment, which may vary in amount.

Combination of Documentary Collection and Down Payment 提预付货款与跟单托收的结合

To ensure that the exporter does not sustain significant losses due to collection, the seller can request the buyer to make a down payment. When the shipment is made, the down payment will be deducted from the amount to be collected. In this way, if the draft is dishonored, the exporter can ship the goods back, and the resulting loss can be compensated by the down payment. However, the exporter must ensure that the goods can be shipped back from the importing country.

Combination of Documentary Collection and Standby L/C
跟单托收与备用信用证的结合

To mitigate risks in documentary collection, the exporter can request the buyer to open a standby L/C. If the payment is dishonored, the seller can then request payment from the issuing bank of the standby L/C.

To use this method, the validity period of the standby L/C must be sufficiently long so that, if the payment is dishonored, the seller has enough time to request payment from the issuing bank. When completing the application form for export collection, the exporter should instruct the remitting bank to notify the collecting bank to provide immediate electronic notice if the draft is dishonored.

8.4 Payment Terms in Contract
合同中的支付条款

Payment can be made in different ways; therefore, it is imperative to clearly stipulate the specific mode of payment and the detailed requirements. The following are some examples of payment terms in a contract.

8.4.1 Remittance
汇付

The Buyers shall pay 100% of the sales proceeds in advance by M/T to reach the Sellers not later than July 15.

All the payment shall be made in the US currency by the Buyer to the Seller, by telegraphic transfer to the Seller's designated account(s) with the bank(s) in(country).

8.4.2 Collection
托收

Document Against Payment at Sight 即期付款交单

- Upon first presentation the Buyers shall pay against documentary draft drawn by the Sellers at sight. The shipping documents are to be delivered against payment only.
- Payment shall be made by net cash against sight draft with bill of lading attached showing the shipment of the goods.
- Payment shall be made by net cash against sight draft with bill of lading attached showing the shipment of the goods. Such payment shall be made through the(bank)of(place). The bill of lading shall not be delivered to the Buyer until such draft is paid.

Document Against Payment After Sight 远期付款交单

- The Buyers shall duly accept the documentary draft drawn by the Sellers at...days sight upon first presentation and make payment on its maturity. The shipping documents are to be delivered against payment only.
- The Buyers shall pay against documentary draft drawn by the Sellers at...days after date of B/L. The shipping documents are to be delivered against payment only.
- The Buyers shall pay against documentary draft drawn by the Sellers at...days after date of draft. The shipping documents are to be delivered against payment only.

Document Against Acceptance 承兑交单

The Buyers shall duly accept the documentary draft drawn by the Sellers at...days sight upon first presentation and make payment on its maturity. The shipping documents are to be delivered against acceptance.

8.4.3 Letter of Credit
信用证

Sight Letter of Credit 即期信用证

- The Buyers shall open through a bank acceptable to the Sellers an Irrevocable Sight Letter of Credit to reach the Sellers...days before the month of shipment, valid for negotiation in China until the 15th day after the month of shipment.
- By Irrevocable Letter of Credit, available by Sellers' documentary draft at sight, to be valid for negotiation in China. until 15 days after the date of shipment. The L/C must reach the Sellers 30 days before the contracted month of shipment.

Time Letter of Credit 远期信用证

- The Buyers shall open through a bank acceptable to them. Sellers an Irrevocable Letter of Credit at...days Sight to reach the Sellers...days before the month of shipment, valid for negotiation in China until the 30th day after the month of shipment.
- By Irrevocable L/G available by Seller's documentary draft at...days sight, to be valid for negotiation in China until 15 days after date of shipment. The L/C must reach the Sellers 30 days before the contracted month of shipment.

8.4.4 Combination of Different Modes
不同支付方式的结合

The Buyers shall open through a bank acceptable to the Sellers an Irrevocable Sight Letter of Credit to reach the Seller... days before the month of shipment, stipulating that 50% of the invoice value available against. Clean draft at sight while the remaining 50% on Documents against Payment at sight (or D/P at...days after sight). The full set of the shipping documents of 100% invoice value shall accompany the collection item and shall only be released after full payment of the invoice value. If the Buyers fail to pay full invoice value，the shipping, documents shall be held by the issuing bank at the Sellers' disposal.

Table 8.2　Sample of Letter of Credit

MT 700		ISSUE OF A DOCUMENTARY CREDIT
SENDER		HSBC BANK PLC，DUBAI, U.A.E.
RECEIVER		HANGZHOU CITY COMMERCIAL BANK, HANGZHOU, CHINA
SEQUENCE OF TOTAL	27：	1 / 1
FORM OF DOC. CREDIT	40A：	IRREVOCABLE
DOC. CREDIT NUMBER	20：	FFF07699
DATE OF ISSUE	31C：	250225
APPLICABLE RULES	40E：	UCP LATEST VERSION
DATE AND PLACE OF EXPIRY.	31D：	DATE 080330PLACE IN U.A.E.
APPLICANT	50：	DIM TRADING CO., LTD. 16 TOM STREET, DUBAI, U.A.E.
BENEFICIARY	59：	ZHEJIANG JINYUN IMPORT & EXPORT CO., LTD. 118 XUEYUAN STREET, HANGZHOU, P.R. CHINA
AMOUNT	32B：	CURRENCY USD AMOUNT 54450.00
AVAILABLE WITH/BY	41D：	ANY BANK IN CHINA, BY NEGOTIATION
DRAFTS AT ...	42C：	60 DAYS AFTER SIGHT
DRAWEE	42A：	HSBC BANK PLC，NEW YORK
PARTIAL SHIPMENT	43P：	PROHIBITED
TRANSSHIPMENT	43T：	ALLOWED
PORT OF LOADING/ AIRPORT OF DEPARTURE	44E：	CHINESE MAIN PORT
PORT OF DISCHARGE	44F：	DUBAI, U.A.E.
LATEST DATE OF SHIPMENT	44C：	250325

continued

MT 700		ISSUE OF A DOCUMENTARY CREDIT
DESCRIPTION OF GOODS AND/OR SERVICES.	45A:	4500 PIECES OF LADIES JACKET, SHELL: WOVEN TWILL 100% COTTON, LINING: WOVEN 100% POLYESTER, ORDER NO. DIM768, AS PER S/C NO. ZJJY0739 STYLE NO.　QUANTITY　UNIT PRICE　　AMOUNT 　L357　　　2250PCS　　USD12.10/PC　USD27225.00 　L358　　　2250PCS　　USD12.10/PC　USD27225.00 AT CIF DUBAI, U.A.E.
DOCUMENTS REQUIRED	46A:	
		+ COMMERCIAL INVOICE SIGNED IN TRIPLICATE.
		+ PACKING LIST IN TRIPLICATE.
		+ CERTIFICATE OF CHINESE ORIGIN CERTIFIED BY CHAMBER OF COMMERCE OR CCPIT.
		+ INSURANCE POLICY/CERTIFICATE IN DUPLICATE ENDORSED IN BLANK FOR 110% INVOICE VALUE, COVERING ALL RISKS OF C.I.C. OF PICC（1/1/1981）INCL. WAREHOUSE TO WAREHOUSE AND I.O.P AND SHOWING THE CLAIMING CURRENCY IS THE SAME AS THE CURRENCY OF CREDIT.
		+ FULL SET（3/3）OF CLEAN 'ON BOARD' OCEAN BILLS OF LADING MADE OUT TO ORDER MARKED FREIGHT PREPAID AND NOTIFY APPLICANT.
		+ SHIPPING ADVICE SHOWING THE NAME OF THE CARRYING VESSEL, DATE OF SHIPMENT, MARKS, QUANTITY, NET WEIGHT AND GROSS WEIGHT OF THE SHIPMENT TO APPLICANT WITHIN 3 DAYS AFTER THE DATE OF BILL OF LADING.
ADDITIONAL CONDITION	47A:	
		+ DOCUMENTS DATED PRIOR TO THE DATE OF THIS CREDIT ARE NOT ACCEPTABLE.
		+ THE NUMBER AND THE DATE OF THIS CREDIT AND THE NAME OF ISSUING BANK MUST BE QUOTED ON ALL DOCUMENTS.
		+ TRANSSHIPMENT ALLOWED.
		+ SHORT FORM/CHARTER PARTY/THIRD PARTY BILL OF LADING ARE NOT ACCEPTABLE.

continued

MT 700		ISSUE OF A DOCUMENTARY CREDIT
		+ SHIPMENT MUST BE EFFECTED BY 1 × 40' FULL CONTAINER LOAD.
		+ THE GOODS SHIPPED ARE NEITHER ISRAELI ORIGIN NOR DO THEY CONTAIN ISRAELI MATERIALS NOR ARE THEY EXPORTED FROM ISRAEL, BENEFICIARY'S CERTIFICATE TO THIS EFFECT IS REQUIRED.
		+ ALL PRESENTATIONS CONTAINING DISCREPANCIES WILL ATTRACT A DISCREPANCY FEE OF USD60.00 PLUS TELEX COSTS OR OTHER CURRENCY EQUIVALENT. THIS CHARGE WILL BE DEDUCTED FROM THE BILL AMOUNT WHETHER OR NOT WE ELECT TO CONSULT THE APPLICANT FOR A WAIVER
CHARGES	71B:	ALL CHARGES OUTSIDE DUBAI ARE FOR ACCOUNT OF BENEFICIARY INCCOUNT.
PERIOD FOR PRESENTATION	48:	WITHIN 5 DAYS AFTER THE DATE OF SHIPMENT, BUT WITHIN THE VALIDITY OF THIS CREDIT.
CONFIRMATION INSTRUCTION	49:	WITHOUT
REIMBURSING BANK	53A:	HSBC BANK PLC, NEW YORK
INFORMATION TO PRESENTING BANK	78:	ALL DOCUMENTS ARE TO BE REMITTED IN ONE LOT BY COURIER TO HSBC BANK PLC, TRADE SERVICES,DUBAI BRANCH, P O BOX 66, HSBC BANK BUILDING 312/45 Al SUQARE ROAD, DUBAI, UAE.

Exercises 练习

I. True (T) or False (F)

1. If the remittance is made by a banker's demand draft, this payment is based on bank credit. (　　)

2. In international trade clean collection is more frequently used than documentary collection. (　　)

3. For a confirmed credit, the confirming bank holds the same liability as the issuing bank. (　　)

4. Under collection though the seller collects payment through banks, it is not guaranteed that he will receive the money as collection is still based on commercial credit. ( )

5. A letter of credit which does not indicate whether it is revocable or not is regarded as irrevocable. ( )

6. Dishonor only refers to the rejection to the presentation for payment, but not rejection to the presentation for acceptance. ( )

7. A letter of credit not mentioning it is non-transferable will be seen as transferable. ( )

8. Open account and payment in advance indicate the minimum and maximum risk for the importer. ( )

9. If the instructions are D/P, the importer's bank will release the documents to the importer only against payment. ( )

10. Since under L/C the seller gets payment from a party independent of the buyer, it is the safest mode for him. ( )

II. Multiple Choice Questions

1. The draft used in collection is ( ).

A. a banker's draft, based on bank credit

B. a commercial draft, based on bank credit

C. a banker's draft, based on commercial credit

D. a commercial draft, based on commercial credit

2. Under collection once the importer refuses to pay, the ( ) will be responsible for the cargo release, customs clearance, warehousing, and reselling in the importing country.

A. drawee   B. collecting bank

C. principal   D. presenting bank

3. The bill of exchange used in D/A must be a ( ).

A. sight bill   B. bank bill

C. bank accepted bill   D. usance bill

4. If there is no specific provision, the draft under a letter of credit

should draw on the (　　).

    A. advising bank　　　　　　B. issuing bank

    C. negotiating bank　　　　　D. applicant

5. If the exporter finds out mistakes on a received L/C, he should contact the (　) at the first place.

    A. advising bank　　　　　　B. negotiating bank

    C. importer　　　　　　　　D. issuing bank

6. A standby credit (　　).

    A. is a special clean credit.

    B. is a documentary credit.

    C. can be a documentary credit as well as a clean credit.

    D. is not a real letter of credit, but a letter of guarantee.

7. If a bank other than the issuing bank guarantees the payment under an L/C, this L/C is (　　).

    A. an irrevocable credit　　　B. a confirmed credit.

    C. non-transferable credits　　D. a negotiable credit

8. (　　) is normally used in processing trade.

    A. revolving　　　　　　　　B. back-to-back

    C. reciprocal credit　　　　　D. red clause

9. Which of the following statements is NOT true about remittance? (　　)

    A. It is cheaper to use than the other terms of payment.

    B. It provides the highest security to the buyer but not the seller.

    C. It may impose high risk either to the buyer or to the credit.

    D. It is based on commercial credit, not bank credit.

10. (　　) is a L/C based financing which will provide the exporter funds before the goods are produced.

    A. packing loan　　　　　　B. factoring

    C. forfeiting　　　　　　　　D. negotiation

III. Case Study

1. On May 1, POP Company signed a contract to export goods to

the US. On May 30, City Bank sent an irrevocable L/C with an amount of USD30,000, The L/C stipulated shipment during June, and Bank of Tokyo to be the reimbursing bank. On June 2, Bank of China advised POP Company of the L/C. But ten days later, POP Company learn that the importer was near bankruptcy. How should POP Company deal with the situation?

2. A company imported steel from abroad under a contract stipulating two separate shipments, each covered by a sight letter of credit (L/C) issued by the Bank of China. After the first shipment, the exporter presented compliant documents to the negotiating bank within the validity period. The negotiating bank **verified** the documents as compliant, paid the exporter, and was subsequently reimbursed by the Bank of China. Upon receiving the first batch of goods, the importer discovered that the quality did not conform to the contract. The importer then demanded that the issuing bank refuse payment under the second L/C, but the issuing bank rejected this request.

证实

Questions: (1) Is the issuing bank justified in refusing this request? Why or why not? (2) How should the importer address the quality issues with the first batch of goods? Can the importer demand that the issuing bank reclaim the reimbursed funds?

3. A **UAV (unmanned aerial vehicle)** manufacturer in China entered into a deal in November 2024 with an American trading company for exporting 30 UAVs for agricultural use under Incoterm CIF, and payment by L/C at sight. The American company opened an L/C through its bank in early March 2025, which was verified to be consistent with the contract. The insured amount was 110% of the invoice amount. When the exporter was busy with production, the American company advised the exporter an amendment to the L/C through the banks, which changed the insured amount to 130% of the invoice amount. The exporter insured and delivered the goods in accordance with the original

无人机

L/C, and submitted the full set of shipping documents to the negotiating bank within the validity of the L/C after shipment. After the negotiation, the negotiating bank sent the full set of documents to the issuing bank, which refused to pay on the ground that the insurance policy was inconsistent with the amendment to the L/C. Is the issuing bank justified in refusing to honor the L/C? Why?

Chapter 9

The General Terms and Conditions in the Contract

第九章　合同中的一般条款

◆ Learning Objectives

• Understand the conditions for breach of contract and settlement of claims;

• Describe ways of stipulating claim clauses in a sales contract;

• Be aware of the consequences of force majeure events;

• Explain ways to stipulate force majeure clauses in a sales contract;

• Realize the importance of arbitration in the settlement of disputes and claims;

• Be aware of the issues to be considered in the negotiation of arbitration;

• Describe the ways of stipulating an arbitration clause in a sales contract.

In international trade, it is ideal that the seller delivers the goods conforming to the contract in respect of quality, specification, quantity, and packing, and hands over the documents concerning the goods at the right time and place stipulated in the contract. On the other hand, the buyer makes payment for the goods and takes delivery of them in the same manner specified in the contract. However, there always exists a gap between ideal and reality. Complaints or claims, sometimes, still arise in spite of well planned and careful work in the performance of a contract. In practice, it is not uncommon that the seller or the buyer neglects or fails to perform any of his obligations, thus giving rise to **breach of contract** and various trade disputes, which, subsequently, leads to claim, arbitration, or even litigation.

In order to avoid disputes or properly handle with their consequences, some **preventive** clauses such as **commodity inspection** clause, **matters of claim, force majeure,** and **arbitration** are usually stipulated in the contract.

9.1 Commodity Inspection
商品检验

9.1.1 A Brief Introduction to Commodity Inspection
商品检验简介

Commodity inspection refers to the examination of the quality, quantity, packaging, etc. of the goods delivered by the seller in the international sale of goods to determine if they conform to the applicable or specified requirements in the contract. Sometimes, technical conditions of shipment, hygiene, epidemics, as well as damages and shortages of the goods in transit shall also be inspected or identified to clarify the causes of accidents and the attribution of responsibilities. Commodity inspection includes **mandatory inspection or quarantine** of certain import and export goods in accordance with the laws or administrative regulations of a country.

Commodity inspection is an indispensable and important part

in the process of transferring goods between buyers and sellers. In international trade, the buyer and the seller are in different countries, and except for the actual delivery of goods under the **E-and D-terms**, the delivery of goods under the **F-and C-terms** is symbolic delivery, which means the seller does not deliver the goods to the buyer in person. Besides, the goods need to be transported over long distances and be loaded and unloaded for many times. Therefore, disputes can be easily aroused if there are quality defects and shortages of the goods arrived. To protect the interests of both parties and avoid disputes, a qualified and authoritative third party independent of the buyer and the seller, namely, a professional inspection body, is required to carry out inspection of the goods delivered by the seller, or to inspect or appraise the conditions of loading as well as damage and shortage of the goods. And a corresponding **inspection certificate** shall be issued by the inspection body to be used as one of the documents for buyers and sellers to hand over goods, make payments, make claims and settlements, **clear customs, impose tariffs,** as well as reduce and be exempt from preferential tariffs.

  E组和D组贸易术语
  F组和C组贸易术语

  检验证书

  清关　征收关税

  In addition, commodity inspection is of particular significance for both import and export of a country, which can not only enhance the competitiveness of the exported goods in the international market by ensuring the quality of them but also protect the interests of people in the imported country by ensuring the quality of the imported goods.

9.1.2 Contents of Commodity Inspection
商品检验内容

9.1.2.1 Quality inspection
质量检验

  Quality of commodity is one of the most important factors in the international sale of goods and the major content for commodity inspection, Quality inspection means to test and identify the quality, specification and grade of import and export commodities by means of **sensory inspection, physical inspection, instrumental analysis, microbiological inspection**, etc. to determine whether they conform to the provisions of the sales contract and relevant standards.

9.1.2.2 Quantity and weight inspection

数量和重量检验

Quantity inspection is to examine the number of the whole batch of goods and the number, length, area and volume of the commodities inside the package to get the exact quantity of the goods. Weight inspection is to carry out inspection and get accurate weight of the import and export commodities by using different weighing methods.

9.1.2.3 Packing inspection

包装检验

Packaging requirements for food, dangerous goods and valuable commodities are particularly strict, which consider not only the general protection of commodities and the safety of the human body and transportation but also the protection of the ecological balance of the environment. There must be corresponding standards to assess the performance of packing materials and packing containers, such as the joints, holes in the corner, moisture content, and adhesive strength of the corrugated box.

9.1.2.4 Sanitary inspection

卫生检验

Sanitary inspection is to check whether the relevant import and export commodities conform to the sanitary conditions for human beings to use, so as to protect people's health and maintain the reputation of the exporters. The **sanitary conditions** of food and animal products directly affect the health and safety of human beings, so the inspection on sanitary conditions is mandatory.

9.1.2.5　Safety inspection
　　安全检验

Safety inspection is the inspection carried out on items of safety performance relating to the import and export commodities, such as quality, performance, and efficiency in accordance with relevant regulations and requirements of sales contract, standards, and national laws and decrees, to ensure the use of commodities and the safety of personal property as well as to avoid accidents damaging the ecological balance.

9.1.3　Inspection Clauses
　　检验条款的主要内容

The inspection clauses cover the follows: inspection time and place; inspection authority; inspection certificate; inspection methods, contents and standards; re-inspection. The following is an example:

"It is mutually agreed that the Certificate of Quality and Weight (Quantity) issued by the Manufacturer (or ×××Surveyor) at the port/place of shipment shall be part of the documents to be presented for negotiation under the relevant L/C. The Buyers shall have the right to reinspect the quality and weight (quantity) of the cargo. The re-inspection fee shall be borne by the Buyers. Should the quality and/or weight (quantity) be found not in conformity with that in the contract, the Buyers are entitled to lodge with the Sellers a claim which should be supported by survey reports, issued by a recognized surveyor and approved by the Sellers. The claim, if any, shall be lodged within ××× days after arrival of the goods at the port/place of destination."

9.1.3.1　Inspection Time and Place
　　检验的时间和地点

The inspection time and the inspection place refer to when and where the inspection is implemented on the goods. The so-called **inspection right** means that the buyer or the seller has the right to 　检验权

exercise inspection on the traded goods, with the inspection result as the evidence for the delivery and the acceptance of the goods. The confirmation of the inspection time and place means confirming which party exerts the inspection right, that is to say, confirming which party's inspection certificate is taken as the final inspection result.

There are the following four ways to regulate the inspection time and place.

(1) Inspection in Export Country

在出口国检验

There are two ways including **the inspection at the manufacturing place (factory) and the inspection at the loading port.**

在产地（工厂）检验和在装运港检验

"离岸品质，离岸重量"

For the inspection at the loading port, it is also called **"Shipping Quality, Shipping Weight"**, which means the inspection authority specified in the sales contracts makes the inspection and appraisal on the cargo's quality, weight (quantity) and the like, and the inspection certificate issued by the authority is taken as the final evidence. The seller is not responsible for the changes of the cargo after the delivery. Therefore, the clause is a great disadvantage to the buyer as it denies the re-inspection right of the buyer.

(2) Inspection in Import Country

在进口国检验

在目的港/地检验和在买方营业处所或最终用户所在地检验

"到岸品质，到岸重量"

It is also divided into **the inspection at the destination port and the inspection at the buyer's business location or the final user's location.**

The inspection at the destination port or discharging port is also called **"Landed quality, landed weight"**, which means that the cargo is inspected by the inspection authority specified in the contract within the specified time on the spot after the cargo arrives in the destination port or place, and the inspection certificate issued by the organization is taken as the final evidence of the cargo delivered by the seller. In the way, the buyer has the right to claim for the compensation with the inspection result made at the destination port or place in case that the quality, weight (quantity) are not in conformity with the involved requirement.

The clause is disadvantageous to the seller. Under the trade term of CIF (CIP, CFR, CRT), the seller is responsible for carrying the goods to the destination, but according to "International Rules for the Interpretation of Trade Terms of 2020", the obligation of the seller has been completed after the goods are loaded on the ship (delivered to the carrier) in the export country, the risk has been transferred to the buyer when the goods are on board. The regulation of the inspection time and place means that the conditions of the goods are subject to the final inspection result in the destination, actually transferring the risks of the cargo losses occurred during the transportation to the seller. During transportation, the goods are out of the supervision of the seller, but under the control of the carrier, so it is quite unfair to the seller with the inspection clause against the regulation of the seller's obligation in the above-mentioned trade terms.

(3) Inspection in Export Country and Re-inspection in Import Country
出口国检验进口国复验

The inspection certificate issued by the exporting country's inspection authority is taken as one of the bank negotiating documents for payment, but not the final inspection proof. After the arrival of the cargo, the inspection certificate issued by the importing country's inspection authority is taken as the final inspection result to confirm if the quantity and the quality of the goods are right and the proof for the buyer's claims.

It is fair and reasonable for the buyer and the seller to regulate the inspection time and inspection place in this way, so it is the way used mostly in international trade, complying with the international usual practice.

(4) Weight Inspection in Export Country and Quality Inspection in Import Country

出口国检验重量，进口国检验品质

It is also called "Shipping Weight, Landed Quality", which means that for the inspection of goods in large quantities, in order to conciliate the conflict between the buyer and the seller on the inspection, the inspection on the weight and the quality are respectively carried out. That is to say, the inspection certificate issued by the inspection authority at the loading port or place is taken as the final proof of the weight of the delivered goods, and the quality inspection certificate issued by the inspection authority at the destination port is taken as the final proof of the commodity quality.

9.1.3.2　Inspection Authority

检验机构

官方检验机构、半官方检验机构和非官方检验机构

The inspection organizations are divided into the following three types, which are **governmental inspection authority, government related inspection authority, non-governmental inspection authority.**

《中华人民共和国进出口商品检验法》（简称《商检法》）

According to the regulation of **"Law of the People's Republic of China on Import and Export Commodity Inspection"** (**"Law of Inspection"** for short) , the General Administration of Customs is in charge of the inspection of the imported and exported commodities throughout the whole country, and the local customs is in charge of the local inspection of the imported and exported commodities.

9.1.3.3　Inspection Certificate

检验证书

An inspection certificate is a kind of testifying document in written form issued and signed by the inspection authority after the inspection and appraisal of the imported and exported commodities.

Functions:

(1) To certify if the quality, quantity, packing and the clean situation of the goods delivered by the seller are complying with the requirements stipulated in the contract;

(2) For customs to release the goods;

(3) For the sellers to settle the payment;

(4) As the evidence of making claims and the settlements.

9.1.3.4　Inspection Bases and Inspection Methods

检验依据和检验方法

(1) Inspection Basis

检验依据

The commodities are usually inspected in accordance with **the confirmed samples, contract by sample,** letters of credit, and standards, etc.　　　　　　　　　　　　　成交样品、标样合同

The inspection standard is the measures and rules adopted for the inspected commodity and inspection process, which are the criteria to appraise and identify if the inspected commodity is complying with the related regulations and requirements.

According to "Law of Inspection", all the imported and exported commodities listed in the catalogue must be inspected according to the governmental technical regulations; for the commodities which are not required by the governmental technical regulations, the inspection can be made in reference to the related standards of foreign countries, stipulated by national commodity inspection body.

(2) Inspection Methods

检验方法

The inspection results are different for the same commodity inspected in different ways. Therefore, it is better to specify in which way to inspect the goods in contract in order to avoid any dispute.

In the business of import and export, the inspection is made according to the following standards:

① According to the requirement in the import contract about the quality, specification, packing, and sampling inspection;

② According to the standard of the manufacturing country, the import country, or the usual standard adopted internationally in case that the standard is not specified in the contract;

③ The law and rules of state and the international practice are prior to the contract clauses;

④ For some international standards such as ISO9000 or the standard of the International Wool Secretariat, it is decided by both seller and buyer to adopt them or not.

9.1.3.5　Re-inspection

复验

The re-inspection right of the buyer is not compulsory, nor the basic condition for the acceptance of goods, depending on the buyer's selection. The buyer must finish there-inspection within a reasonable time if the re-inspection is needed. The reasonable time is regulated in the contract.

The time for re-inspection shall be specified in the contract according to the specific property of the cargo.

9.2　Claim

索赔

9.2.1　A Brief Introduction to Claim

索赔简介

Claim refers to the legal demand or assertion by a claimant for compensation, payment, or reimbursement for a loss under a contract, or an injury due to negligence. And claim settlement means to deal with the claims of the aggrieved party by the defaulting party. Claim and settlement are two aspects of the same problem with claim being for the aggrieved party and settlement being for the defaulting party. Claims about performance of sales/purchase contract arise mainly because of the breach of contract by the relevant parties. Claims in international trade can be generally classified as follows:

9.2.1.1　Claims against the seller

针对卖方的索赔

The buyer can lodge a claim against the seller for the buyer's losses caused by the seller's breach of contract. For example, the seller failed to prepare the goods required by the contract in time or delivered goods that are not in accordance with the contract of quality, specifications, etc., or the attached shipping documents are incomplete and inadequate.

9.2.1.2　Claims against the buyer

针对买方的索赔

Cases of claims against buyers are rare. However, it constitutes the seller's claim against the buyer that the buyer breaches the contract, especially in cases that the buyer refuses to open the relevant letter of credit if the seller has prepared the goods that are highly specific according to the contract, and that the buyer uses improper means to transfer the goods to other areas restricted by the seller. And the seller may also lodge a claim against the buyer if the buyer wrongfully refuses to accept goods or fails to pay for the goods when payment is due.

9.2.1.3　Claims against shipping companies

针对航运公司的索赔

Claims against shipping companies, or transportation claims, include claims caused by the delay of shipping companies in dispatching the ship, cargo damage during transportation, unauthorized change of route and detour, delay of the ship's arrival at the port of destination, and short unloading.

9.2.1.4 Claims against insurance companies
针对保险公司的索赔

Any loss that occurs within the insurance coverage can be claimed for compensation against the insurance company.

9.2.2 Claim Clause in Contract
合同中的索赔条款

<small>异议和索赔条款 处罚条款</small>

There are two kinds of claim clauses in contracts of import and export: one is **the clause of dispute and claim for compensation**, the other is the **penalty clause**. Generally speaking, there is only dispute and claim clause in most of sales contracts, but in the contracts about the goods in large quantities or large mechanical equipment, there are dispute and claim clause as well as penalty clause.

9.2.2.1 Dispute and Claim Clause
异议与索赔条款

<small>索赔的依据、索赔期限、索赔损失的办法和赔付金额。</small>

The clause includes, unless otherwise stipulated that one party is entitled to lodge a claim against the other party who breaches a contract, **the proofs for lodging a claim and the effective period for filing a claim, the ways to compensate for the loss, and the compensation sum**, etc...

<small>法律依据和事实依据</small>

The proofs for lodging a claim are mainly covering the necessary proofs or certificates for claims, and the relevant certificate issuing authorities. Proofs for claims include **legal proof and fact proof**. The former refers to the trade contract and the related national laws and regulations while the latter refers to the facts and the written evidence of the breach to verify the truth of the breach.

The effective period for filing a claim means the period in which the claimant can make a claim against the party who is in breach of contract. The party in breach of contract can refuse a claim made after the effective period. Therefore, the effective period for a claim shall be stipulated reasonably according to different commodities, the warranty period shall be added in the contract for the commodity with quality warranty. The warranty period can be one year or more. In conclusion, the period for lodging a claim shall be dependent on the nature of the commodity and the inspection time, etc., in order to avoid extra obligation undertaken by the seller, the stipulated claim period shall not be too long except for some special commodities such as mechanical equipment, and to assure the time for buyers to file a claim, the stipulated claim period shall not be too short either.

The ways of settling claims and the compensation sum will be stipulated in the contract in general. It is very difficult to estimate the exact compensation sum and the losses caused prior to the breach of contract, so there is no specific stipulation about the compensation sum.

The clause of dispute and claim is a restriction for the seller to fulfill the contract as well as for the buyer, No matter which party is in the breach of contract, the other party suffering the losses has the right to make a claim for compensation against the party in breach.

9.2.2.2 Penalty Clause

罚金条款

The clause is applicable to the situations including the delayed delivery of goods by the seller or the buyer, the deferred issuance of L/C, the delayed payment etc.. One party shall make payment in a certain sum of money to the other party in loss as the compensation when the party fails to fulfill the contract. **The penalty is also called as the fine for the breach of contract.** The sum of penalty is dependent on **the breach time** with a maximum amount.

罚金亦称"违约金"或"罚则"

违约时间

违约金的起算日期有两种：一种是合同规定的交货期或开证期终止后立即

There are two ways to calculate the due time of the penalty: one is to calculate from the end of the deliver time in the contract or the end of the L/C issuance time; the other is to stipulate one period extended after the end of the relevant time in the contract, and the penalty is exempt

起算；另一种是规定优惠期，即在合同规定的有关期限终止后再宽限一段时间，在优惠期内免于罚款，待优惠期届满后起算罚金。

within the extended time and the penalty sum will be calculated from the end of the extended time. The seller shall not be exempt from the obligation to fulfill the contract after paying the penalty.

In the Law of Contract of our country, it is stipulated about the penalty as follows: the parties involved may agree in the contract, that one party shall pay a penalty to the other party when he is in breach of contract; or both parties agree the way of calculating the compensation sum for the losses arising from the breach. However, when the agreed penalty sum is much lower or higher than the losses resulting from the breach of contract, the party involved may ask the court or the arbitration organization to make a proper increase or reduction. Meanwhile, it is stipulated that, the party involved whoever pays the penalty for the delayed fulfillment of contract shall continue to fulfill the contract after paying the penalty.

Generally, only the clause of dispute and claim will be stipulated in the contract for import and export, and for the contracts of the goods in large amount with delivery in installments or mechanical equipment, the penalty clause will be added to the contract.

9.3 Force Majeure
不可抗力

9.3.1 A Brief Introduction to Force Majeure
不可抗力简介

Force Majeure, also called Act of God, refers to an event that can neither be anticipated nor be preventable, avoidable, and controllable after the conclusion of the contract. It does not result from the fault or neglect of the parties involved, leading to the failure or the delay of the fulfillment of the contract; the party who fails or delays to fulfill the contract due to such event can be free from the liabilities, or to be given an option of terminating the contract or postponing the performance of the contract.

Force Majeure clause is an **escape clause** in a contract, a **legal principle** as well. In international trade, different laws and rules have their own regulations and rules about it. In the United Nations Convention on Contracts for the International Sales of Goods of 1980, the exemption is regulated as follows: "A party is not liable for a failure to perform any of its obligations if it proves that the failure was due to an impediment beyond its control and that it could not reasonably be expected to have taken the impediment into account at the time of the conclusion of the contract or have avoided or have overcome it or the consequence of it." The Convention has pointed out that the party who fails to perform the contract due to the occurrence of an impediment beyond his control, which cannot be expected, avoided or overcome, can be free from the liability.

免责条款
法律原则

The definitions of a Force Majeure event in different laws and rules are not explanatorily unified, nor its descriptions, however the basic principles are the same generally, which include the following points:

① The occurrence of a Force Majeure event is after the conclusion of the contract.

② The event is not resulting from the **fault or neglect** of the parties involved.

过失或疏忽

③ The event is beyond the control of the parties involved, such as the market risk, fluctuation of commodity prices, change of foreign exchange rates, etc.

9.3.2 Consequences of Force Majeure
不可抗力的后果

According to relevant laws and international practice, if the contract cannot be performed in whole or in part because of the occurrence of force majeure events, the parties concerned can modify or terminate the contract based on the impact of the force majeure events to exempt them from corresponding liabilities. If the performance of a contract is delayed by a force majeure event temporarily or for a short time, the contract may be suspended. And the contract should be resumed after the force majeure event finishes. For example, if there is a delayed shipment because of an industrial strike, the contract will be suspended. But when the strike is over, the contract should continue, and the seller has to go on to ship the goods. If the force majeure event has damaged or destroyed the basis of the contract, for example, the flood has damaged or destroyed the goods ready for shipment, the contract can be terminated.

The party that is free from the liability according to the force majeure clause should meet two requirements. First, the party should timely inform the other party right after the accident so that the latter is able to take necessary remedial measures. Otherwise, the former will still be held responsible for the losses or extended losses thus caused. Second, the party that failed to perform the contract should provide effective documentation describing the frustrating events and their consequences. If he fails to do this, or if the facts identified are not in conformity with his descriptions, he will not be exempted or exempted totally from the liability of his failure to perform the contract.

9.3.3　Force Majeure Clause in the Contract
　　　　合同中的不可抗力条款

The force majeure clause in the contract usually includes the scope and consequences of the force majeure events, the time limit for notifying the other party of the contract, the certificate that needs to be presented and the issuer of the certificate, etc.

The force majeure clauses in China's import and export contracts can be expressed either vaguely or in details. But the best way is to list the force majeure events added with **supplementary explanations**, 补充解

such as "and other force majeure events agreed by both parties". The clause stipulated in this way is clear, specific, and flexible because other unexpected events that may occur in the performance of the contract have been considered. The following is an example:

"The Seller shall not be held responsible for failure or delay to perform all or any part of this contract due to war, earthquake, flood, fire, storm, heavy snow, or other causes of Force Majeure. However, the seller shall advise the buyer immediately of such occurrence and within 10 days thereafter, shall send by registered airmail to the buyer for their acceptance a certificate issued by the competent government authorities of the place where the accident occured as evidence thereof. Under such circumstance, the seller, however, is still under the obligation to take all necessary measures to hasten the delivery of the goods. In case the accident lasts for more than 4 weeks, the buyer shall have the right to cancel the contract."

9.4 Arbitration
仲裁

9.4.1 A Brief Introduction to Arbitration
仲裁简介

In most cases, the claim is not able to be settled successfully as expected of many reasons. Therefore, in international trade practice, when disputes arise between sellers and buyers, they usually can be settled by negotiation, arbitration, or **litigation**. Through negotiation, 诉讼 the disputes can be settled in an amicable way. But it is often the case that disputes cannot be amicably settled by negotiation, and then it is necessary to resort to arbitration or litigation. However, litigation, which is time-consuming and follows a formal procedure that is open to the public, can be detrimental to the relationship between the parties involved. Therefore, arbitration has become a popular method in international trade to settle disputes in that it brings about a friendly atmosphere and is more flexible, less expensive and quicker in handling cases than litigation. What is more, the arbitration award is final and binding on both parties.

9.4.1.1 Definition and features of arbitration
仲裁的定义和特点

(1) Definition of arbitration

仲裁的定义

Arbitration is a means of settling a dispute between parties through a third party who is not partial to either of the parties involved in the dispute, and whose decision on the dispute is final and binding. It is a formal and organized process for dispute resolution that applies a substantive law selected by the parties while following procedures established by the parties or the arbitral institution.

(2) Features of arbitration

仲裁的特点

Settling disputes by arbitration has the following features:

① Submission to arbitration is based on the voluntary consent of both parties;

② Arbitration is a way for an impartial third party to resolve disputes;

③ Arbitration awards are final and binding without the recourse to appeal or retrial;

④ Arbitration is flexible and convenient;

⑤ Arbitration is highly confidential.

9.4.1.2 Arbitration form and body
仲裁形式和机构

(1) Arbitration form

仲裁形式

临时仲裁
机构仲裁

Arbitration includes **ad hoc arbitration** and **institutional arbitration**. Ad hoc arbitration refers to the arbitration conducted in an ad hoc arbitration tribunal organized by arbitrators jointly appointed by both parties to the dispute. Ad hoc arbitration is formed to hear a specific case. After the hearing of the case is finished, the **arbitration tribunal** is automatically dissolved. Institutional arbitration means that both parties agree to submit an application to a permanent arbitration institution and conduct arbitration in accordance with the arbitration rules of the arbitration institution or the arbitration rules selected by both parties. In general, if the parties agree to arbitrate by a permanent arbitration institution, arbitration will be conducted in accordance with the arbitration rules of that institution. However, the parties involved are also allowed by many countries to choose the arbitration rules that they think are appropriate. In recent years, institutional arbitration has been adopted in most international commercial arbitrations.

仲裁法庭

(2) Arbitration body

仲裁机构

If both parties agree to resolve their disputes by arbitration, they shall specify which arbitration institution will be chosen. Internationally, there are some permanent arbitration bodies, such as the *International Court of Arbitration of International Chamber of Commerce (ICC), the American Arbitration Association (AAA), the London Court of International Arbitration (LCIA), the Arbitration Institute of the Stockholm Chamber of Commerce (SCC), the International Center for the Settlement of Investment Dispute (ICSID)*, etc.

国际商会国际仲裁法院（ICC）、美国仲裁协会（AAA）、伦敦国际仲裁法院（LCIA）、斯德哥尔摩商会（SCC）、国际投资争端解决中心（ICSID）

In China, the most welcomed arbitration body is the *China International Economic and Trade Arbitration Commission (CIETAC)*, which is one of the major permanent arbitration institutions in the world. Set up in April 1956, CIETAC independently and impartially resolves economic and trade disputes as well as investment disputes by means of arbitration. Headquartered in Beijing,

中国国际经济贸易仲裁委员会（CIETAC）

CIETAC has several sub-commissions/arbitration centers in different cities of China. They adopt the same set of Arbitration Rules and have the same Panel of Arbitrators. In accordance with the New York Convention, CIETAC awards are recognized and enforceable in 159 countries.

9.4.2 Arbitration Clause in Contract
合同中的仲裁条款

The arbitration place is the main content and the key element in an arbitration clause since the arbitration place generally determines the arbitration rules and the relevant laws. The selection and arrangement of arbitration place in international practice are generally in the following ways: the country of buyer, the country of seller, the third country, **the country of defendant, the country of complaint,** the location of the goods, etc. There are three ways to stipulate the arbitration place according to our country's law.

<small>被告所在国，原告所在国</small>

9.4.2.1 Arbitration in Our Country
规定在我国仲裁

For example, "Any dispute, controversy or claim arising out of or relating to this contract, or the breach, termination or invalidity thereof, shall be settled amicably through negotiation. In case no settlement can be reached through negotiation, the case shall then be submitted to the China International Economic and Trade Arbitration Commission of the China Council for the Promotion of International Trade, Beijing, for arbitration in accordance with its Rules of Arbitration. The arbitral award is final and binding upon both parties."

9.4.2.2 Arbitration Tribunal Formation and Arbitrators Appointment
组织仲裁庭与仲裁员的指定

The stipulation about the number of arbitrators and the appointment ways varies in indifferent countries. In most countries, an arbitration tribunal is composed of three arbitrators, but there is sole-arbitrator tribunal in the U.K., and the U.S.A., and there is also arbitration tribunal composed of two persons or **even numbers** in a few countries. In a temporary arbitration, the sole arbitrator is appointed by both parties in the arbitration agreement. For an arbitration tribunal with three arbitrators, two of them are appointed by both parties respectively, and the third arbitrator so called chief arbitrator is appointed by the two arbitrators together. The arbitrator can also be appointed by the chairman of the arbitration body and the **chief arbitrator** is chosen by the chairman from the panel of arbitrators. In order to have the case settled fairly and reasonably, the arbitrators appointed by both parties respectively shall neither have any interest in the case, nor represent any party's interest. If the appointed arbitrator has any interest in the case, it shall ask for abstaining from the arbitration. It is decided by the arbitration body if the arbitrator shall abstain from the case. When the arbitrator abstains from the case or fails to fulfill the duty, a new arbitrator shall be appointed according to the procedures.

双数

首席仲裁员

9.4.2.3 Proceedings of Case

审理案件

There are two forms of proceedings of an arbitration case: one is a closed proceeding. It is usually required or agreed by the parties involved that the arbitration tribunal may examine the case and issue an award on the basis of documents only; the other one is an open proceeding. The arbitration is usually not in public according to the arbitration rules. Upon the request of both parties involved, an open proceeding can be exercised dependent on the decision of the arbitration tribunal.

9.4.2.4 Award Issuance

做出裁决

To issue an award is the last section of the whole arbitration process. After an award is issued, the procedure of arbitration has come to an end, so the judgment is final. According to the Arbitration Rules of our country, the arbitration tribunal may issue an intermediate award or a partial award with respect to any problem of the case. An **intermediate award** means an award temporarily issued for the dispute which has been examined and handled clearly, in favor of further handling of the case; a **partial award** is a final one issued separately for some problems which have been handled clearly in the case, and the partial award is regarded as the part of the final award for the whole case.

中间裁决

部分裁决

An award of arbitration must be issued in written form within 45 days after the closing of the case. Except for the verdict issued through mediation, an arbitration award shall specify the reasons for issuing the award, and state that the award is final with the date and place of award issuing as well as the signature of the arbitrators. The parties involved shall enforce the award within the time limit stipulated in the award. For the award without a time limit, the award shall be enforced immediately. In case that one party fails to fulfill the award, the other party may have recourse to the court of China to apply for the enforcement in accordance with the law of China, or settle it according to the relevant international convention and practice.

In the arbitration clause of a sales contract, the arbitration rules of which country or region and arbitration body are adopted shall be specified. For the applicable arbitration rules in China, it refers to China International Economic and Trade Arbitration Commission Rules. There are different arbitration rules in different countries and regions. It should be noted that the adopted arbitration rules must not be in compliance with the arbitration place though the arbitration rules of the arbitration place are usually adopted according to the international practice. It is also allowed in law to adopt the arbitration rules of other countries or regions rather than the arbitration place based on the agreement of both parties.

In addition, about the cost of arbitration, which party shall bear the arbitration cost is usually specified clearly in the arbitration clause. Usually, it is stipulated that the arbitration cost is borne by the losing party, or depending on the arbitration tribunal's decision.

Exercises 练习

I. Ture (T) or False (F)

1. Reasons for disputes in international trade can be classified into three categories: breach of contract by the seller, breach of contract by the buyer and breach of contract by both the seller and the buyer. (   )

2. One of the ways to stipulate period for claim is: "Claim should be filed within 90 days after shipment". (   )

3. The best way to stipulate force majeure events in the Force Majeure Clause of a contract is to stipulate them in a synthesized way. (   )

4. The arbitration award is final and binding on both parties, therefore should been forced without any doubt. (   )

5. There are two main types of arbitration body: governmental body and non-governmental body. (   )

6. Inspection on import and export commodities in China falls into two categories: statutory inspection and non-statutory inspection. (   )

7. If a claim is well supported, the claimant shall pay a fine, a certain percentage of the total contract value. (   )

8. The main ways to settle disputes in international trade are negotiation, mediation, arbitration and litigation. (   )

9. When a force majeure event takes place, the party concerned has no choice but to terminate the contract. (   )

10. The arbitration tribunal has the power to decide that the losing party shall pay the winning party the arbitration fee incurred in dealing with the case. (   )

II. Multiple choices.

1. The disagreement resulted from one party of a transaction being totally or partially unable to perform the obligation and liability stipulated in the contract is_____.

   A. claim
   B. dispute
   C. breach of contract
   D. settlement of disputes

2. Which of the following may possibly result in disputes between sellers and buyers?

   A. Breakage of the package
   B. Rising of price
   C. Fluctuation of exchange rate
   D. Quota

3. Which of the following is a clause in a contract and meanwhile a law itself?

   A. Arbitration Clause
   B. Claim Clause
   C. Dispute Clause
   D. Force Majeure Clause

4. The main arbitration body in China is_____.

   A. MOFTEC   B. CCPIT   C. CIETAC   D. ICC

5. According to usual practice, the penalty of a contract shall not exceed _____ of the total value of the goods.

   A. 3%   B. 4%   C. 5%   D. 5.5%

6. Force Majeure Clause is a clause that mainly_____.

   A. protects the right of the seller

   B. protects the right of the buyer

   C. enables the seller to avoid his contractual obligations

   D. enables the buyer to avoid his contractual obligations

7. After a dispute, in case that the parties concerned are unable to reach an agreement, they can ask a third party to help settle the dispute. But the result has no binding effect on either party. This action is called_____.

   A. negotiation   B. mediation   C. arbitration   D. litigation

8. Before going for arbitration, both parties involved in a dispute need

to make an arbitration agreement in written form, in which they agree to refer the subject in dispute to a third party. This indicates the _____ nature of arbitration.

  A. flexible B. simplified C. compulsory D. voluntary

  9. The award of arbitration is final and binding on both parties. This shows the _____ nature of arbitration.

  A. flexible B. swift C. enforceable D. voluntary

  10. The best way to stipulate the place and time of inspection is_____.

  A. inspection at the factory

  B. inspection at the port of shipment

  C. inspection at the port of destination

  D. inspection at the port of shipment and re-inspection at the port of destination

  11. In the event of _____, the defaulting party may invoke the Force Majeure clause to claim exemption of contractual obligations.

  A. a war

  B. international price fluctuations

  C. currency devaluation

  D. mistakes in production

  12. Claims in international trade include_____.

  A. trade claims   B. transportation claims

  C. insurance claims   D. all the above

  13. Which one of the following is an INCORRECT statement about the function of the inspection certificate?

  A. It determines the standards and methods of inspection.

  B. It is the certificate required for customs clearance.

  C. It is one of the documents to be presented by the exporter for negotiation.

  D. It is evidence that the goods delivered by the exporter conform to the provisions of the contract.

14. When deciding the place of arbitration for an import and export contract, which of the following country do traders generally believe to be fair to both the importer and exporter?

A. A third country   B. China

C. The importer's country   D. The exporters country

15. Which is the CORRECT statement about "Inspection in the exporting country, re-inspection in the importing country"?

A. It is favorable to the importer.

B. It is favorable to the exporter.

C. It considers the interests of both the importer and the exporter.

D. It is favorable to the insurance company.

III. Case Study.

1. One trader abroad placed an order with a domestic manufacturer at FOB price, it is stipulated in the sales contract that the manufacturer shall pay 5% of the total payment as the penalty to the buyer if the goods are not delivered by the end of July. Later, the manufacturer delayed the delivery for 5 days, leading to the buyer's claim for 3% penalty against the trader.

Question:

In this case, shall the trader make lodge claim against the manufacturer? For 5% or 3%?

2. A Chinese exporter signed a CFR contract with an importer in America on canned meat for an amount of US $50000, with payment by D/P at sight. On the morning of May 5, 2023, the goods were all loaded onto the named vessel. The Chinese salesperson in charge of this contract was so busy that he forgot to send the buyer the shipping advice until the next morning. Unexpectedly, when the American importer went to the local insurance company to insure the goods, the insurance company had already learned that the ship suffered a wreck on May 6 and refused to insure the shipment. The American importer immediately

sent a fax to the Chinese exporter saying "owing to your delayed shipping advice, we are unable to insure the goods. Since the vessel has been destroyed in a wreck, the loss of goods should be on your account. At the same time, you should compensate our profit and expense losses which amount to US $50000." Soon all the shipping documents sent through the collecting bank were returned to the Chinese exporter, for the reason that the importer refused to take up the shipping documents.

Question:

Who should be responsible for the loss and why?

3. The Chinese furniture manufacturer Okart Furniture Co., Ltd concluded an export contract for 200 sets of dining tables and chairs with an American company AllNature Furniture Trading Co., Ltd., under Incoterm CIF New York. The contract stipulated the time of shipment in December 2024. At the end of November, however, Okart's warehouse caught fire, resulting in the burning of about half of the furniture. It asked the AllNaure to **exempt** its responsibility of delivery on the ground of a force majeure event. The US importer disagreed and insisted on it making delivery on time. It had no choice but managed to deliver the goods in early January 2017, and the importer made a claim for late delivery.

免除，豁免

Questions:

(1) Is it reasonable for Okart to ask for an exemption from the delivery responsibility? Why?

(2) Is Allnature's claim reasonable? Why?

Chapter 10

The Performance of Export and Import Contract

第十章 进出口合同履行

◆ Learning Objectives

- Be familiar with the process of export and import
- Be familiar with the performance of export and import contract
- Be familiar with the main documents for settlement

出口和进口

外汇

限制

For most nations, **exports and imports** are the most important international activities. Each country has to import the articles and commodities it does not produce itself, and it has to earn **foreign exchanges** to pay for them. It does this by exporting its own manufactured articles and surplus raw materials. Thus the import and export trades are two sides of the same coin, and both can have beneficial effects on the home market. Imports create competition for home-produced goods; exporting gives a manufacturer a larger market for his products, so helping to reduce the unit cost. In each case the effect is to keep prices in the home market down.

But there may be factors that compel governments to place **restrictions** on foreign trade. Imports may be controlled or subjected to a custom duty to protect a home industry, or because the available foreign exchange has to be channeled into buying more essential goods and exports, too, may be restricted, to conserve a particular raw material required by a developing home industry.

These factors mean that importing and exporting are subject to a lot of formalities, such as customs entry and exchange control approval, from which the home retail and wholesale trades are free. They also mean that the procedure of foreign trade is much more complicated than that of domestic trade, the latter involves specialized knowledge and highly trained personnel.

All or most of the following organizations are involved in an export and import transaction:

- The exporters
- The shipping agents at the port or airport of loading
- The railways (in some cases) in the exporters' country
- The road hauler (in some cases) in the exporters' country
- The port authority
- The shipping company (for sea freight)
- The airline (for air freight)
- The insurance company or brokers
- The exporters' bank
- The importers' bank
- The railways (in some cases) in the importers' country
- The road hauler (in some cases) in the importers' country
- The shipping agent at the port or airport of discharge
- The importers

Many specialists may be involved in export and import transaction, including:

- A shipping agent and/or freight forwarder (forwarding agent) will take responsibility for the documentation and arrange for the goods to be shipped by air, sea, rail, or road. These services may be carried out by the supplier's own export department, if they have the expertise.

- Airlines, shipping lines, railway companies or haulage contractors will actually transport the goods.
- Both the importer's and exporter's banks will be involved in arranging payments if a letter of credit or bill of exchange is used.
- Customs and Excise officers may need to examine the goods, check **import or export license** and charge duty and/or **VAT**.
- A **Chamber of Commerce** may need to issue a **certificate of origin**, if this is required by the importer's country.
- An insurance company insures goods in transit.
- A lawyer if a special contract has to be drawn up.

Many import or export deals are arranged through an **exporter's agent or distributor** abroad, in this case the importer buys from a company importing goods in his own country. Alternatively, the deal may be arranged through an **importer's buying agents** or a buying house acting for the importer, or through an export house based in the exporter's country. In these cases, the exporter sells, directly to a company in his own country, the latter will then export the goods.

An export or import business is so complicated that it may take quite a long time to conclude a transaction. Varied and complicated procedures have to be gone through in the course of an export or import transaction. From the very beginning to the end of the transaction, the whole operation generally undergoes four stages: preparing for exporting or importing, business negotiation, implementing the contract, and settlement of disputes (if any). Each stage covers some specific steps. Since the export and import trades are two sides of the same coin, and one country's export is another country's import, hence, we will take the procedures of export transaction in the following diagram to illustrate the

Chapter 10 The Performance of Export and Import Contract

general procedures of export and import transaction. Before proceeding to the following units, it is advised that this general picture be kept in mind.

This Chapter tries to present a general picture and a brief introduction to export and import trades for the purpose of clarifying their complicated procedures.

10.1 General Procedures of Export Transaction
出口业务流程

Different countries have different **economic policies or systems**. 经济体系或经济政策
So before doing business with foreign countries, one has to understand the whole procedures of exporting. Take the contract on the basis of CIF and payment by L/C as an example, you can refer to Figure 10.1.

As can be seen from Figure 10.1, the export business process is divided into four parts: preparation for exporting, business negotiation, implementation of contract, and settlement of disputes. Among these, the preparation for exporting includes market research, trade plan making, knowledge of trade laws and regulations, and obtaining trade qualification, for more details, please refer to Chapter 1. As for business negotiation, it typically involves inquiry, offer, counteroffer, and acceptance, as discussed in Chapter 2. Sometimes complaints or claims arise after the fulfillment of a contract by the exporter and importer, these issues may stem from reasons such as more or less quantity delivered, wrong goods delivered, poor packing, inferior quality, discrepancies between samples and delivered goods, delay in shipment, etc. Once disputes arise, arbitration is generally advised over litigation. Chapter 9 discusses these issues in detail. The following part will focus on introducing the process of contract performance.

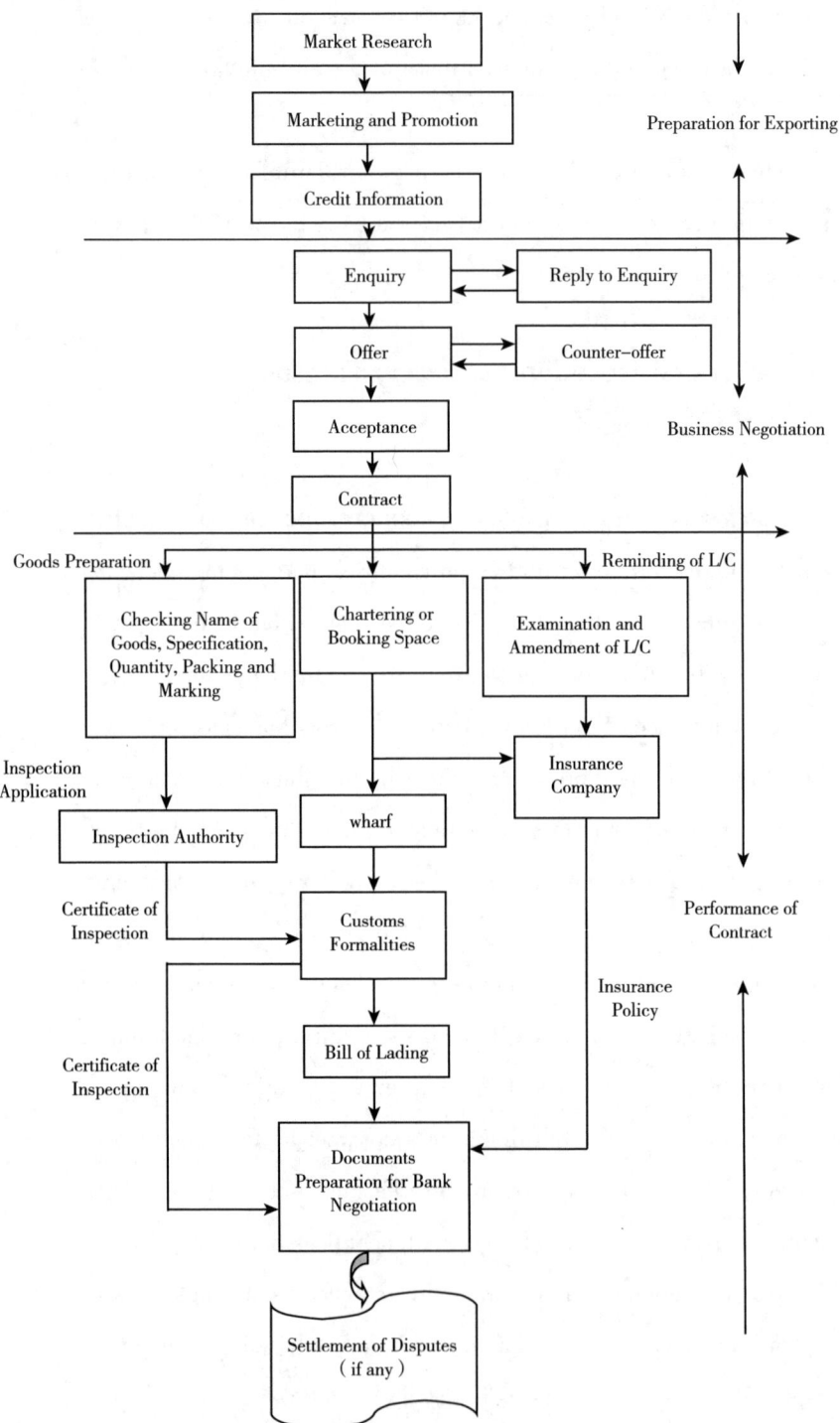

Figure 10.1

Chapter 10 The Performance of Export and Import Contract   **283**

Under CIF contract with terms of payment by L/C, the implementation of an export contract usually goes through the steps of goods preparation, inspection application, reminding of L/C, examination and modification of L/C, chartering and booking shipping space, shipment, insurance, documents preparation for bank negotiation and the settlement of claims, etc.

10.1.1 Preparing Goods for Shipment
备货

After a contract is made, it is the main task for the exporter to prepare the goods for shipment and check them against the terms stipulated in the contract. The quality, specification, quantity, marking and the packing should be **in line with** the contract or the L/C, the date for the preparation should agree with the shipping schedule. 　与……一致

10.1.2 Inspection Application
检验

If required by the stipulations of the states or the contract, the exporter should obtain a certificate of inspection from the institutions concerned where the goods are inspected. Usually, the commodity will be released only after the issuance of the **inspection certificate** by the inspection organization.　检验证书

10.1.3 Reminding, Examining and Modifying L/C
催证、审证和改证

In international trade, a banker's **letter of credit**, is commonly used for the payment of the purchase price. In the course of the performance of contract, one of the necessary steps for the seller is to **urge** the buyer to **establish L/C**. According to the contract, the buyer should establish the L/C on time, but sometimes he may delay 　信用证

催促，开立信用证

it for various reasons. For the safe collection of payment, the seller has to urge the buyer to expedite the opening of L/C. Upon receipt of a letter of credit, the seller must examine it very carefully to make sure that all terms and conditions are stipulated **in accordance with** the contract. If any **discrepancies** exist, the seller should contact the buyer immediately for necessary **amendments** so as to guarantee the smooth execution of the. contract.

10.1.3.1　L/C Reminding

催证

If the payment is effected by L/C, **the exporter is not to make the shipment until after he has received the L/C.** Sometimes it is necessary to remind the buyer of the L/C. The buyer should also open the L/C ahead of schedule. Because of financial difficulties or other reasons, the buyer might not be able to open the L/C in time. The seller might feel it necessary to give him some time as a grace period, and meanwhile retain the right of claim against the buyer.

10.1.3.2　Examine the L/C

审证

Having received an L/C, the **beneficiary** should examine the L/C to see if it **fully corresponds with** the sales contract and the **Uniform Customs and Practice for Documentary Credit**. If any discrepancy happens, the seller should ask the importer to require the opening bank to make corrections. The seller cannot make the shipment until he has received an effective, complete, and acceptable L/C. The examination can be overall examination or only of the specified clause.

10.1.3.3　Make Overall Examination

总体审查

An L/C should be opened by a bank of a country or an area which keeps economic relations with our country. This principle is applicable even if the L/C has been opened by a branch bank of such nations or areas. The L/C must be **in conformity with** the trade agreements between the two trading nations, and finally the L/C should not carry **deprecatory clauses** or clauses which contain political bias.

与……一致

反对条款

The **notifying bank** should examine the seal or the test of the L/C to see if it is a false one, if the L/C has been delivered to the seller directly, he should present it to the notifying bank for such an examination. If the notifying bank doubts the credit status of the **opening bank**, certain measures should be adopted accordingly, such as asking the applicant to have the L/C **confirmed** by a bank of good reputation, having the paying bank to confirm the payment and add a payment insurance clause to the L/C, demand partial shipment and partial settlement if the consignment is of great quantity, and add a cable reimbursement clause to the L/C.

通知行

开证行

保兑

The beneficiary should also examine if the clauses on the L/C are **self-contradictory**, such as in the case when a B/L is required for negotiation but transshipment is not allowed; the price term is CFR, but **insurance policy** is required for negotiation, etc.

自相矛盾

保险单

Finally, the beneficiary should check if there are any misspelt words, if he can fulfill all requirements (such as in the case when the L/C requires a particular vessel for shipment) or if he can get all the documents ready within a given time, etc.

10.1.3.4　Examine Individual Clauses

个别条款审查

By this we mean to examine the individual clauses of the L/C one by one. The beneficiary of the L/C should examine the L/C to see the relevant clauses covering the name, specifications, quantity, packing, unit price, time for shipment, loading and unloading port, etc. correspond with those as listed in the sales contract. Particular attention should **be devoted to** the following:

专注于……

·Expiry date of the L/C 信用证到期日

Take "Expiry Date: June 15, 2025, in China for negotiation" for example, it gives the last date by which negotiation at a bank in the exporter's country should be done. Unless there are more secure means to avoid relevant risks, it is advisable for the beneficiary not to accept other clauses.

·The amount to be given 信用证金额

溢短装条款

The amount given in the L/C should correspond with that given in the sales contract, and in the same currency. If a **"more or less" clause** is given for the quantity of the goods in the sales contract, **the L/C should bear a similar quantity clause** and the amount of the L/C should be flexible accordingly or the amount of the draft and the invoice should not be any more than that given in the sales contract.

信用证中应载明相应数量条款

·Time of loading, time of validity, and time for surrender of the shipping documents 交货期，信用证有效期，运输单据提交日期

装货期

The time of loading should be the same as that given in the sales contract. But it is acceptable if the time of loading given in the L/C is longer than that given in the sales contract. The seller should ask for the extension of the time of loading if he cannot make the shipment on time because of various reasons, such as the late arrival of the L/C, the delay in the preparation of the goods, etc.

到期日

The L/C should have **a time of validity**, which is generally 10 to 15 days after the time of shipment so that the seller might have sufficient time to prepare the required **shipping documents** for payment settlement.

装运单据
提示单据、交出单据

The time of surrendering the shipping documents is sometimes given in the L/C. This is given in the case when the time of validity of the L/C is rather long and the buyer wants to get the required shipping documents in time to take the delivery of the goods. It is usually given that the "surrender of the shipping documents should be made xxx days after the date of **the bill of lading**". If no such time is given, the shipping documents should be made within 21 days after the shipment has been made. If the time for the surrender of the shipping documents is too short, such as two days, it is, usually unacceptable.

· Transshipment and partial shipment 转船和分批装船

If the sales contract states that **transshipment** and **partial shipment** are allowed, while the L/C does not bear such a clause, it should be taken that transshipment and partial shipment are allowed.

· Applicant and beneficiary 开证申请人和受益人

The exporter must make sure that the name and the address of the **applicant** and the **beneficiary** are correctly given and spelt in the L/C. Sometimes the **deliverer of the consignment** is someone else other than the exporter, e.g., the **branch agency** or some **other manufacturer**, then the L/C should be **transferable**, in this way to avoid the trouble of different beneficiary and deliverer.

· Examination of terms 检查其他条件

The exporter should also examine other terms item by item and think about if they correspond with the sales contract or pose **unnecessary barriers** to the deal, or if they **conflict with each other**.

· Time of payment 支付时间

The **time of payment** must correspond with that given in the sales contract. If the L/C is a **usance L/C** and the sales contract states that the buyer should **bear the interest thereupon**, the LC must bear similar clauses.

10.1.3.5 Amendment of the L/C
改证

Once the exporter has found some **flaws** with the L/C, he should think about whether it is necessary to make the **amendment**. If the flaw poses a great barrier to the settlement of payment and **hinders** the performance of the sales contract, the exporter should ask for the importer to require the **opening bank** to make an amendment in time. If the flaw is of minor significance and the deal can be performed smoothly accordingly, perhaps it will not be necessary to make the amendment, so as to save time and expenses.

If more than one clause should be amended, the exporter should ask for the amendment at once. **The importer is obliged to accept or reject all of them**, he cannot accept the amendment of one clause while rejecting the other (or others) . Once the amendment is made, it becomes part of the L/C and the deal is to be executed accordingly.

10.1.4　Chartering and Booking Shipping Space 租船订舱

After receiving the relevant L/C, the exporter should contact the **ship's agents** or the shipping company for the chartering and the booking of shipping space and prepare for the shipment in accordance with the importer's **shipping instruction**. Chartering is required for goods in large quantities which need a full shipload; and for goods in small quantities, space booking would be enough.

10.1.5　Customs Formalities 报关手续

Before the goods are loaded, certain procedures in customs formalities have to be completed. As required, completed forms giving particulars of the goods exported together with the **copy** of the contract of sale, invoice, packing list, weight. Memo, commodity inspection certificate and other relevant documents, have to be lodged with the Customs. After the goods are **on board**, the shipping company or the ship's agent will issue a **bill of lading** which is a receipt evidencing the loading of the goods on board the ship.

10.1.6 Insurance
保险

The export trade is subject to many risks. For example, ships may sink or consignments may be damaged in transit, exchange rates may alter, buyers default or governments suddenly impose an embargo, etc. It is customary to insure goods sold for export against the **perils** of the journey. The cover paid for will vary according to the type of goods and the circumstances. If the exporter has bought insurance for the goods, he will **be reimbursed for** the losses.

危险、风险

报销、被返还

10.1.7 Documents Preparation for Bank Negotiation
制单结汇

After the shipment, all kinds of documents required by the L/C shall be prepared by the exporter and the importer and presented, within the validity of the L/C to the bank for negotiation. As to the shipping documents, they include commercial invoice, bill of lading, insurance policy, packing list, weight memo, certificate of inspection, and, in some cases, consular invoice, certificate of origin, etc. Documents should be correct, complete, concise and clean. Only after the documents are checked to be fully in conformity with the L/C, does the opening bank makes the payment. Payment shall be **disregarded** by the bank for any **discrepancies** in the documents.

拒付

不符点

10.1.8 Getting Tax Refund
获得出口退税

Once your transaction is verified by the Customs and the revenue is reported to SAFE, the State Taxation Administration refunds a certain amount of the **value-added tax (VAT)** that you have already paid if your category of product is eligible. This refund is known as the **tax**

增值税

退税

国际双重征税

关税总协定

ASOne：中国国家外汇管理局开发的外汇管理网上服务平台，用于企业申报跨境收支、外汇收入结汇等外汇相关业务。

STA: 国家税务总局

协调系统代码

世界海关组织

关税表

refund/tax rebate/tax drawback for export, which exists to avoid **international double taxation** and is allowed by the WTO as per **General Agreement on Tariffs and Trade (GATT)** as long as the amount of refund does not exceed the VAT that the exporter has paid. Once you have shipped the cargo, collected the payment, and reported your exchange revenue on **Administrative Service Online (ASOne)**, you go to the **State Taxation Administration (STA)** to file for this refund. After a while, this money will be credited to your bank account. For specific refund rate, you need to know **the Harmonized System Code (HS code)** of your product category. The Harmonized System is a unified coding system for goods and services developed by **the World Customs Organization** to facilitate import and export. Participating countries are required to use this code when describing their **tariff schedules**. Nearly all international trade occurs under the Harmonized System.

10.2 General Procedures of Import Transaction 进口合同的履行

So far we have studied the general procedures of export transaction and dealt with different stages and steps, from the point of view of an exporter. Having been familiar with the process of the export business, we find it much easier to understand how an importer handles his import business. After all, the export and import trades are two sides of the same coin. When handling an import trade, the trade conditions and terms you are striving for are sometimes just the opposite to those you do in an export trade. The terms of delivery remain the same regardless of whether you work as an importer or an exporter. A bill of lading is a bill of lading no matter who uses it for some practical purposes. The knowledge we have acquired from the previous sections is also applicable to import procedures. With the fundamental knowledge of export procedures, we can grasp the essential points of import procedures easily and manage import trade well and smoothly.

The general procedures of import transaction (take FOB contract with terms of payment by L/C as an example, the procedures shown in Figure 10.2) can be summarized as follows:

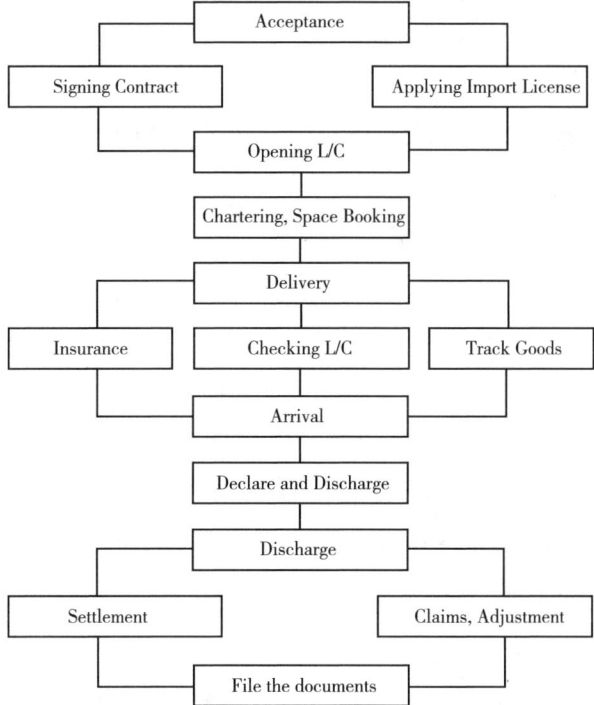

Figure 10.2 Procedures of Import Transaction

- to conduct market investigation;
- to formulate import plan for a certain commodity;
- to send inquiries to the prospective sellers overseas;
- to compare and analyze the offers or quotations received;
- to make counter-offers and decide on which offer is most beneficial;
- to sign a purchase contract;
- to apply to a bank for opening a letter of credit;
- to book shipping space or charter a carrying vessel for taking over

the cargoes, if the contract is in terms of FOB;
- to effect insurance with the insurance company upon receipt of shipping advice;
- to apply for inspection if necessary;
- to attend to customs formalities to clear the goods through the Customs;
- to entrust forwarding agents with all the transport arrangements from the port to the end-user's warehouse;
- to settle disputes (if any).

10.3 Documents Needed in Export and Import Transaction
主要进出口单证

单据交易 象征性交货

物权凭证

International trade attaches so great importance to shipping documents that, to a certain degree, it can be called **trade of documents,** or **"symbolic" trade.** This is because shipping documents represent **the title to the goods.** For example, under letter of credit, the buyer cannot take the delivery of the goods until he obtains the shipping documents; on the other hand, only if the seller releases the shipping documents can he receive the payment. What documents are used and how to carefully and accurately complete them deserve our adequate attention. As a rule, every contract of sale stipulates the kinds of shipping documents required. The slightest negligence in these documents might result in serious problems, which are not infrequent in practice. It is, therefore, imperative for both an exporter and an importer to abide by such stipulations. Generally, commercial invoice, bill of lading, insurance policy or certificate, packing list, and weight memo, etc., are called shipping documents. In addition, other documents required by the buyers and related to the matter of duty to be paid on the imported goods, sometimes, are also included in shipping documents, such as the proforma, consular invoice, certificate of origin, certificate of value, certificate of inspection. Commercial invoice, bill of lading and insurance policy constitute chief shipping documents in international trade. They are indispensable in almost every instance of export or import consignment. This unit mainly deals with commercial invoice, proforma invoice, bill of lading, packing list, weight memo, inspection certificate, and insurance policy.

10.3.1　Commercial Invoice
商业发票

Definition of Commercial Invoice 商业发票的定义

An invoice is a statement sent by the seller to the buyer giving particulars of the goods being purchased, and showing the sum of money due. Different parties require such statements for different purposes. There are various invoices, such as commercial invoices, banker's invoices, consular invoices, customer invoices and proforma invoices. Among these, the commercial invoice is the most common one and has to be provided for each and every consignment as one of the documents evidencing shipment. When speaking of an invoice covering a certain shipment, we usually refer to commercial invoice. It is a document which contains **identifying information** about 身份信息 merchandise sold for which payment is to be made. All invoices should show the name and address of the debtor, terms of payment, description of items, the price. In addition, the invoice should show the manner of delivery.

Contents of the Commercial Invoice 商业发票的内容

Commercial invoices vary in forms. However, no matter what forms they may take, the contents must be in full accordance with the contract. In general, a commercial invoice summarizes contract terms, and declares that shipments have been made on the basis of them. It contains, first of all, the names and addresses of the seller and the buyer; next, a full description of the goods dispatched, including the weights and numbers and marks of all the packages; thirdly, the price per unit and the total cost of the consignment. The commercial invoice will also state the port of shipment and the date, the terms of sale, such as CIF, and the terms of payment, such as by sight draft, perhaps under a letter of credit. Finally, it must be signed by an authorized employee of the seller, and may even quote import or export license numbers.

Sometimes the invoice price is **broken down** into such things as the cost of materials, the cost of processing and manufacture and the cost of packing and transport. The amount of detail on an invoice depends on the rules of the importing country. Some countries require a more detailed breakdown of the price.

Some foreign governments have special regulations for commercial invoices, such as requiring them to be translated into the local language or requiring the use of metric weights and other measurements. Several customs authorities and other regulatory agencies also insist on complete consistency between the different documents. Thus, the numbers and marks on the commercial and consular invoices, the insurance certificate, and the bill of lading must agree exactly.

Originals of commercial invoices must bear the signature of the seller, who is usually the shipper. The abbreviation "E. & O. E." standing for "Errors and Omissions Excepted" is usually printed at the foot of the invoice form. It means that the shipper is prepared to make correction in case errors and omissions are found.

Functions of Commercial Invoice 商业发票的作用

The invoice functions mainly as a record of the export transaction for buyers, sellers, and customs authorities. **Copies of the invoice** are used by the exporters, their bank, the paying bank, the receiving agents at the port of discharge, the customs in the exporting country and the importers. The importer needs it to check up whether the goods consigned to him are in compliance with the terms and conditions of the respective contract. The banks need it together with the Bill of Lading and the Insurance Certificate to effect payment. The customs need it to calculate duties, if any. The exporters and importers need it to keep their accounts. In the absence of a draft, the commercial invoice takes its place for drawing money.

Illustrations of a Commercial Invoice 商业发票范例

To understand and be able to write an invoice you should think about these points:

- Customer's name.
- (1) The office address; (2) The delivery address.
- The invoice number (for your records).
- The order number.
- The reference number and/or description of each item.
- The quantity.
- The price of each item.
- The total price of items and total of all items.
- The amount of discount allowed and the conditions.
- The method of freight, insurance and cost.
- The delivery address.
- The number of parcels, packages or crates.
- The markings on the parcels, packages or crates.
- Any other points.

To know the format of Commercial Invoice, please refer to Figure 10.3.

```
                    上海进出口贸易公司
            SHANGHAI IMPORT & EXPORT TRADE CORPORATION.
                    1321 ZHONGSHAN ROAD SHANGHAI, CHINA
                          COMMERCIAL   INVOICE
    TEL : 021-65788877                              INV NO : TX0522
    FAX : 021-65788876                              DATE :   JUN. 01
                                                    S/C NO : TXT264
          TO :                                      L/C NO :  XT173
          TKAMLA CORPORATION
          6-7, KAWARA MACH OSAKA
          JAPAN
    FROM      SHANGHAI PORT           TO     OSAKA PORT
```

MARKS & NO	DESCRIPTIONS OF GOODS	QUANTITY	U/ PRICE	AMOUNT
T.C TXT264 OSAKA C/NO. 1-66	CHINESE GREEN TEA ART NO.555 ART NO.666 ART NO.777 Packed in 66 cartons	100 KGS 110 KGS 120 KGS	CIF OSAKA USD 110.00 USD 100.00 USD 90.00	USD 1100.00 USD 1100.00 USD 10800.00 USD 32800.00

TOTAL AMOUNT: SAY US DOLLARS THIRTY TWO THOUSAND EIGHT HUNDRED ONLY.

WE HEREBY CERTIFY THAT THE CONTENTS OF INVOICE HEREIN ARE TRUE AND CORRECT.

Figure10.3　Illustration of a Commercial Invoice

10.3.2　Proforma Invoice
形式发票

The Definition of Proforma Invoice 形式发票的定义

Proforma, in Latin, means "for the sake of form". A proforma invoice is a document such as an invoice, issued as a **temporary statement**，but ultimately to be replaced by a final statement which can only be issued at a later date. Outwardly, except the marked "proforma", it is like an ordinary

临时情况

commercial invoice containing the general particulars, for example, marks, number of goods, descriptions, quantities, quality, price, etc. However, in nature, it is a different form of the invoice which treats "hypothetical" sales as though they had actually and contractually taken place. It is not a formal document but a document without engagement, which is binding neither on the importer nor the exporter.

假设的

Functions of proforma Invoice 形式发票的作用

Proforma invoices are required for various reasons. Primarily the importer requires them to comply with the regulations in force in his country. Moreover, the importer can require them in advance for information, or letter of credit purposes.

In many countries, especially in the developing countries of the Third World, foreign trade is under strict control. The governments of such countries usually enforce an **Import License System** or an **Import Quota System**. Importers must apply for the necessary Import License or **Foreign Exchange** and they may not import any goods without the approval of Import License or the allocation of Foreign Exchanges. Often their application has to be supported by an informal invoice, a proforma invoice, issued by the foreign exporter showing the name of commodity, specifications, unit price, etc.

进口许可证制度

进口配额制

外汇

The importer who asks for a proforma invoice is in fact making an enquiry, and the exporter who sends the proforma invoice is actually making an offer. If the exporter wants to make a firm offer, he must mention the term of validity in the covering letter when sending the proforma invoice.The sample of proforma invioce please refer to Figure 10.4.

10.3.3 Bill of Lading
  提单

Definition of Bill of Lading 提单的定义

The most important shipping document is the Bill of Lading(B/L or

Blading). It is a document given by a shipping company, representing both a receipt for the goods shipped and a contract for shipment between the shipping company and the shipper. It is also a document of title to the goods, giving the holder or the assignee the right to possession of the goods.

Contents of Bill of Lading 提单的内容

A Bill of Lading is, firstly, a contract between the shipper and the shipping company; secondly, a receipt for the consignment; and thirdly, a document of title. A Bill of Lading does not only contain a full description of the consignment—numbers and weights and marks of packages—but a lot of other information as well. It quotes the name of the shipper and the carrying vessel, the ports of shipment and destination, the freight rate, the name of the consignee (unless the B/L is "**to order**", like a check), and the date of shipment, which is very important from a contractual point of view. 凭指定

It may also contain a number of other clauses. Some bills of lading are marked "**freight paid**", when a shipper is selling CIF or CFR, others may allow transshipment, which means that the cargo may be transferred from one ship to another at some intermediate port. It is often important to a shipper that his bill of lading should be "clean" rather than "dirty", that is, that the shipping company should not have made any qualifications about the quantity or condition of the cargo actually shipped. This is because the shipper's letter of credit may insist on clean bills, just as it may insist on "**on board**" as opposed to "alongside" ladings. Sometimes a **mate's receipt** is given to the shipper in advance of the B/L, which takes time to issue. 运费已付 / 已装船 / 大副收据

A Bill of Lading is usually made out in sets of three or four originals. The shipper may ask for several extra copies for his files. One copy of the Bill is kept for the ship. The other copies are sent to the exporters or directly to their bank. These negotiable Bills of Lading are used for

Chapter 10 The Performance of Export and Import Contract

payment. They pass to the buyers or their agents in the importing country.

Then the Bills and the other shipping documents are presented to the shipping company when the ship arrives. The shipping company can then compare the negotiable Bills with their copy on the ship. In this way the importers can show their legal right to the goods and obtain them from the ship.

In recent years, a considerable simplification of documentary practices has been achieved. Bills of Lading are frequently replaced by non-negotiable documents similar to those which are used for other modes of transport than carriage by sea. These documents are called "**sea waybills**", "**liner waybills**", "**freight receipts**", or variants of such expressions. "海运单" "班轮运单" 货运收据

Illustrations of a Bill of Lading 提单范例

To understand and be able to draw up a Bill of Lading you should consider these points:

- How the goods are to be sent.
- Who will pay the freight charges.
- The name of the shipper.
- The name of the consignee.
- The vessel and port of lading.
- The port: of discharge.
- Type of packing, numbers and marks, gross weight and measurements.
- Any other points.

If a Bill of Lading only contains those particulars mentioned above, it is called a "**short form B/L**". However, if a Bill of Lading includes those particulars on the face of it, together with various clauses dealing with the rights and duties of the shipowner and shipper on its back, such a Bill is called "**long form B/L**". The long form B/L is used much more frequently than short form B/L in international trade. To know the format of Bill of Lading, please refer to Figure 10.4. 短提单、略式提单

全式提单

1. Shipper ZHEJIANG LIFANG DOWN PRODUCTS CO., LTD. 6 YILE ROAD, HANGZHOU, P.R.CHINA	B/L No. NGBFXT006329 中海集装箱运输(香港)有限公司 CHINA SHIPPING CONTAINER LINES (HONGKONG) Cable: CSHKAC Telex: 87986 CSHKAHX Port-to-Port or Combined Transport
2. Consignee TO ORDER	**BILL OF LADING**
3. Notify Party (carrier not to be responsible for failure to notify) RAM TRADING CO., LTD. 9 SMITH STREET, LITTLEBOROUGH, OL15, 8QF, U.K. TEL: 0044-845-6012288 0044-845-6012289	RECEIVED in external apparent good order and condition, except otherwise noted. The total number of containers or other packages or units shown in the Bill of Lading receipt, is said by the shipper to contain the goods described above, which description the carrier has no reasonable means of checking and is not part of the Bill of Lading. One original Bill of Lading should be surrendered, except clause 22 paragragh 5, in exchange for delivery of the shipment. Signed by the consigned or duly endorsed by the holder in due course. Whereupon the other original(s) issued shall be void. In accepting this Bill of Lading, the Merchants agree to be bound by all the terms on the face and back hereof as if each had personally signed this Bill of Lading. WHEN the place of Receipt of the Goods is an inland point and is so named herein, any notation of "ON BOARD", "SHIPPED ON BOARD" or words to like effect on this Bill of Lading shall be deemed to mean on board the truck, trail car, air craft or other inland conveyance (as the case may be), performing carriage form the Place or Receipt of the Goods to the Port of Loading. SEE clause 4 on the back of this Bill of Lading (Terms continued on the back hereof Read Carefully)

4. Pre-carriage by	5. Place of Receipt	
6. Ocean Vessel Voy. No. CMA CGM VELA, V. FL600W	7. Port of Loading SHANGHAI	**ORIGINAL**
8. Port of Discharge SOUTHAMPTON, U.K.	9. Place of Delivery	10. Final Destination (of the goods-not the ship)

11. Marks & Nos. Container Seal No.	12. No. of Containers or Packages	13. Description of Goods	14. Gross Weight	15. Measurement
RAM LD20100318 A001/A002 SOUTHAMPTON C/NO.:1-372	1×40GP FCL 372CTNS FREIGHT PREPAID	WHITE DUCK FEATHER AND DOWN DUVET L/C NO.: LC-520-046704 NAME OF ISSUING BANK: BANK OF CHINA, LONDON BRANCH DATE OF ISSUE: MAR.25, 2010 ON BOARD MAY 22, 2010 CHINA SHIPPING CONTAINER LINES (HONGKONG) 王力	6845KGS	59.520M³

16. Description of Contents for Shipper's Use Only (CARRIER NOT RESPONSIBLE)						
17. Total Number of containers and/or packages (in words): ONE CONTAINER ONLY.						
18. Freight & Charges	19. Revenue Tons	20. Rate	21. Per	22. Prepaid		23. Collect
24. Ex. Rate:	25. Prepaid at SHANGHAI	26. Payable at		27. Place and date of issue MAY 22, 2010		
	28. Total Prepaid	29. No. of Original B(s)/L THREE (3)		Signed for the Carrier CHINA SHIPPING CONTAINER LINES (HONGKONG) 王力		

Figure10.4 Illustration of a Bill of Lading

10.3.4 Packing List
装箱单

Packing list is a document made out by a seller when a sale is effected in international trade. It shows numbers and kinds of packages being shipped, total of gross, legal, and net weights of the packages, and marks and numbers on the packages. It is used to make up the deficiency of an invoice. It also enables the consignee to declare the goods at the customs office, distinguish and check the goods when they arrive at the port of destination, thus, facilitates the clearance of goods through customs. What's more, packing lists can facilitate settling insurance claims in case of loss or damage. To know the format of Packing List, please refer to Figure 10.5.

	GUANGDONG HUANYA IMPORT AND EXPORT CO., LTD. 118 XUEYUAN STREET, GUANGZHOU, P.R. CHINA TEL: 0086-020-86739178 FAX: 0086-020-86739178
	PACKING LIST
To:	DIM TRADING CO., LTD. 16 TOM STREET, DUBAI, U.A.E.		Invoice No.:		GH08018
			Invoice Date:		APR. 10, 2025
			S/C No.:		GDHY0739
			S/C Date:		FEB. 15, 2025
From:	GUANGZHOU, CHINA	To:		DUBAI, U.A.E.	
Letter of Credit No.:	FFF07699	Issued By:		HSBC BANK PLC, DUBAI, U.A.E.	
Date of Issue:	FEB. 25, 2025				
Marks and Numbers	Number and kind of package Description of goods	Quantity	Package	G.W	N.W	Meas.
DIM S/C no.: ZJJY0739 Style no.: L357/ L358 Port of destination: DUBAI, U.A.E. Carton no.: 1-502	LADIES JACKET Style no. L357 Style no. L358 PACKED IN 9 PCS/CTN, SHIPPED IN 40'FCL.	2250PCS 2268PCS	250CTNS 252CTNS	2500KGS 2520KGS	2250KGS 2268KGS	29.363M³ 29.597M³
	TOTAL:	4518PCS	502CTNS	5020KGS	4518KGS	58.96M³
SAY TOTAL:		FIVE HUNDRED AND TWO CARTONS ONLY.

Figure10.5　Illustration of a Packing List

10.3.5　Weight Memo
重量单

Weight memo is a document made out by a seller when a sale is effected in foreign trade. It indicates the gross weight and net weight of each package. It is used to make up the deficiency of an invoice. It is also used to facilitate the customs formalities and the general check of the goods by the consignee on their arrival at the destination. Packing list and weight memo usually come out in a combined form. To know the format of Weight memo, please refer to Figure 10.6.

	WEIGHT MEMO 重量单	
Name of the Company 公司名称: Address 公司地址:		P/L NO.: 包装单号码: DATE: 制单日期:
SHIPPER: 托运人公司资料 托运人地址		
BUYER: 买方公司资料 买方地址		
COMMODITY: 商品 SHIPMENT BY: 运输公司资料 SHIPPED PER: 船只资料 FROM: 出口地(港) TO: 进口地(港) SAILING ON OR ABOUT: 装船日		
MARKS &NOS. DESCRIPTION QTY N.W. G.W. MEASUREMENT 唛头箱号 商品名称 数量 净重 毛重 尺寸体积		
总计：总数量 总净重 总毛重 总尺寸体积		
总箱数(英文大写) Name of the Company 公司名称 Signature 签名 (签名英文正楷-职称) SHIPPING MARKS 正侧唛资料		

Figure 10.6　Illustration of a Weight Memo

10.3.6　Inspection Certificate
　　　　　检验证明

检验证明　调查报告

　　Inspection certificate or survey report is a document which shows the quality or quantity or other elements of the goods. It is issued by the manufacturer of the goods, chambers of commerce, surveyors, or government institutions. It mainly performs two functions: Firstly, as a document of quality or quantity, it can decide whether the quality or quantity of the goods shipped by the seller is in conformity with that stipulated in the contract. It is an important proof at the time of refusing payment, lodging, or settling a claim. Secondly, it is one of the shipping documents used at the time of negotiating payment.

For the import commodities that are subject to inspection by the inspection authorities as stipulated in the foreign trade contract, upon their arrival, the receivers, and users or forwarding agents should apply to the inspection authorities at the arrival port/station in due time. A survey report or inspection certificate shall be issued to the applicant after inspection. These commodities shall be checked and released by the customs upon presentation of the seal of the inspection authorities affixed on the customs declaration.

For export commodities which are subject to inspection as stipulated in the contract or by law, the manufacturers or suppliers should apply for inspection before shipment. If they are proved up to the standard, the inspection authorities shall issue inspection certificates for them to clear the goods through customs. If vessels and containers are used for carrying perishable goods, such as cereals, oils, foodstuffs, and frozen products for export, the carriers and container stuffing organizations should apply for inspection of the holds or tanks and containers to the inspection authorities at the port. They shall be permitted to carry the goods only after a certificate is issued after examination which proves that they conform with the technical condition for shipping. To know the format of inspection certificate, please refer to Figure 10.7.

10.3.7 Insurance Policy or Certificate
保险单或保险证明

An insurance policy or an insurance certificate is issued when goods are insured. An insurance policy (or a certificate) forms part of the chief shipping documents. A policy also functions as collateral security when an exporter gets an advance against his bank credit.

保险人　　　　　Insurance policy, issued by the **insurer**, is a legal document setting out the exact terms and conditions of an insurance transaction—the name

ENTRY-EXIT INSPECTION AND QUARANTINE
编号 No.: XXX　正本 ORIGINAL
QUALITY INSPECTION CERTIFICATE

发货人 Consignor	TIANJIN BINHAI IMPORT & EXPORT CO., LTD.	
收货人 Consignee	SINGAPORE WONKA TRADING COMPANY LTD.	
品名 Description of Goods	SWIMMING SUITS	标记及号码 Marks & No.
报检数量/重量 Quantity/Weight Declared	-3,000- PIECES/1,200 KGS (N.W.)	SWTC SINGAPORE NO.1-30 TBIM-SWTC-09
包装数量及种类 Number and type of packages	-30-CARTONS	
运输工具 Means of Conveyance	S. S. DONG FENG V.133	

检验结果:
RESULTS OF INSPECTION:

IN ACCORDANCE WITH THE RELEVANT STANDARD, THE REPRESENTATIVE SAMPLE WERE DRAWN AT RANDOM AND INSPECTED WITH RESULTS AS FOLLOWS:
　　OF NORMAL QUALITY
THE QUALITY OF THE GOODS IS IN CONFORMITY WITH THE RELEVANT REQUIREMENTS.

印章 Official Stamp	签证地点 Place of Issue	TIANJIN, CHINA	签证日期 Date of Issue	JUNE 13, 2022
	授权签字人 Authorized Officer	GUO SIRAN	签名 Signature	

中华人民共和国检验检疫机关及其官员或代表对本证书的任何财经责任。No financial liability with respect to this certificate shall attach to the entry-exit inspection and quarantine authorities of P. R. of China or to any of its officers or representatives.

Figure10.7　Illustration of Inspection Certification

中国平安保险股份有限公司
PING AN INSURANCE COMPANY OF CHINA, LTD.

NO. 1000005959

货 物 运 输 保 险 单
CARGO TRANPORTATION INSURANCE POLICY

NO.S OF ORIGIAL: TWO(2)

被保险人：Insure CHINA NATIONAL LIGHT IND. PRODUCTS I/E CORP., NINGBO BRANCH

中国平安保险股份有限公司根据被保险人的要求及其所交付约定的保险费，按照本保险单背面所载条款与下列条款，承保下述货物运输保险，特立本保险单。

This Policy of Insurance witnesses that PING AN INSURANCE COMPANY OF CHINA, LTD., at the request of the Insured and in consideration of the agreed premium paid by the Insured, undertakes to insure the under mentioned goods in transportation subject to the conditions of Policy as per the clauses printed overleaf and other special clauses attached hereon.

保单号
Policy No.

赔款偿付地点
Claim Payable at NEW YORK IN USD

发票或提单号
Invoice No. or B/L No.   INVOICE NO. GMS-025

运输工具
per conveyance S.S. MAYER V.225

查勘代理人
Survey By: PICC NEW YORK BRANCH,
666 CARNEY STREET, NEW YORK, U.S.A.
001-65432143

起运日期
Slg. on or abt.   AS PER B/L

自   From   NINGBO
经   VIA
至   To   NEW YORK

保险金额
Amount Insured
USD55000.00(SAY US DOLLARS FIFTY-FIVE THOUSAND ONLY.

保险货物项目、标记、数量及包装：
Description, Marks, Quantity & Packing of Goods:
PEN, AS PER INV. NO. GMS-025, 110CTNS

承保条件
Conditions:
COVERING MARINE INSTITUTE CARGO CLAUSES (ALL RISKS) AND WAR CLAUSES AND SRCC FOR 110% INVOICE VALUE.

签单日期
Date: OCT.15,2015

For and on behalf of
PING AN INSURANCE COMPANY OF CHINA, LTD.
authorized signature 签名

Figure10.8   Illustration of Insurance Policy

of the insured, the name of the commodity insured, the amount insured, the name of the carrying vessel, the precise risks covered, the period of cover and any exceptions there may be. It also serves as a written contract of insurance between the insurer and the person taking out insurance. To know the format of insurance policy, please refer to Figure 10.8.

10.3.8　Certificate of Origin and GSP FORM A
　　　　一般原产地证和普惠制产地证

普惠制产地证明表格A

Two types of certificates of origin exist in export—a general certificate of origin and a **Generalized System of Preference Form A**.

证明

Like an identity card, the certificate of origin is a document **attesting** to the origin or place of manufacture of the goods when they enter the international market. It is used mainly for the customs of the importing country to adopt differentiated trade policies and treatments toward different countries. In countries where customs or consular invoices are not used, certificates of origin are often required for determining the tariff rates applicable to the imported goods. Countries that restrict the import of goods from a certain country or region also require the document to verify the origin of the goods. It can be issued by notary firms, chamber of commerce in the place of export, the **Entry-**

出入境检验检疫局
中国对外贸易促进委员会

Exit of Inspection and Quarantine (EEIQ) under the Customs or **China Council for the Promotion of International Trade (CCPIT)**. As for who shall issue the document or what kind of certificates shall be issued, it should be handled in accordance with the provisions of the contract or the letter of credit if any.

普惠制是发达国家给予发展中国家出口制成品和半制成品普遍的、非歧视的、非互惠的一种关税优惠制度。普

The Generalized System of Preferences is a universal, non-discriminatory, and non-reciprocal preferential tariff system provided by developed countries to developing countries on the latter's export of finished and semi-finished products, aiming to help the latter increase export and foreign exchanges, and promote their industrialization and economic growth.

The certificate of origin under GSP, also known as G.S.P FORM A, is a document required by the preference granting countries that attests the beneficiary country as the origin of manufacture and entitles the goods to preferential tariff in the preference-granting country. To know the format of G.S.P FORM A, please refer to Figure 10.9.

惠制产地证又称GSP证书或格式A证书，是依据给惠国要求而出具的能证明出口货物原产自受惠国的证明文件，并能使货物在给惠国享受普遍优惠的关税待遇。

ORIGINAL

1. Goods consigned from (Exporter's business name, address, country) FUJIAN ZHONGYI IMPORT & EXPORT CO.,LTD. R 18 FUXIANG BUILDING NO.119 WUSI FUZHOU FUJIAN P.R.CHINA	Reference No: **GENERALIZED SYSTEM OF PREFERENCES** **CERTIFICATE OF ORIGIN** (Combined declaration and certificate) **FORM A** Issued in THE PEOPLE'S REPUBLIC OF CHINA (country)
2. Goods consigned to (Consignee's name, address, country) STURM HANDELS GMBH D-72108 ROTTENBURG GARTENSTR.88 GERMANY	
3. Means of transport and route (as far as known) FROM FUZHOU TO HUMBURG BY SEA	4. For official use

5. Item Number	6. Marks and numbers of packages	7. Number and kind of packages; description of goods	8. Origin criterion (see Notes overleaf)	9. Gross weight or other quantity	10. Number and date of invoices
01	STURM ZY02TB08 019 HAMBURG C/No.1-550	550CTNS (SAY FIVE HUNDRED AND FIFTY CARTONS) 3 ITEMS OF RUCKSACK (CANVAS&NYLON BAGS) ***************	"P"	14740.00KGS	INVOICE NO.: ZY07540 INVOICE DATE: JULY 20,2008

11. Certification It is hereby certified, on the basis of control carried out, that the declaration by the exporter is correct. 中华人民共和国 福建出入境检验检疫局 （盖章） FUZHOU. 5-AUG-2008 Place and date, signature and stamp of certifying authority	12. Declaration by the exporter The undersigned hereby declares that the above details and statements are correct, that all the goods were produced in **CHINA** (country) and that they comply with the origin requirements specified for those goods in the Generalized System of Preferences for goods exported to **GERMANY** (importing country) FUJIAN ZHONGYI IMPORT & EXPORT CO.,LTD. FUZHOU , 5-AUG-2008 Place and date, signature of authorized signatory

Figure 10.9   Illustration of G.S.P FORM A

Exercises 练习

I. True (T) or False (F)

1. You cannot open a L/C with a bank if the underlying transaction is not real. ( )

2. When you agree to an amendment to the L/C advised from the exporter, you should notify your consent both to the exporter and the issuing bank. ( )

3. Since stipulations concerning documents may not appear in every contract documents are not so important in an international trade transaction. ( )

4. For import, we need to arrange for a ship to pick up the goods at a foreign port if the deal is concluded under FOB. However, under CIF, the exporter shall book the space and ship the goods to a Chinese port. Therefore, the cargo risk we assume under FOB is greater than that under CIF. ( )

5. Export documents should be made out based on the information either in the sales contract or in the L/C. ( )

6. The commercial invoice serves as a record of the essential details of a transaction. ( )

7. The CIF price includes the sea freight and insurance premium which covers the distance till the named port of destination, but the exporter is under no obligation to make sure the goods reach the port of destination. ( )

8. Among the methods of payment, L/C is more reliable to exporters, while D/P and D/A are more popular with importers. ( )

9. An inspection for import could only be conducted at the port of destination. ( )

10. A Certificate of Origin can be used to certify the time of the export commodities. ( )

II. Multiple Choice Questions

1. Which of the following documents grants you the fundamental right to import and export? (　)

   A. The import license.

   B. The import quota.

   C. The Form for Registration as a Foreign Trade Dealer.

   D. The duty exemption certificate for import.

2. Which of the following quotations is the CORRECT syntax of Incoterms rule for import to China? (　)

   A. $55 per carton FOB Shanghai

   B. $90 per carton CIF Tianjin

   C. $55 per carton FCA Zhengzhou

   D. $90 per carton FAS Ningbo

3. Which of the following is NOT a possible reason for the wide adoption of FOB for import to China? (　)

   A. The exporter doesn't want to bear the risk of the freight rate rising.

   B. The exporter doesn't want to bear the trouble of international transport.

   C. It helps the importer save on foreign exchange

   D. It helps the exporter save on foreign exchange.

4. Which one of the following practices regarding the time of opening an L/C is NOT appropriate? (　)

   A. The L/C should be opened within the deadline if any such deadline is stipulated in the contract.

   B. The L/C should be opened when the exporter notifies his/her readiness for shipment.

   C. The L/C should be opened when the exporter confirms the time of shipment.

   D. The L/C should be opened at the importer's convenience.

5. If a transaction is concluded on (　) term, the exporter is

obliged to obtain an insurance policy or certificate.

  A. EXW   B. FOB/FCA   C. CFR/CPT   D. CIF/CIP

6. For all export transactions, documents required need to be prepared largely on the basis of the (　　)

  A. sales contract   B. letter of credit

  C. commercial invoice   D. packing list

7. A (An) (　　) is the first document a seller has to prepare when he intends to export commodities that are under the export control of his country.

  A. commercial invoice   B. export license

  C. proforma invoice   D. customs invoice

8. (　　) is a document made out by the seller as a supplementary document to the commercial invoice to make up the deficiency of an invoice by giving all the necessary particulars of the goods.

  A. consular invoice   B. pro forma invoice

  C. packing list   D. customs invoice

9. A (　　) is dispatched by the carrier or the agent to inform the exporter of the particulars of shipment arrangement after the shipping space is booked.

  A. booking note   B. bill of lading

  C. shipping advice   D. shipping order

10. A (An) (　　) is a document indicating the results of the inspection of the goods in terms of the quality, quantity or any other element that has been specified.

  A. inspection certificate   B. inspection application

  C. certificate of origin   D. inspection certificate of quality

III. Case Study

1. One of our trade companies establishes an export contract of garment with a foreign businessman. The contract stipulates that the payment should be made against the irrevocable L/C payable by

sight draft. The buyer issues the L/C to the advising bank within the contractual stipulated issuing time. The L/C has been transferred to us through the advising bank. After we audit the L/C, we find that the stipulations of the shipping date and the prohibited transshipment on the L/C are not in accordance with those on the contract. In order to save the time and amend the L/C for shipment, we cable the issuing bank to amend the L/C without delay. We require the issuing bank to send us the amendment notice directly after they amend the L/C. Questions: (1) What is the consequence of our action? (2) What is the correct channel of the amendment of ?

2. One of our trade companies established an export contract of Christian gifts with a foreign businessman. The contract stipulated that the delivery should be on the CIF basis and the date of delivery was on or before Dec. 1, 2001. However the buyer did not stipulate the issuing date of the L/C in the contract, The buyer began to urge for the establishment of the L/C at the beginning of November, After several urges for establishment. the L/C which is opened by the buyer reached us on Nov. 25. We completed the shipment on Dec. 5 for the late L/C, When we offered the documents to the bank, the bank dishonored to us for the discrepancies of the L/C. Questions: (1) Is the bank's dishonor reasonable? why? (2) What are our mistakes in this case?

3. One of our foreign trade companies received a sight documentary L/C from a foreign buyer through the issuing bank. The L/C stipulated that the shipment could not be effected later than March 15, 2001. However, we couldn't effect shipment duly for the shortage of shipping space, We cabled to the buyer to extend the shipment to April 15 on March 5. The validity of the L/C was extended at the same time. We received the buyer's cable on March 10 that they agreed to accept the cable of March 5, the shipment was changed to be not later than April

15. The validity of the L/C was extended for one month We arranged for shipment immediately on receipt of their cable. We completed our shipment on April 12 and prepared the full set of documents to negotiate with the bank But the bank refused to collect the document. Question: What is the reason for the bank to collect the documents? Why?

Chapter 11
Digital Trade Practice
第十一章　数字贸易实务

◆ Learning Objectives

- Understand the historical development of digital trade
- Be familiar with and grasp the concept of cross-border e-commerce
- Understand the Pattern of cross-border e-commerce

Digital technologies are transforming economic and societal processes. Major improvements in internet connectivity have enabled businesses and households to exchange and transfer information with greater variety, in increasing volume, and at higher velocity. Computing power and data storage have surged as costs have declined, boosting the development of software tools as well as of advanced technologies and analytical techniques. Consequently, the number of new business models, products, and modes of delivery that exploit digital technologies is rapidly increasing.

The most **transformative impact** that **digitalization** has had on trade has been a rapid reduction in the costs of international transactions, which has made it affordable for firms to reach global markets. In much the same way that reductions in transport and coordination costs enabled the fragmentation of production along global value chains, falling costs

颠覆性的影响，数字化

of sharing information are powering this digital trade revolution. The lower costs of storing and sharing information are reducing some of the traditional constraints associated with engaging in international trade, such as asymmetric information, delays in delivery, or contract enforcement. This is encouraging a greater number of businesses and consumers to connect globally, as well as leading to a faster diffusion of knowledge and ideas across borders.

电子商务

The impact of digitalization on international trade is multifaceted. Digitalization has enabled the emergence of **E-commerce**. Many services that traditionally required proximity between producers and consumers can now be traded remotely. Online platforms play a transformative role in many industries. These are the development of **digital trade**.

数字贸易

11.1 Overview of Digital Trade
数字贸易概述

11.1.1 The concept of digital trade
数字贸易的概念

There is no single recognized and accepted definition of digital trade, and the WTO Work Programme on Electronic Commerce, established in 1998, defines e-commerce as the "production, distribution, marketing, sale or delivery of goods and services by electronic means". More recently, the work of López-González and Jouanjean (2017) proposes a framework for digital trade, by which all **digitally enabled transactions** are considered to be in scope for digital trade.

数字化赋能的交易

数字贸易测度手册

Building on all of the above, the **Handbook on Measuring Digital Trade** (OECD, WTO, and IMF, 2019) defines digital trade as trade that is **digitally ordered** and/or **digitally delivered**. This definition reflects the multi-dimensional character of the phenomenon by identifying the nature of

数字化订购 数字化交付

the transaction as the defining characteristic of digital trade and acknowledges the overlap that may exist between digitally ordered and digitally delivered trade. The conceptual framework of digital trade shows as Figure 11.1.

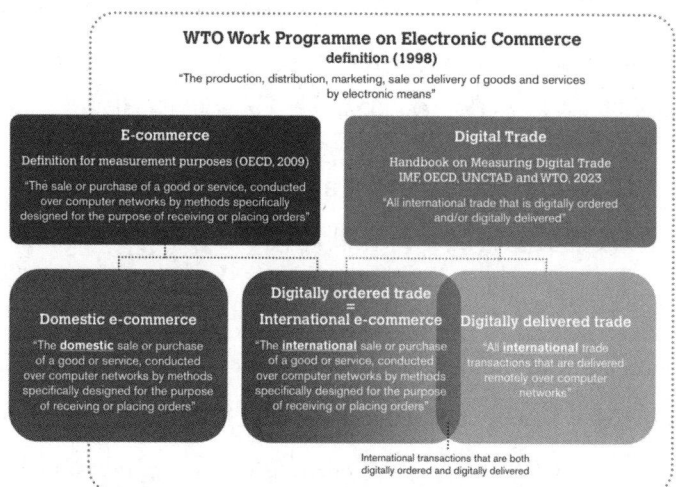

Figure 11.1　The Conceptual Framework of Digital Trade

Digitally ordered trade 数字化订购的贸易

Digitally ordered trade, the international sale or purchase of a good or service, conducted over computer networks by methods specifically designed for the purpose of receiving or placing orders, echoes the OECD definition of e-commerce (OECD, 2011). Digitally ordered trade, as defined here, is therefore equivalent to international e-commerce and as such it is a subset of total e-commerce.

Digitally delivered trade 数字化交付的贸易

Digitally delivered trade, which **only covers services**, is defined as "all international trade transactions that are delivered remotely over computer networks" and builds on the concept of ICT-enabled services transactions developed by TGServ (UNCTAD, 2015). It covers any form of digital delivery, not only delivery methods "specifically designed for the purpose of delivering services".

仅包含服务贸易产品

The value of global exports of digitally delivered services reached

US$ 3.82 trillion in 2022, capturing an estimated 54 per cent share of total global services exports and accounting for 12 percent of total goods and services exports. Between 2005 and 2022, the estimated average annual growth rate of digitally delivered services reached 8.1 per cent, outpacing those of goods exports (5.6 per cent) and other services exports (4.2 per cent)(WTO, 2023b).

11.1.2　Digital trade ushers in a new era of globalisation 数字贸易开启全球化新时代

The digital transformation is fundamentally changing the international trade landscape. The age of digitally enabled trade is not just about digitally delivered trade, it is also about more physical, traditional or GVC, trade enabled by growing digital connectivity increasing access to foreign markets for firms in a way that would previously have been unimaginable.

Digitalisation changing how we trade 数字化改变了贸易方式

比较优势

Trade is still subject to **comparative advantage**, and informational asymmetries and barriers to trade both at-the-border and behind-the-border. However, new business models are changing how we trade:

在线平台

- The growth of **online platforms** has led to a rising number of small packages crossing international borders.

- New technologies are also changing how services are produced and supplied, blurring already grey distinctions between modes of delivery and posing new challenges for the way international trade and investment policy is made.

分布式账本（区块链）增材制造（3D打印）

- Emerging technologies, such as **distributed ledgers** (Blockchain) or **additive manufacturing** (3D printing) have the potential to further change how we trade in the future.

Digitalisation changing what we trade 数字化改变贸易内容

Digitalisation is also changing what we trade:

- New | "information industries" supplying, for example, "big data" analytics, cybersecurity solutions, or at-a-distance quantum computing services across borders are emerging.
- At the same time, digitalisation is also changing the tradability of already established service industries and enabling a greater bundling of goods and services.

Digital trade underpinned by the movement of data 数据构建了数字贸易的基础

The movement of data, or information, across borders underpins this digital trade environment.

- It is at the core of new and rapidly growing service supply models such as cloud computing, the IoT and additive manufacturing.
- It also underpins trade less directly: by enabling control and coordination along international production networks or by enabling the implementation of trade facilitation measures.
- Data flows are thus a means of production, an asset that can itself be traded, the means through which some services are traded, and the means through which GVCs are organized.

As international trade practice focuses on trade in goods, which are generally challenging to be delivered digitally, this chapter emphasizes digital ordered trade, specifically cross-border e-commerce operations.

11.2 Overview of Cross-Border E-commerce 跨境电商概述

On May 22, 2020, when Premier Li Keqiang made the **government work report** at the **National People's Congress**, he proposed to "accelerate the development of **cross-border e-commerce** and other **new formats**, and enhance the international freight transport capacity. In particular, we should speed up the development of cross

政府工作报告

全国人民代表大会

跨境电商

外贸新业态

border e-commerce, a new form of foreign trade, and accelerate the development of China's foreign trade.

11.2.1 The concept of Cross-Border E-commerce
跨境电商的概念

Cross-border Electronic Commerce refers to as the Cross-Border E-commerce and means a kind of international business transactions that trade subjects belonging to different customs areas make deals and conclude payment and settlement through e-commerce platform and deliver goods and complete deals via **cross-border logistics**.

跨境物流

Cross border e-commerce can be divided into **broad cross-border e-commerce** and **cross-border e-commerce in a narrow sense**.

广义跨境电商
狭义跨境电商

In a narrow sense, the cross-border e-commerce is substantially equivalent to the **cross-border retail** as a matter of fact. Cross-border retail refers to the transaction process that trade subjects belonging to different customs areas make deals, pay and settle through computer network and deliver goods to consumers via cross-border logistics by way of express mail, small packets and other luggage and mail. The popular way of cross-border electronic commerce in the international arena is cross-border e-commerce which refers to cross-border retail actually. Generally, from the perspective of customs, the cross-border retail is equivalent to the online trading packet, both basically for consumers. In a strict sense, with the continuous development of cross-border e-commerce, consumers in cross-border retail will also include a portion of B-class business users with fragmented and small-amount transaction; however, it is quite difficult to distinguish such B-class businesses and C-class individual consumers and to identify the strict boundaries between the two. So, generally speaking, this part of sales targeting at B-class also attributes to cross-border retail.

跨境零售

Broadly speaking, the cross-border e-commerce is substantially identical to the foreign trade e-commerce which refers to an international business transaction that trade subjects belonging to different customs areas electronic the links of display, negotiations and transaction in traditional import and export trade via e-commerce means and deliver goods and conclude deals through cross-border logistics. In a broader sense, the cross-border e-commerce refers to **applications of e-commerce in import and export trade,** being the electronic, digital, and networking version of traditional international business processes. It involves many activities in varied aspects, including electronic trading of goods, online data transfer, electronic fund transfer, electronic freight documents and others. In this sense, any aspect that involves e-commerce applications in international trade links can be included within this statistical category.

电子商务在进出口中的运用

11.2.2 The Characteristics of the Cross-Border E-commerce 跨境电商的特点

Compared with the traditional international trade, cross-border e-commerce presents five new features: global, intangible, anonymous, instant, and paperless.

Global 全球性

Cross-border e-commerce depends on the e-commerce platform as the basis for international trade, which determines its characteristic of globalization. When compared with the traditional trade, cross-border e-commerce breaks the geographical restrictions and time limits: the sellers in one country can post information about products and services, and communicate, negotiate and make deals with buyers in another country through the Internet; what's more, buyers in one country can search for sellers through the Internet, and then make an inquiry, bargaining, payment and settlement, and ultimately purchase inexpensive products or services. The global feature of cross-border e-commerce brings information sharing to global buyers and sellers to the greatest extent; however, there are some risks of payment and settlement as well. Anyone who masters a certain basic knowledge of network can enter the network information and perform online transactions whenever and wherever he is. For example, a smaller Chinese foreign trade company can offer products and services to businesses or consumers in any country through an e-commerce platform once they have access to the Internet and meet corresponding demands. Such a way largely facilitates international trade, but meanwhile, it brings some troubles to national tax.

Intangible 无形性

The traditional foreign trade is mainly for barter trade, but with the development of Internet, transactions on a number of digital products and services (such as e-books, movies and copyrights, etc.) becomes more and more. Digital transmission is conducted in a global network environment, being intangible; while cross-border e-commerce develops based on network, thus it inevitably possesses the invisible feature of the network. Take books deal as an example: traditional foreign trade makes the deal by treating a book (physical items for transaction) as the subject matter, while in cross-border e-commerce transactions, buyers in one country can simply purchase the right to data of the book online so as to get the appropriate information, being convenient. The intangible characteristic of e-commerce brings new challenges to a country's tax authority and legal department: its transaction records are in the form of data code, making relevant authorities difficult to define the trading activities, thus they cannot carry out effective monitoring and taxe collection.

Anonymous 匿名性

Due to the globalization and intangibility of cross-border e-commerce, both parties of the transaction can use the Internet to trade anytime and anywhere. Consumers, who use e-commerce platform for trading, usually do not expose their true information, such as real name and the exact geographic location, for the purpose to avoiding transaction risks. But this does not affect their trading smoothly: the anonymity of the Internet provides consumers with such favorable conditions, allowing them to do so. The anonymity of cross-border e-commerce causes the extreme asymmetry between consumers' rights and obligations. Consumers can enjoy maximum rights and interests in a virtual network environment, but they bear minimal responsibilities and obligations, and even some of them are trying to evade responsibilities, all of which make relevant authorities impossible to learn the true interest income and trading conditions of traders, thus they cannot calculate the tax payable and tax the taxpayer legitimately.

Instant 即时性

In traditional foreign trade, two trading subjects communicate mostly by mail and fax; the sending and receiving of information pose different levels of time difference, and there may be some obstacles during the transfer process, making the information not able to transfer in a smooth and timely way and affecting the international trade to some extent. Unlike the traditional mode of foreign trade, cross-border e-commerce has real-time transmission of information, that is to say, regardless of how far away between the actual locations, sellers' sending message and buyers' reception of information are almost simultaneous, there being no time difference, which is equivalent to face-to-face communication in traditional foreign trade to a certain degree. For transactions of some digital goods (such as software, movies, etc.), placing orders, payment, delivery and settlement can be done through the network instantly, bringing great convenience to both parties.

The real-time feature of cross-border e-commerce reduces the middleman link in traditional foreign trade and makes exporters directly face the end consumers, which improves the efficiency of trade, but also hides legal crisis. Such crisis is presented in the taxation area as follows:

due to the immediacy of e-commerce activities, buyers and sellers can start, change, and terminate trading activity at any time, which increases the randomness of trade while reducing the effectiveness of trade. This makes the tax authorities unable to ascertain the real situation of transactions by the parties and supervise ineffectively, bringing some difficulties to the collection of taxes in tax authorities.

Paperless 无纸化

In traditional foreign trade, the whole process, from the inquiry, bargaining, negotiations, contracting and payment settlement, requires a series of written documents as the basis for the transaction. While in e-commerce, trading subjects mainly employ the paperless operation, which is the typical characteristic of cross-border e-commerce being different from the traditional trade. Sellers send information through the network, and buyers receive information through the network, thus the entire electronic information transmission process is paperless. Paperless trade, on the one hand, makes information transmission get rid of the limitation of paperwork, being more efficient; on the other hand, it also causes chaos in the legal system. Since the majority of existing laws and regulations are based on "paper-trading" as a starting point, and do not apply to cross-border e-commerce "paperless" transactions.

The "paperless" transactions in cross-border e-commerce replace the written documents (such as a written contract, settlement documents, etc.) in traditional foreign trade for trading; in the context where no data is available, the tax authorities cannot be informed the real situation of taxpayers, which increases the difficulty for tax authorities to acquire taxpayer operating conditions, making a large part of tax revenues lost and not conducive to international tax policy. For example, stamp duty, as one of the traditional taxes levied universally, should be levied on the basis of written contract provided by trading parties. However, in the "paperless" e-commerce environment, there are no legal contracts and written confirmation in physical form, due to which the taxation of stamp duties by the nation is out of nowhere and lawless.

11.2.3　Operational Modes of the Cross-Border E-commerce 跨境电商运营模式

According to the different status and role of China's cross-border e-commerce enterprises in the cross-border e commerce transaction and circulation, as well as the different business models, the operational modes of cross-border e-commerce can be divided into the following categories: **B2B, B2C, C2C, O2O**, etc.

> Business to Business, Business to Consumer, Consumer to Consumer, Online to Offline

B2B Mode　B2B模式

B2B refers to the marketing relationship between enterprises. With B2B mode, enterprises apply e-commerce with priority to use of advertisement and information release, due to its deals and customs clearance process are fulfilled in an offline manner, it is still in the essence of the traditional trade, incorporated into the customs statistics of general trade. **DHgate, Alibaba** is a typical third-party B2B platform. Figure 11.2 shows the procedures of B2B mode.

> 敦煌网，阿里巴巴国际站

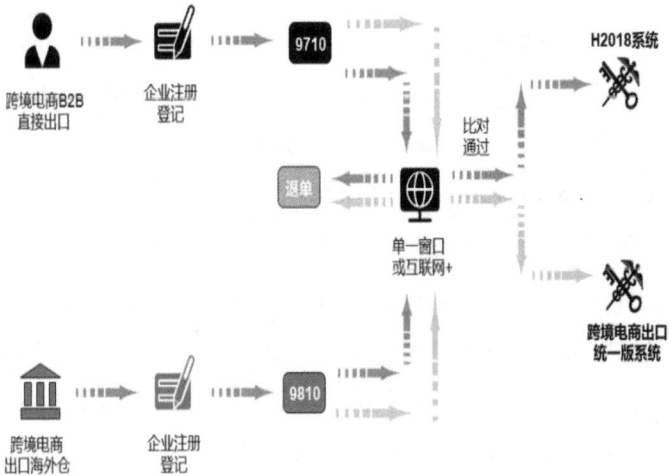

Figure 11.2　The Procedures of B2B Mode

B2C Mode B2C模式

B2C is the e-commerce of enterprises to consumers, that is, enterprises provide consumers with a new shopping environment through the Internet online stores Consumers shop online and pay online through the Internet. According to the Report on the Development Trend of China's Cross-border E-commerce Retail Export Industry 2014 released by eBay, China's cross-border e-commerce retail export industry has a strong development momentum. In terms of export products, the top five categories of products with the highest turnover are electronics, fashion, home & garden, auto parts, and collection. Among them, electronics and fashion products are the traditional export blockbusters, while home & garden and auto parts are the two fastest growing categories. According to the data on eBay platform, the trend of destination market of China's cross-border e-commerce is obvious, with the United States, the United Kingdom, and Australia as the three main markets. **Amazon, AliExpress, Wish, eBay, JD Global, and VIP Overseas Selec**t are regarded as this mode.The procedures of B2B mode please refer to Figure 11.3

亚马逊，速卖通 Wish，易趣网，京东全球购，唯品会海外精选

C2C Mode C2C模式

C2C is e-commerce between consumers. Under this mode, the e-commerce website provides an online trading platform for both buyers and sellers, on which the sellers can publish information of the goods to be sold, while buyers can choose among them and make a purchase. **Taobao Global** is a typical C2C mode.

淘宝全球购

O2O Mode O2O模式

O2O mode is to carry out online marketing promotion through the Internet platform and attract foreign consumers to offline stores in the country where the consumers are located, that is, online to offline; or to move consumers from offline to online through offline marketing promotion, that is, offline to online. It can improve the user experience of consumers, ensure the authenticity of products, and facilitate cross-border commodity sales. **OSell** is the representative of the O2O platform mode of cross-border e-commerce. 　　大龙网

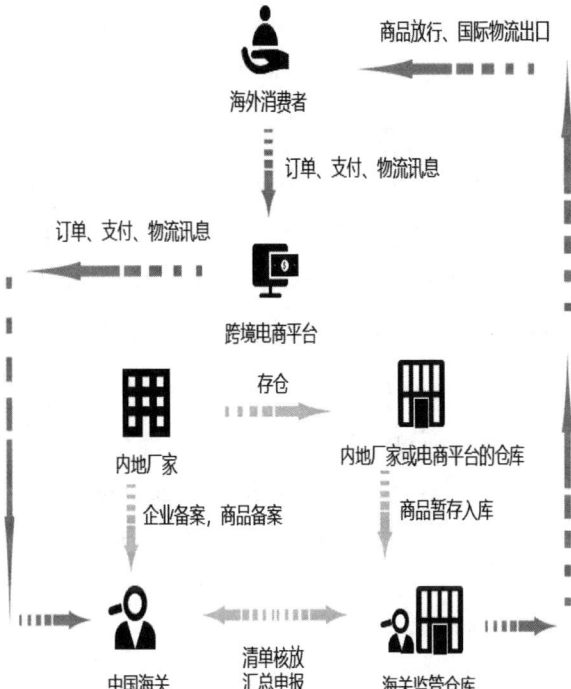

Figure 11.3　The Procedures of B2C Mode

11.2.4　The World's Major Cross-Border E-commerce Platforms
主要跨境电商平台

Currently, the main cross-border e-commerce platforms around the world are AliExpress, Wish, DHgate, eBay and Amazon.

AliExpress 速卖通

AliExpress was officially launched in April 2010. It is a foreign trade online transaction platform that Alibaba helps medium and small enterprises to connect with overseas terminals, to expand profit space and creates for integrating order, payment and logistics, which is called by sellers as "international version of Taobao". Currently, AliExpress is the largest B2C transaction platform in China, covering more than 220 countries and districts. The current average daily order volume exceeds 5 million.

From the launch in 2010 to 2014, the annual turnover of AliExpress grew rapidly. The GMV in 2023 was approximately 30 billion US dollars. The number of active shoppers on AliExpress is more than150 Million. On November 11, 2014, it was the first time that AliExpress participated in global November 11, 6.84 million transaction orders were created within 24 hours. The valid orders in that day cover 211 countries and districts. As for the ranking of flow, Brazil, Russia and Turkey rank the second in shopping website, the US tanks the fifth, Spain ranks the first, and Indonesia ranks the sixth. And the monthly flow is about 600M, the main distributions are mainly in these several countries, and the proportion of flow is about 50% of the total amount.

The home page of AliExpress as shown in Figure 11.4.

Figure 11.4　The home page of AliExpress

Wish

Wish was founded on December 1, 2011 in Silicon Valley of San Francisco in the US, and it is a commercial platform based on mobile App. At first, Wish platform is used to communicate and share, which does not involve product transaction. In March 2013, Wish online transaction platform is officially launched, and mobile APP is launched in June 2013. Wish becomes a rising star in cross-border e-commerce mobile terminal platform. The GMV in 2023 was approximately 2 billion US dollars.

Wish is now active in 60+ countries around the world. Currently, Wish has 1 billion registered users. And the daily active users are 1.2 million. The main consumer group of Wish is 15 to 28 years old, and the proportions of men and women are 3:7. The proportions of Wish merchants in Asia and Europe are 81:19, which means Wish is dominated by Chinese sellers. Wish ranks the first in download amounts in the US. And its founder is named as one of the best founders, and APP is rated as the best APP for Android.

Compared with other e-commerce platforms like Amazon, eBay, and AliExpress, Wish will not charge additionally through key words to recommend products for users. The system of Wish is calculated by data of buyers' behaviors to evaluate the hobby of buyers, interesting product information and choose corresponding product recommendation for buyers.

Figure 11.5 Mobile application page of Wish

Mobile application page of Wish as shown in Figure 11.5.

DHgate 敦煌网

DHgate(*www.dhgate.com*)is the first B2B cross-border e-commerce platform in China, which was founded in 2004. It helps medium and small enterprises in China to enter into global market through e-commerce platform. Currently, it has more than 2.6 million domestic suppliers with more than 33 million products in 225 countries and districts around the world and with the scale of 77 million online buyers. Each order is created within 1.39 seconds in average. It has 188 global logistics routes and 14 overseas fulfillment centers. DH gate mainly uses profit modes like commission, value-added service and advertising. The advantageous programs of DHgate are cell phone and electronic products.

With the mission of "promoting global trade and creating entrepreneurial dream", DHgate helps medium and small enterprises utilize e-commerce platform by a large scale and seek for new development space for Chinese foreign trade and expand new picture of foreign trade and transaction. The values of DHgate bringing to small and medium enterprise customers lie in two aspects: the first one is "to pay for success", which makes medium and small enterprises pay few commissions for transaction and not pay for high annual fees; the second one is the DHgate helps enterprise customers to look for overseas buyers and helps customers to solve the problems of overseas marketing. At the same time, DHgate has professional marketing teams of foreign staff from Facebook, YouTube and Google for promotion, uses the latest marketing method——community marketing for customers from medium and small enterprises to look for overseas buyers.

The home page of DHgate as shown in Figure 11.6.

Figure 11.6　The home page of DHgate

eBay 易趣网

eBay is an online auction and shopping website for global citizens to buy and sell products. It was founded on September 4, 1995 by Pierre Omidyar using the name of Auctionweb in San Jose, California. The initial purpose of eBay is to help founder's girlfriend to find out the fans of Pez candy box in the US for communication. It was surprising that eBay became popular soon. At the beginning of establishment, eBay is positioned as an online auction and shopping website for global net citizens to buy and sell products.

There are two main selling methods for sellers to release products in eBay platform: "auction" and "fixed price". eBay charges sellers differently due to different selling methods, it is usually calculated as "publication fee" plus "transaction fee", which is: production release fees and transaction commissions.

The home page of eBay as shown in Figure 11.7.

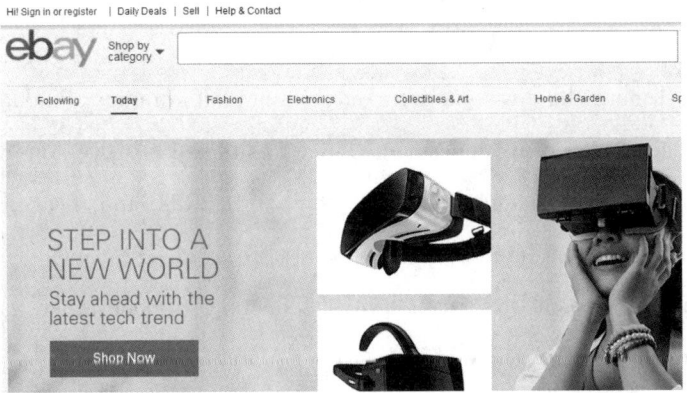

Figure 11.7　The home page of eBay

Amazon 亚马逊

Amazon is the largest e-commerce company, which was founded in the US in 1995. Its initial position was an online bookstore selling books and audio-visual products. In 1997, it transformed to the largest comprehensive network retailer. Until 2025, Amazon has 19 overseas sites, more than 400 fulfilment centers and more than 2 billion Prime

Members. Amazon can deliver goods to over 200 countries and regions.

Currently, Amazon mainly sells brand new, refurbished and used items, including books, digitals, home furniture, cookers, household appliances, beauty makeup, food, drinks, maternity stuff, toy, apparel and automotive supplies.

The home page of Amazon as shown in Figure 11.8.

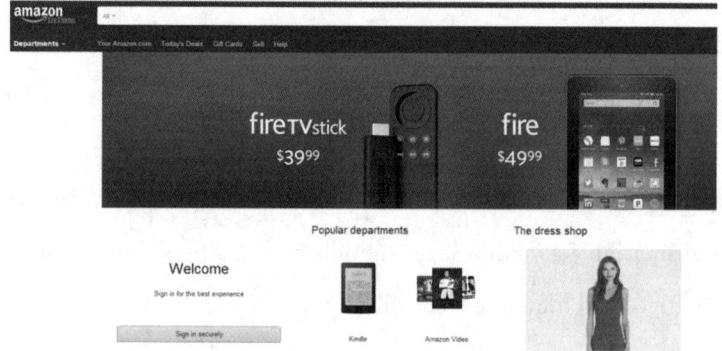

Figure 11.8　The home page of Amazon

Temu 拼多多海外版

Temu, the cross-border e-commerce platform under Pinduoduo, is headquartered in Guangzhou, China. Positioned to serve mid-range users, Temu was launched on September 1, 2022, and is owned by Shanghai Yucan Information Technology Co., Ltd. The name "Temu" stands for "Team Up, Price Down", reflecting its model where prices decrease as more people purchase. As of March 2024, Temu sells goods in more than 50 countries and regions worldwide.

Temu offers a wide range of product categories, including: Apparel and footwear, Bags and accessories, Jewelry, Maternal and child products, Kids' clothing and toys, Sports and outdoor gear, 3C electronics (computers, communication, consumer electronics), Small home appliances, Mobile phones and accessories, Auto and motorcycle parts, Office and pet supplies, Home goods and furniture, Musical instruments, Industrial tools.

The home page of Temu as shown in Figure 11.9.

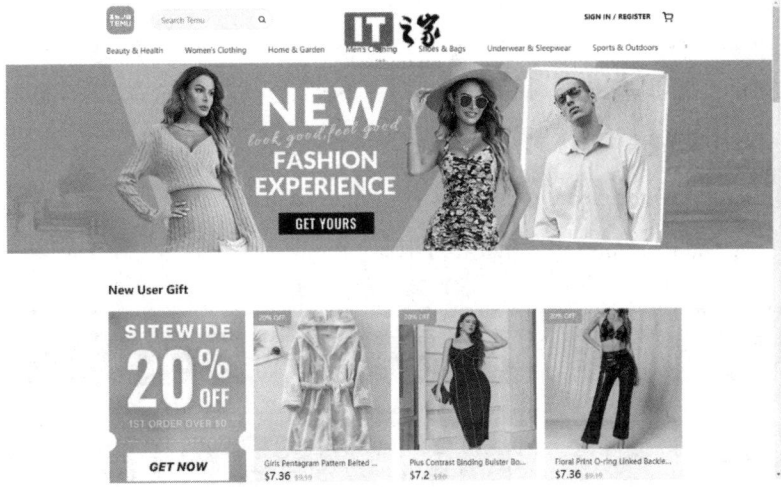

Figure 11.9 The home page of Temu

Shopee 虾皮

Shopee, a leading e-commerce platform in Southeast Asia, operates across over ten markets including Singapore, Malaysia, the Philippines, Thailand, Vietnam, Brazil. In 2023, Shopee achieved 8.2 billion total orders, with a robust 24% year-on-year growth in total order volume during Q3 2024. Shopee partnered with Chinese cross-border sellers to achieve record-breaking sales during major shopping festivals. On 11.11, 2024, localized fulfillment warehouse orders surged to six times the daily average, while cross-border short video orders skyrocketed to 20 times the daily average.

According to the authoritative mobile data analytics platform data.ai, Shopee ranked first globally in user time spent on shopping apps on Google Play during the first half of 2024. It also dominated Southeast Asia and Brazil across key metrics: user time spent, average monthly active users, and total downloads in the shopping app category. Additionally, Shopee's brand influence remains extensive, securing the top position in Kantar Brand Z's 2023 ranking of Southeast Asia's most valuable retail brands.

Committed to building an integrated cross-border ecosystem, Shopee empowers sellers through cost-effective logistics solutions, precision marketing strategies for traffic conversion, and comprehensive operational support spanning system integration, language services, payment solutions, and third-party partnerships—unlocking limitless possibilities for global expansion.The home page of

Temu as shown in Figure 11.10.

Figure 11.10　The home page of Shopee

11.3　Differences between Cross Border E-commerce and Traditional Trade
跨境电商与传统贸易的区别

Different Ways of Negotiation 交易磋商方式的不同

In the traditional international trade, our buyers and sellers contact each other by means of telephone, e-mail, and other instant communication tools and software. They usually go through the process of preparation (Market Research), inquiry, quotation, counter-offer acceptance, contract signing, goods preparation, chartering and space booking, insurance purchase, customs declaration and inspection, transportation of goods, buyer's receipt and payment, etc. Compared with the traditional national trade model, cross-border e-commerce frequency and low cost. It has the characteristics of mobility, multilateral, small order, high frequency and low cost. And can do: (1) Delivery before trading, trading mode from offline to online, greatly reducing the transaction time and cost, improving the efficiency of the transaction. (2) It omits many links of middlemen, which can make manufacturers and consumers directly linked, and has the characteristics of fewer links, low cost, high efficiency, high profit and high frequency. (3) The whole process of cross-border e-commerce can be operated on the cross-border e-commerce platform from the initial transaction negotiation to the transaction. For example, bank transfer, freight forwarding, commodity inspection, customs declaration and other businesses all adopt online application and offline processing, which greatly saves time, speeds up the processing time, simplifies the negotiation process and improves efficiency.

Different Modes of Transportation 运输方式的不同

The traditional modes of national trade transportation mainly include ocean transportation, air transportation, railway transportation, container transportation and so on. Among them, the container ocean transportation mode accounts for nearly 80%. Among the cross-border e-commerce, the most common mode of transportation is international express in postal transportation. According to the data of the national e-commerce Research Center, the number of cross-border e-commerce is increasing 70% of the export business is international express.

Different Types of Transportation Insurance 运输保险险别的不同

In the traditional trade, the insurance clauses for marine transportation are ICC formulated by London Insurance Association and C.I.C. clauses issued by China. These clauses include W.P.A., F.P.A., all risks, and war risks. In cross-border e-commerce, the main mode of transportation is postal transportation. Obviously, the contents of these terms are no longer applicable. For postal transportation, express insurance is more used.

Different Payment Methods 支付方式的不同

In traditional trade, after delivery, the buyer and the seller will directly accept payment by letter of credit, remittance, and collection, There are many intermediate links, complicated procedures and complicated bills involved, In cross-border e-commerce platform transactions most of them are online or electronic payment methods, such as credit cards, online banking. Electronic transfer, mobile phone payment, third party payment PayPal and China Alipay. The new payment method is not only low cost, but also fast. It also greatly improves the efficiency of the transaction, enhances the trust of both sides, and helps the seller to facilitate the completion of the transaction.

Different Order Completion Efficiency 订单完成效率的不同

In traditional international trade, exporters usually spend a lot of money to participate in exhibitions around the world, search for information about relevant companies on the international official website or get yellow pages from commercial counselors, and then make business contact with each other, which is inefficient, In the cross-border e-commerce mode. The buyer and the seller do not need to negotiate for a long time. As long as the online communication is conducted, and the online buyers basically have demand, the transaction time is short, the cost is very low and the efficiency is greatly improved.

❯ Exercises 练习

I. True (T) or False (F)

1. Cross-border e-commerce is a good way for every product to go

global. (　)

2. Most international buyers use PayPal or Alipay for cross-border e-commerce. (　)

3. Overseas warehouse is applicable for every product for export through cross-border e-commerce. (　)

4. Lazada and Shopee are popular platforms for South East Asian countries. (　)

5. Some cross-border e-commerce platforms acquire traffic and sales through livestreaming, such as TikTok Shop. (　)

6. Managing customer review of your online store requires you to achieve enough sales and positive reviews for your store. (　)

7. Analyzing data about your online store is mostly done manually and very exhausting. (　)

8. When you conduct social media marketing, posting engaging content is critical. (　)

9. Online marketing campaign can be conducted both on and outside a platform for cross-border e-commerce. (　)

10. When you buy foreign products from online, your order is probably fulfilled in one of the following ways: directly mailed to you, mailed from a bonded warehouse located in China, or directly sold to you with duty paid. (　)

II. Multiple Choice Questions

1. Which one of the following mainly adopts a buyer model for cross-border e-import? (　)

A. Ymatou.com.　　　　B. JD Worldwide.

C. Xiaohongshu.　　　　D. Tmall Global.

2. Which one of the following platforms mainly adopts a self-running model for cross-border e-import? (　)

A. Ymatou.com.　　　　B. Tmall Global.

C. JD Worldwide.　　　　D. Kaola.com.

3. Which one of the following platforms for cross-border e-import acquires traffic and sales through shared contents of social media influences and online word of mouth?（　）

A. Ymatou.com. B. Tmall Global.

C. Xiaohongshu. D. TikTok Shop.

4. Which one of the following platforms for cross-border e-import offers shopping guides and rebates to customers?（　）

A. Mia.com. B. 55haitao.com.

C. Xiaohongshu. D. Tmall Global.

5. Under which model is return and replacement most difficult for cross-border e-import?（　）

A. The direct sale model.

B. The bonded warehouse model.

C. The transshipment model.

D. The direct sale with duty paid model.

6. Which of the following factor（s）should be considered when you run a cross-border e-business?（　）

A. Product.　B. Price.　C. Promotion.　D. Place.

7. Which one of the following is the correct order of preferred payment services for cross-border e-commerce by most European buyers?（　）

A. Visa, PayPal, Mastercard. B. PayPal, Alipay, Visa.

C. PayPal, Visa, Mastercard. D. PayPal, Visa, Alipay.

8. Which of the following factor（s）influence（s）how much you price your product online?（　）

A. Your pricing goal. B. Your target market.

C. Your cost. D. Your competitors' prices

9. According to the textbook, which of the following online platforms are preferred by Russian and Brazilian customers respectively?（　）

A. EBay and Amazon. B. EBay and Alibaba.

C. Amazon and AliExpress.   D. AliExpress and AliExpress.

10. If you do not consider overseas warehouse, what logistics option (s) do you have for cross-border e-export? ( )

A. Postal package service.   B. Foreign couriers.

C. Domestic couriers.   D. Special line logistics.

III. Web Page Clipping

1. Log into the listed platforms for cross-border e-commerce, find out which one you like, clip a web page and talk about why.

2. Log in to TikTok Shop or Instagram Shopping, select a vertical category (e.g., yoga apparel), access the flagship stores of three brands, and compare their respective online marketing strategies. Visit platforms like AliExpress, Amazon, or Shopee, select a popular cross-border e-commerce category (e.g., smart wearables/eco-friendly tableware), review product detail pages of similar products from three sellers, and analyze:

- Keyword structure in product titles
- Main product videos and contextual displays
- Payment/logistics options
- Review management strategies
- Propose three actionable optimizations for these pages.

References

参考文献

[1] 冷柏军,李洋.国际贸易实务双语教程[M].北京:中国人民大学出版社,2021.

[2] 易露露,陈新华,尤彧聪.国际贸易实务双语教程(第五版)[M].北京:清华大学出版社,2024.

[3] 王小娟.国际贸易实务双语教程[M].北京:对外经济贸易大学出版社,2024.

[4] 周瑞琪,王小鸥,徐月芳.国际贸易实务(英文版)(第五版)[M].北京:对外经济贸易大学出版社,2020.

[5] 傅龙海、丛晓明、陈剑霞.国际贸易实务双语教程(第四版)[M].北京:对外经济贸易大学出版社,2022.

[6] 姜艳艳.国际贸易实务(双语版)第2版[M].上海:上海财经大学出版社,2024.

[7] 杨贵章.国际贸易实务双语教程(第二版)[M].大连:大连理工大学出版社,2022.

[8] 马述忠,陈珉,孙金秀等.跨境电商理论与实务[M].北京:高等教育出版社,2023.

[9] 覃娜,符白薇.国际贸易实务中英双语教程[M].浙江:浙江大学出版社,2025.

[10] 蔡玉斌,龙游宇.国际贸易理论与实务(第三版)北京:高等教育出版社,2012.

[11] 张靓芝. 国际贸易实务（英文版）[M]. 北京：对外经济贸易大学出版社，2013.

[12] 田运银. 国际贸易实务精讲（第六版）[M]. 北京：中国海关出版社，2014.

[13] 孙智慧. 国际贸易实务（双语）[M]. 对外经济贸易大学出版社，2018.

[14] 帅建林. 国际贸易实务（英文版）（第三版）[M]. 成都：西南财经大学出版社，2015.

[15] 中国国际贸易学会商务专业培训考试办公室. 进出口货物贸易单证实务[M]. 北京：中国商务出版社. 2014

[16] 李鹏博. 揭秘跨境电商[M]. 北京：电子工业出版社，2015.

[17] 翁晋阳，Mark，管鹏，文丹凤. 再战跨境电商[M]. 北京：人民邮电出版社，2015.

[18] 丁晖. 跨境电商多平台营运[M]. 北京：电子工业出版社，2015.

[19] 肖旭. 跨境电商实务[M]. 北京：中国人民大学出版社，2015.

[20] 张炳达，顾涛. 海关报关实务（第三版）[M]. 上海财经大学出版社，2015.

[21] López González, J. and M. Jouanjean. Digital Trade: Developing a Framework for Analysis [J]. OECD Trade Policy Papers, No. 205, OECD Publishing.2017.

[22] OECD. Measuring Digital Trade: Toward a Conceptual Framework [J]. OECD Working Party on International Trade in Goods and Trade in Services Statistics, 2017.

[23] Casalini, F. and López González, J. Trade and Cross Border Data Flows [J]. OECD Trade Policy Papers No. 220, Paris: Organisation for Economic Co-operation and Development (OECD), 2019.

[24] Anderson, R. D., Muller, A. C., KovaC.I.C., W. E. and Sporysheva, N. Competition Policy, Trade, and the Global

Economy: Existing WTO Elements, RTA Commitments, Current Challenges and Issues for Reflection [J]. Geneva: Staff Working Paper No. ERSD-2018-12, Geneva: World Trade Organization (WTO), 2018.

[25] International Monetary Fund (IMF), Organization for Economic Co-operation and Development (OECD), United Nations Conference on Trade And Development (UNCTAD) and World Trade Organization (WTO) (2023), Handbook on Measuring Digital Trade (Second Edition) Geneva: WTO, 2023.

[26] 中华人民共和国海关总署网站 http://www.customs.gov.cn/

[27] 海关信息网 http://www.haiguan.info/

[28] 中国人民财产保险股份有限公司网站 http://www.piccnet.com.cn/

[29] 全球银行间金融电讯协会 http://www.swift.com

[30] 马士基航运公司网站 htttp://www.maerskline.com

[31] 阿里巴巴国际站 htttp://www.alibaba.com

[32] 全球速卖通网站 http://www.aliexpress.com

[33] 国际商会网站 http://www.iccwbo.org

[34] 锦程物流网 http://www.jctrans.com/

[35] 中国国际贸易仲裁委员会网站 http://www.cn.cietac.org/

[36] 全关通信息网 http://www.qgtong.com

[37] 中华人民共和国商务部网站 http://www.mofcom.gov.cn/

[38] 维基百科网站 http://en.wikipedia.org